Critical Essays on Henrik Ibsen

Critical Essays on World Literature

Robert Lecker, General Editor
McGill University

Critical Essays on Henrik Ibsen

Charles R. Lyons

G. K. Hall & Co. • Boston, Massachusetts

Library of Congress Cataloging in Publication Data

Critical essays on Henrik Ibsen.

(Critical essays on world literature)
Bibliography: p. 239
Includes index.
1. Ibsen, Henrik, 1828–1906 — Criticism and
interpretation. I. Lyons, Charles R. II. Series.
PT8890.C75   1987   839.8'226   86-29541
ISBN 0-8161-8835-1 (alk. paper)

This publication is printed on permanent/durable acid-free paper
MANUFACTURED IN THE UNITED STATES OF AMERICA

For my students,
past and present

CONTENTS

INTRODUCTION

IBSEN'S DRAMA AND THE COURSE
OF MODERN CRITICISM

Today the publication of its text usually accompanies the premiere production of a new play by Samuel Beckett. Within a short period of time the play is published in several languages and performed in theaters around the world. The major events of the avant-garde are international, and playwrights like Beckett, Pinter, and Handke address a wide-ranging audience of spectators and readers who experience the text in their own languages. This phenomenon first occured in the 1890s, when Ibsen's controversial plays were appropriated by experimental theaters in Germany, France, and Britain, and he became the dominant figure of an international avant-garde. Even though Ibsen's realistic plays detail the bourgeoisie of his native Norway, their innovative structure and ideology helped to define the radical program of art theaters on the continent and in Britain. Antoine's production of *Ghosts* in 1890 marks an important event in the history of the *Théâtre Libre*, a small experimental house whose highly realistic productions pointed up the artificiality and superficiality of the dramatic fare and conventional scenography of the commercial Parisian theater. This theater became the model for Otto Brahm's *Freie Bühne* in Berlin, which opened with *Ghosts* in 1890, and J. T. Grein's Independent Theatre in London, which he founded with a private performance of the same play in 1891. As I discuss later, when the French avant-garde shifted from realism to symbolism in 1893 with the establishment of the *Théâtre de l'Oeuvre*, Lugné-Poe's production of Ibsen's *Rosmersholm* became the vehicle for a symbolist production that signaled a new style.

The translated works of Ibsen form part of the history of modern drama in several countries. The French text of *Ghosts* is, surely, as important a document in the history of dramatic modernism in France as the work of any French playwright, and in the development of modern English drama only Shaw rivals the significance of Archer's English translations of Ibsen. The German translations of Ibsen, influencing the

1

development of Hauptmann and others, made an equally striking impact on the drama of that language. Understandably, the criticism of Ibsen, as well, has not been confined to specialists of Scandinavian literature, although it has been richly fed by them. Ibsen has become a useful subject for a variety of critical perspectives and theoretical arguments.

At midpoint in the 1980s, the cacophony of differing critical voices forms an appropriate, if problematic, context for a reconsideration of Ibsen criticism. The practice of dramatic criticism itself seems to be in a state of crisis. For the past fifty years, with few exceptions, the major critical strategies have been either explicitly or implicitly nonmimetic.[1] The confident voice of the Neo-Aristotelians, insisting on the primacy of action and character, has been all but silenced by arguments that emphasize the dramatic text as a verbal structure that conveys its meaning through the operation of highly charged language rather than through formal schemes that produce a value-laden imitation of human behavior.

In the 1930s and 1940s, the antimimetic strategies of the New Criticism disassembled the literal sequence of texts to reconstruct networks of intersecting metaphoric systems that unify individual literary works and convey their meaning.[2] In the 1950s and 1960s, the proponents of the Geneva School, building models of the psyche based upon an existential phenomenology largely derived from Heidegger, erased the boundaries of the individual text and worked with the idea of an oeuvre that reveals a structure composed of conceptual paradigms that form the conscious and unconscious processes of the poet's psyche throughout his or her writing.[3] Phenomenological and psychoanalytic criticism, in related but different ways, demanded that the text be seen not as the representation of its ostensible subject matter but as the cryptic expression of the structure of the psyche. In these terms, the reader or spectator apprehends a text that appears to represent the objective world but, in fact, only pretends to be directly mimetic. Phenomenological criticism celebrates the uniqueness of a subjectivity that determines its own structure. Psychoanalytic criticism appropriates that subjectivity to an archetypal model of the unconscious drawn from Freud, Jung, Laing, or others whose work defines itself against Freud.[4]

In the 1960s and 1970s, the arguments of those influenced by structural anthropology, linguistics, and Russian formalism began to speak of the text as a synthetic container of multiple linguistic and visual codes.[5] More recently, post-structuralism has worked to diminish the connection between writer and text in a programmatic attempt to see the text as the product of the processes of writing and reading rather than of the subjectivity of the writer.[6] Recently, however, the efforts of the deconstructionalists to dissolve the connection between the language of a text and reality have provoked a reactionary call for a return to mimetic criticism.[7]

Throughout this time literary historians have continued to speak of texts in positivist terms as the representation of ideas external to the poet, situating the individual writer within an ideological context.[8] However, more radical voices have defined the biases of this type of scholarship by identifying its arguments as the manifestation of highly conventionalized notions of intellectual history that systematically fulfill their own expectations and work to perpetuate the dominant, institutionally determined values of the history they address. In recent years, working toward a redefinition of the practice of historical analysis, others have returned to the relation of text and history, but these scholars, under the influence of Foucault, have abandoned the positivist attitude, and offer more speculative arguments.[9] As they attempt to perceive the previously unwritten, unauthorized history that counters the orthodox narrative of men and events, these "new historians" examine the text as the oblique evidence of unspoken cultural biases. Their analyses expose either the subverted or subversive social energies that direct the writing of the texts they examine.

Ibsen, as much as any major modern writer whose works have achieved the status of classics, provides a screen on which the major transitions in criticism display themselves. The twentieth century has offered up a variety of ways to read the classic texts, and the same freedom operates in the theater, where the demand to offer the public new interpretations of the classics is even more relentless than in the academy. The producer may choose any point along a hypothetical continuum between an attempted reconstruction of the theatrical conventions of its original production or an adaptation that uses the text merely as the starting point for an original creative exercise. The increasing authority of the producer, director, or *regisseur* in the twentieth century permits the reshaping of the classics to suit the aesthetic or ideological concerns of the immediate moment. Today the director may use the published script as a stimulus to the imagination rather than as a constraint formed by notions of authorial intention or historical authenticity. Until criticism itself became involved in the playful reconstitution of the text, literary scholars opposed performance-generated revision of the classics, because these aesthetic experiments seemed antithetical to the scholarly object of fixing the relationship of text, meaning, and context. Because performance delivers the play to its spectators through the interpretative agency of actors, directors, and designers, the text has always been a transitive object in the theater, vulnerable to both deliberate and accidental revision. But scholars and critics, until recently, tended to view the authorized text as sacrosanct and perceived the more radical interventions of performance as "violations" of the text. Their objections frequently ignored the fact that their own readings of the authorized text often incorporated accumulated conventions of performance that originated in the idiosyncratic interpretations of specific actors and directors, which then became institutionalized as traditions of performance.

The radical difference between the activities of reading a text and experiencing a play in performance has always complicated the project of dramatic criticism. Even the most sophisticated and skillful of analysts have vacillated among various rhetorical strategies that do not always clarify whether they consider the dramatic text as a literary work equivalent to poetry or fiction, as the score for a hypothetical performance, or as a written document that has been subject to a history of theatrical production and is encumbered with unofficial appendices of critical glosses and established conventions of performance. While the idea of performance persistently intervenes in the critical project, commentators rarely define the nature and function of that performance precisely. The critic who deals well with the nuances and complexity of the playwright's language may lack the spatial sensibility required to comprehend the implicit visual signs that become explicit in performance. Textual critics are subject to the limitation of their experience in the theater, and while attempting a new interpretation of a text they may imagine it within a conventional staging, unaware of the potential for new modes of design and performance. They may well be unaware that the conventional staging they imagine constrains their perception of the language of the text because it fixes statement in a specific context.

Ibsen criticism began as journalistic controversy when the production of his realistic plays was, indeed, news. By midcentury, the discussion of his plays had become an academic pursuit, subject to the shifting trends of aesthetic and literary theory. Consequently, the diversity of opinion represented by this anthology of essays represents a variety of Ibsens — the realist, the iconoclast, the successful or failed idealist, the poet, the psychologist, the romantic, the antiromantic. Ibsen, of course, is no one of these, nor is he the sum of these predications. For a time, literary studies assumed that it was possible to reconstruct or to restore the work of a writer whose texts had been distorted in the sequence of interpretations that intervened between their publication and the present moment. Nowadays we recognize that current systems of interpretation invariably shape our efforts to understand the texts of the past, and we know what we see is, to a large degree, determined by what we look for and the language in which we discuss it.[10] In his lifetime Ibsen was either celebrated as a social reformer or vilified as an immoral radical. Those who found him a skillful and significant artist discovered that value in his realistic confrontation with social issues. The British Ibsenites, led by William Archer and Bernard Shaw, declared that the purpose of Ibsen's representation of human behavior and social environment was to expose social injustice and the absence of moral significance in the institutions of the middle class. In their view, the mimetic image, intensified in the compression of theatrical performance, forced the audience to confront themselves. The Ibsenites, of course, saw the literal surface of the text, either read or witnessed in performance, as complete and self-contained. That is, the truth represented in Ibsen's realistic texts is literal, verifiable, and immediately accessible. Shaw's collection of his essays on Ibsen, published as *The Quintessence of Ibsenism*, built an image of Ibsen the social realist that remained firm for decades:

> Ibsen saw that . . . the more familiar the situation, the more interesting the play. Shakespear [*sic*] had put ourselves on the stage but not our situations. Our uncles seldom murder our fathers, and cannot legally marry our mothers; we do not meet witches; our kings are not as a rule stabbed and succeeded by their stabbers; and when we raise money by bills we do not promise to pay pounds of our flesh. Ibsen supplies the want left by Shakespear. He gives us not only ourselves, but ourselves in our own situations. The things that happen to his stage figures are things that happen to us. One consequence is that his plays are much more important to us than Shakespear's. Another is that they are capable both of hurting us cruelly and of filling us with excited hopes of escape from idealistic tyrannies, and with visions of intenser life in the future.

This statement comes from the chapter titled "The Technical Novelty in Ibsen's Plays," which is the first essay in this collection. Shaw assumed that Ibsen's drama shows the audience its own potential image translated into the fictive world of the stage, and he believed that this image is immediately accessible. In Shaw's view the Ibsen play *is* its literal form.

William Archer's judgment that *When We Dead Awaken* reveals the failure of Ibsen's skill documents the Ibsenites' concentration on the literal. Archer, Ibsen's editor and English translator, published a complete edition of the plays in 1907. His introduction to Ibsen's last play devalues the work on the basis of its violation of plausibility. Archer's argument claims that it would be physically impossible for Rubek's statue to develop from a single figure into a group composition:

> This is an abandonment of the fundamental principle which Ibsen over and over again emphatically expressed — namely, that any symbolism his work might be found to contain was entirely incidental, and subordinate to the truth and consistency of his picture of life. Here . . . without any suggestion of the supernatural, we are confronted with the wholly impossible, the inconceivable. How remote is this alike from his principles of art and from the consistent, unvarying practice of his better years! So great is the chasm between *John Gabriel Borkman* and *When We Dead Awaken* that one could almost suppose his mental breakdown to have preceded instead of followed the writing of the latter play.

At the end of the nineteenth century and the beginning of the twentieth, *When We Dead Awaken*, like Shakespeare's last romances, seemed to present the evidence of the playwright's aesthetic and intellectual deterioration because an increasing complexity of language and visual image accompanied an unexpected simplification of referential detail and an apparent inattention to notions of plausibility. Ibsen's final play seemed to Archer to be a failure because the text was not vulnerable to the critical strategies he valued. Archer could not respond positively to a text that appeared to subordinate character and situation to language.

Archer's introduction was published seven years after the eighteen-year-old James Joyce confronted this central aesthetic problem in his review of a production of Ibsen's final play. Joyce's essay has achieved a kind of retrospective fame in its anticipation of a revaluation of Ibsen that would not take place in academic studies until almost mid-century. As the novelist's first published writing, this article holds interest both as a contribution to Ibsen criticism and as a significant document in Joyce studies. While his critical insights develop slowly as he performs a rather orthodox analysis of the characters and action, his discussion culminates in a paragraph in which the simplicity of his statement almost obscures Joyce's surprising rejection of conventional mimetic theory: "Ibsen's plays do not depend for their interest on the action, or on the incidents. Even the characters, faultlessly drawn though they be, are not the first thing in his plays. But the naked drama — either the perception of a great truth, or the opening up of a great question, or a great conflict which is almost independent of the conflicting actors, and has been and is of far-reaching importance — that is what primarily rivets our attention." Joyce suggests that the primary object of aesthetic communication in Ibsen's drama is the interaction of perceptions, presented through the convention of characters who fulfill the function of housing or grounding this conceptual dynamic. The characters, and their behavior, are not significant in themselves but operate as instruments to embody these sudden, illuminating recognitions.

Joyce's youthful essay offers no theory to explain how the "perception of a great truth" or the "opening up of a great question" actually functions "almost independent" of the presentation of characters. Joyce does claim that the conceptual complexity of such a drama operates more successfully in performance than in a text that is read, re-read, and "pondered." Joyce's sense of the difference between the experience of confronting these illuminations in the theater and pondering them in the study provides one of the most important points of the essay. Joyce proposes that the performance of Ibsen succeeds not because of its cohesive, unified explica-tion of a concept or ideology, nor because of the authenticity of its representation of human experience, but because the performance is the vehicle for the confrontation with ideas or perceptions — sudden insights that do not necessarily add up to a highly integrated argument or fully realized representation. Here Joyce anticipates the nonmimetic course that criticism would take later in the twentieth century although he does not, like those who defined the nonmimetic nature of Ibsen's drama, see a cohesive sub-structure that orders the work in a nonrepresentational form. It is not surprising that James Joyce, as a young man concerned with writing itself, would perceive the dramatic text nonmimetically since the practice of fiction and drama, with painting and sculpture, was at this very moment being released from the traditional obligation to hold the mirror up to nature. It would be almost a generation before criticism freed itself from the notions of character and action as the mimetic objects of writing.

The separate histories of critical theory and experimental fiction and drama intersect in curious but understandable correspondences. At the end of the nineteenth century, Edward Dowden, A. C. Bradley, and others approached the Shakespearean text with an interest in the representation of human behavior that coincided with the importance of psychological motivation in the emerging realism that marked the new drama of this period.[11] A generation later the New Criticism, which self-consciously attacked Bradley's method of character study, emphasized the operation of the unconscious in the creative process and thereby showed itself to be responding to concepts of representation more related to the avant-garde literary and theatrical practices of symbolism, expressionism, and surrealism than to the kind of realism practiced in the late nineteenth century by Ibsen and others. When painting, sculpture, fiction, and drama abandoned representation as the principal objective of art, criticism needed to develop analytic strategies that discovered significance in aesthetic processes other than imitation. Expressionism and surrealism provoked theorists to find aesthetic value in non-literal processes; and, consequently, criticism also began to address texts that were previously considered representational with a different critical language.

In a passage I quote more fully below, Hugh Kenner's phrase, "superficially thorough documentation," voices the attitude of those who see the language of the text as a surface that both hides and discloses layers of significance that underlie the explicit meaning of its language. Joyce, before his own experimentation with nonmimetic uses of languages, saw the nonliteral functions of Ibsen's drama before professional critics identified them. The avant-garde theatre of the 1890s, also on the edge of experimentation that would explode the conventions of realism, identified Ibsen as a practicing symbolist even before he wrote the controversial *When We Dead Awaken*. But in the major documents of Ibsen criticism, the image of Ibsen the realist held relatively firm, with some exceptions such as Joyce's youthful essay, until after World War II. However, in production, the conflict between Ibsen the realist and Ibsen the symbolist emerged as early as 1893, only two years after Shaw framed his definition of Ibsen's realism cited above. Naturalism and realism dominated the avant-garde theater of France and Germany only briefly, and Lugné-Poe's defection from Antoine's *Théâtre Libre* to develop the symbolist program of the *Théâtre de l'Oeuvre* illustrates the rapidity with which the experimental theater of the 1890s shifted into anti-realistic modes of production. Ibsen's texts were vulnerable to conflicting visions of their representational nature in the theater even before this question became a major issue in criticism.

In 1951, Kenner confronted the problematic relationship of Ibsen,

Joyce, realism, and symbol. Kenner's essay focuses on the significance, to both Ibsen and Joyce, of the artist-myth, the thematic centrality of vocation. His argument suggests that the Irish novelist's affinity for Ibsen is the result of Joyce's ability to perceive that Ibsen's use of realistic detail is not, as the Ibsenites thought, to speak the truth about social conditions, but, rather, to reveal the drama of man's grappling with the significant issues of modern life. According to this essay, Joyce identifies with Ibsen's use of realistic detail both as an instrument of symbolism and as an aspect of the ironic play between knowledge and incomprehensibility:

> It ought to be said that for the mature artist the use of the "naturalist" convention will invariably involve and permit an irony of this kind, because of the insistent indication, beneath the superficially thorough documentation, of what is being left. Joyce and Ibsen display this irony on inspection, though it will scarcely carry its full weight to a reader unable to realize their implications, in the charged handling of language, of what a very different convention, like the Shakespearean, would permit.

Kenner's article, which was published in *Sewanee Review*, the principal organ of American New Criticism, identifies itself with the new critical strategies in its use of T. S. Eliot and its reference to L. C. Knights' essay, "How Many Children Had Lady Macbeth?", one of the first volleys of the New Criticism's attack on Bradley's literal sense of Shakespearean character. Kenner's invocation of Knights' facetious article suggests that Archer's critique of *When We Dead Awaken* is as conceptually inadequate in its discussion of Ibsen as Bradley's hyper-mimetic criticism of Shakespeare.

Critical Essays on Henrik Ibsen includes Joyce's provocative article on Ibsen's last play, Archer's critical introduction, and Kenner's New Critical response to both. While these essays provide ideas useful to the study of Ibsen's plays, they also demonstrate that Ibsen studies, like commentary on any major writer, constitutes a highly self-referential body of writing in which individual critics see and identify themselves in relationship to earlier interpretators. Joyce's article, which would have remained an obscure bibliographic item if its young author had not become one of the principal experimental writers of his generation, has become a critical emblem. Those who emphasize Ibsen's poetic vision and diminish the significance of his realistic style often hoist their quotations from Joyce to exhibit the supreme modernist's affinity for Ibsen and, thereby, support their own rhetorical strategy.

Kenner's application of the principles of New Criticism was not atypical of the moment. In the period immediately following the Second World War, the dramas of Ibsen were subjected to the strategies of analysis that the New Criticism had evolved, principally, at least, in close readings of the Shakespearean text in the 1930s and 1940s. In fact, Muriel Bradbrook, whose primary work centered on Shakespeare and Renaissance Drama, published a study of Ibsen in 1946 that demonstrates the impact of the New Criticism on Ibsen studies. The conclusion of *Ibsen the Norwegian: a Revaluation* discusses the final lines from *The Wild Duck*: "The examination of such a passage serves to shew that close reading can still extract new meanings from Ibsen, such as are characteristic of poetry rather than of prose. It is the poetic quality of his imagination which offers, to the actor and to the attentive reader alike, an opportunity to enter the work and relive it from within; thus, by an ever-renewed act of creation, making it into something that is reborn with each occasion."[12] Shaw saw the performance of an Ibsen text as the reflective surface of an image of the spectator's reality. Bradbrook focused upon the kind of experience the language of the text can provide for the actor and the reader—significantly *not* the spectator—as his or her imagination penetrates, processes, and appropriates that language. The opposition between the concept of the language of the text as reflective surface and the image of that language as a surface to be penetrated and appropriated by the reader defines the clear difference between the mimetic criticism of the late nineteenth and early twentieth century and the New Criticism.

The conflict between the image of Ibsen the realist and Ibsen the poet provided the principal problem of Ibsen criticism at the middle of our century. While the nonmimetic direction of criticism in the last fifty years has attempted to drive the image of Ibsen the realist out of Ibsen studies, the playwright's seminal contribution to the development of realism as a mode of dramatic writing and performance has complicated the project of constructing the image of Ibsen as a maker of theatrical poetry. From *Pillars of the Community* through *John Gabriel Borkman*, Ibsen exploited the developing scenographic resources of the theater and the potential for referentiality in dramatic language to posit an aesthetic image that appeared to correspond to the world of his spectator's experience. That is, the physical spaces his fictional characters inhabit, the objects they use, the clothes they wear, the language they speak, clarify the socioeconomic coordinates in which they live, the familial and sexual relationships they exercise, and the intellectual and emotional strategies they employ in conceptualizing their experience. Each of these facets of the representation displays itself in relationship to the intended spectator's conception of the normative, presenting itself as typical or exceptional according to the received scale of values that underlay the social system at this given moment. Each reference to categories the spectator would recognize—and the accumulated patterns of reference—works to build images of character and place that the spectator may situate within his or her understanding of social reality. Recall Bernard Shaw's claim that Ibsen developed a veridical image that reflects back the form and substance of the spectator—"ourselves in our own situations."

For those critics who see the Ibsen text as a highly complex but subtly unified structure of images, the presence of that veridical image is a source of embarrassment, and the detail of Ibsen's "superficially thorough documentation" must be justified on grounds other than verisimilitude. Consequently, those who read Ibsen primarily in terms of the structure of his imagery have attempted in some way to excuse or to explain the presence of the referential details of late nineteenth century realism. John Northam's ground-breaking study, *Ibsen's Dramatic Method*, moves from textual analysis to the consideration of the metaphoric quality of Ibsen's use of scenography and properties. Northam's perceptive understanding of the theatrical function of scene and objects in Ibsen anticipates the more theoretically self-conscious analyses of the semiotics of theatrical performance. Northam's interpretations do not deny the realistic mode but suggest its vulnerability to the signifying processes of visual and textual metaphor. Inga-Stina Ewbank's essay, "Ibsen's Dramatic Language as a Link between His 'Realism' and His 'Symbolism,' " brilliantly demonstrates that the individual realistic detail emphasized in individual speeches functions as a dramatic image that simultaneously contributes to both the realistic surface and the poetic substructure: "Ibsen's language takes us under the photographic surface of realism; in which it helps us to see *through* the literal superstructure to the inner dramatic form of the play, through the physical landscape into a spiritual one." Ewbank focuses upon the idea of perception, however, and — like Joyce — sees the image of character as secondary to representation of conflicting visions of reality. The development of the analytic strategies of close reading gave Professor Ewbank the methodological tools to examine that process, critical strategies that didn't exist for Joyce.

My own discussion of Ibsen's realism in *Henrik Ibsen: The Divided Consciousness* claims that the demands of realism to make the individual symbol plausible forced Ibsen to invest the metaphoric detail with amplified meaning: ". . . the multiplicity of detail, especially in the re-creation of an illusion of natural environment which realism demands, affected the development of Ibsen's language, making his imagery assume a narrower focus. In that increased specificity, each individual image informed the larger metaphoric structure more richly, giving the inner structure a greater density and scope." The implication here, of course, is that the pressures of the newly forged conventions of realism forced Ibsen to ground his basic metaphoric structure in rich contextual detail that, in turn, invested those images with amplified significance. In other words, the stringencies of realism disciplined the playwright's language.

The differences in the ways in which Ibsen's text has been interpreted develops, as this essay has already suggested, from a diversity of ideas about language itself. Shaw assumed, with some confidence, that dramatic language has the power to articulate a clearly perceived vision of experience. The next generation of Ibsen commentators saw the text as a matrix that suspends multiple perceptions that do not align themselves in a single vision but, rather, in their simultaneity, refuse to be unequivocal. In this sense, dramatic language does not communicate a comprehensive perception of experience but a dynamic interplay of ideas. To experience the play, in the theater or in the study, is to confront its language as an opacity, an obscurity, a puzzle that yields its multiple significance only through the processes of identifying patterns of relationship between the concrete and the metaphoric. The interpretative strategies of Shaw and Archer demand intelligent but not analytic reading; the mandate they impose upon the reader or spectator is to attend to the text or performance as a descriptive or ideological statement. The influential Marxian critic, Georg Lukács, who—like Shaw—believed in the possibility that language can represent objective reality, does not see the text as a statement but rather as an instrument of analysis that both reflects and mediates the social relations that constitute the principal component of reality.

While Lukács was drawn to the dramas of Henrik Ibsen, which he found superior to the other literature of this moment, he declared these plays to be admirable but "problematic." He based his critique upon his identification of two apparent failures in Ibsen's writing—one structural and one ideological. Lukács's formal criticism of the Norwegian playwright derives from his clear differentiation between the structural possibilities of the historical novel and the historical drama. The potential for detail in the novel, which allows an extended examination of the relationship of character and social situation, provides an opportunity for the novelist to represent the dynamic interaction between the forces of the social world and the ordinary individual. Lukács's famous essay on historical drama, part of which is included in this collection, argues that "world historical figures," whose willed action embodies and exemplifies those forces, should remain on the periphery of the novel. In the economy of drama, that kind of exploration cannot take place because there is insufficient time to use the minutiae of detail that would represent the impact of the socioeconomic situation upon the ordinary individual. The form of drama demands the theatrical representation of the collision of social forces as specific actions that embody the wills of "world historical individuals:" ". . . the fully developed, plastic personality of the 'world historical individual' . . . is portrayed in such a way that he not only finds an immediate and complete expression for his personality in the deed evoked in the collision—without losing or weakening in the least either his personality or its immediacy."

Lukács recognized that this simplification of the hero's psychology and, even more significantly, the abstraction of the social forces at play, caused the playwright "to do violence to important manifestations of life which are closely connected with his heroes' psychology and the nature of his collisions for the sake of dramatic form." He believed that playwrights who, like Ibsen, are concerned with the nature of their own time, wrote characters and placed them in situations that are more appropriate to the novel. He focused upon the scene in which Rebekka West confesses to

Rosmer that she willed Beate's suicide, that over an extended period of time she gradually came to realize that she desired the woman's death and could not force herself to take the necessary steps to prevent it. Lukács argued that the material Ibsen used could never become a real drama because Rebekka's will could not be presented as a single action that expresses her character, but, instead, voices itself in a narrative that describes a series of psychological gestures that constitute the interaction between her desire and Beate's will.

Peter Szondi expanded Lukács's critique of Ibsen's novelistic technique in a work that has not been translated into English, *Theorie des Modernen Dramas.* This discussion, translated for this collection, begins with Lukács's notation of the difference between the representation of time in Sophocles and Ibsen. In the Lukács-Szondi argument, the analytical structure of Sophocles's drama exercises a moment of recognition, the Aristotelian *anagnorisis*, in which the hero confronts the truth of the past which is fully present as "objective nature." In Ibsen, however, truth— which has no objective presence that equates with the unequivocal facts of Oedipus's history— manifests itself only within the subjectivity of introspection. Ibsen's characters, who find their identity primarily through their idiosyncratic perception, cannot survive the exposure of their idea of truth because that conceptual structure disintegrates when it becomes objectified in shared language. These characters can only survive by transforming subjective truth into the "*consumptive* 'life-lie.' " The representation of this psychological process would be appropriate to the novel which can detail the mental processes of its characters. According to Szondi, when Ibsen attempted to make the exposure of his characters' secret lives dramatic through dialogue, he was forced to dramatize their movement into death because their being could not survive this exposure.

Lukács's later criticism of *The Wild Duck* bases itself upon his description of the ways in which the increasingly decadent voices of capitalism had appropriated, on a superficial level, the idealism of the revolutionary spirit. Lukács believed that Ibsen's embodiment of the exploitative capitalist class, Grosserer Werle and his cynical bride, Fru Sorby, achieved the kind of marriage, based upon truth and honesty, that the idealist son, Gregers, wishes for Hjalmar and Gina. His essay quotes Marx's statement that the function of comedy is to allow humanity to part with its past *cheerfully*, and the argument suggests that Ibsen, despite his own criticism of Gregers Werle, was unable to free himself sufficiently from the "contents of Gregers Werle's proclamations" and, therefore, was unable to represent this character in the rich comic form that the character's anachronistic idealism deserves.

Lukács's perception of the ideological failure of this play forced him to see its symbolism as superficial. The symbols of the wild duck and the garret, in his opinion, constitute an aesthetic attempt to unify and to resolve an ideological conflict that the play cannot solve. The metaphoric language of the play, resounding with images of the forest, sea, and mythical voyages, does not, in Lukács's opinion, constitute the surface layer of a complex substructure but, rather, a superficial network that imposes a unity upon a representation of reality that the content of Ibsen's drama has not adequately realized.

Lukács and Szondi find Ibsen problematic for the reason that critics like James E. Kerans, James Hurt, and Charles R. Lyons find his plays fascinating. Those who read the texts as the exploration or manifestation of psychic processes see the literal action and language of these dramas as either the displacement or the physical enactment of highly subjective conceptual or psychic paradigms. In these discussions of Ibsen, we confront ideas of human behavior, notions of the function of representation, and conceptions of the nature of dramatic language that differ radically from the assumptions of Ibsen's Marxian critics. Because Lukács and Szondi saw human behavior as both the manifestation and the consequence of a social process, they believed that drama should represent human action as the manifestation of a social dynamic—not presenting characters as the victims of their history but as plausible images of an intricate interaction between individual will and the objective truth of social relations. The psychoanalytic and phenomenological perspectives put the idea of *objective truth* within quotation marks. While the objective world has presence, it can be known, perceived, experienced— and, hence, represented—only through the subjective processes of the human mind. Even if an aesthetic work, like a text by Ibsen, presents itself within the conventions of what we call realism, the work exercises those conventions to produce an enigmatic artifact that must be processed by the reader or spectator. The Freudian would claim that the unconscious voices itself only through the puzzle, the enigma, the text as equivalent to dream. The unconscious, where actual determination exists, has no language that the consciousness can understand and, therefore, must speak through the agency of the symbol. Kerans's essay, exercising these assumptions, offers a Freudian reading of *Little Eyolf* that isolates the processes in which the content of the unconscious surfaces in the representation of speech and action. Hurt articulates a substructure that derives from R. D. Laing's psychoanalytic analysis of the schizoid personality. Lyons relates the Ibsenian triad—the man and two women—to a model that encompasses the hero's failure to contain phenomenological experience within a comprehensive vision of a reality. Here the image of the hero divides between the desire to engage with experience and the antithetical desire to fix reality, and personal identity, within a formal vision. Neither Kerans, Hurt, nor Lyons would deny the vitality of Ibsen's representation of character and situation, but they do not see these dramatic figures as the principal objects of representation. From their perspectives, Ibsen's dramatic figures function as the means by which a paradigmatic dramatic conflict, realized in metaphoric language, works itself out.

In the last thirty years, serious attention has been directed to Ibsen's dramatic structure. Essays in this collection represent several of these valuable formal studies. P. F. D. Tennant's clear and articulate chapter on exposition from *Ibsen's Dramatic Technique* has facilitated later studies that examine the affective voice of the past in Ibsen's drama. I have already noted the significance of John Northam's discussion of the functional value of scene and properties in *Ibsen's Dramatic Method.* Daniel Haakonsen's essay, which uses the model of the overheard conversation between Oswald and Regine as a play-within-a-play, outlines the potential significance of moments that appear to reenact the past and defines this model as an Ibsenian structural convention.

Oliver Gerland's essay, published for the first time here, adapts Haakonsen's idea of the reenactment of the past as a play-within-a-play. He focuses on Rubek's narrative descriptions of the statuary group that the public perceives as his masterpiece. The sculpture itself, of course, is not present on the stage, and the audience has access to its image only through the language that describes it. Rubek uses his detailed, spoken image of the sculpture as the centerpiece of the narrative account of his history. In Gerland's terms, that narrative, of course, provides his self-identification and yet confines him within the limits of that definition. Gerland discusses Rubek's action in the third act as an attempt to reenact the narrative contained in the description of the statuary group and, in that reenactment, to revise his image of himself in relationship to Irene. Rubek wishes to alter the relationship that is fixed first in the marble of the sculpture and then in the language in which he describes and conceptualizes that absent object. Gerland defines Rubek's narrative account of the statue and his new image of the self as *texts* that the character *writes* and in which he is bound. This essay, which uses some of the rhetorical strategies of post-structuralism, bridges, in some sense, mimetic criticism and the current formalistic examination of dramatic language. This discussion of *When We Dead Awaken* does examine representation even if it deals with representation as the rhetorical / psychological strategy in which Ibsen reveals the character inventing himself.

Clearly Ibsen criticism was freed by the nonmimetic or nonliteral approaches to the text, and this freedom has increased our understanding of the processes in which the verbal and visual languages of the texts convey meaning. However, despite the work of the New Critical, psychoanalytic, phenomenological, and formalist studies of Ibsen, we need to continue our interrogation of Ibsen's plays. What we do not understand as well as we should is the interaction of nonmimetic systems of signification and the basic conventions of dramatic realism. At this point in the history of Ibsen criticism we need to consider more thoroughly the function of the realistic style through which these textual and visual images voice themselves. Ibsen's plays may, indeed, perform an inner psychic drama as they reenact an Oedipal crisis or manifest the processes of consciousness in which the self constructs, revises, and destroys its image of itself. The plays may also voice the principal ideological issues of the moment of their origin, and — in Joyce's terms — burst forth with sudden illuminations free of their realistic form. However, the dramas from *Pillars of the Community* through *John Gabriel Borkman* ground themselves, through specific references, to the concrete geographic, sociological, historical, and psychological schemes by which the late nineteenth century perceived and discussed itself. While we no longer consider the literal surface to be the *complete* text, Ibsen's drama operates as drama through the representation of a fictional world that, by careful use of correlative detail, points self-consciously to the moment in time it shares with its original audience. We need to understand more fully the aesthetic processes involved in the representation of a fictional world that sets itself up to be perceived as the equivalent to the world immediately outside of the theater.

One of the problems of the criticism that discusses the poetic value of Ibsen's language is that, as it focuses upon the individual image or metaphoric complex, the analysis does not deal with the overriding stylistic convention of realism itself. The realistic style constitutes an aesthetic ground that holds the individual detail in a framework and allows the word or image to function referentially both within the realistic style and as a metaphor. Ibsen criticism needs to explore the ways in which that aesthetic ground signifies as a whole and not merely as a framework for individual images. In many ways, the nonmimetic critical strategies of the past fifty years have played themselves out, and criticism will now undoubtedly move toward a more informed sense of mimesis, although A. B. Nuttall's *A New Mimesis: Shakespeare and the Representation of Reality* seems more a restatement of a sentimentalized Bradleian approach than a new vision of the function of representation and does not give us useful strategies for dealing with the texts of Ibsen (or Shakespeare).[13] The kind of mimetic criticism that would be healthy at the moment would — first of all — confront the conventionality of Ibsen's plays, the various dramatic techniques and strategies he borrows or develops, and relate these aesthetic processes to the hypothetical realities from which the plays were originally witnessed.

E. H. Gombrich's formal analysis of representation in painting has influenced literary and theatrical studies in the clarity of his definition of the conventionality of aesthetic perception.[14] Gombrich examines the relationship between matching (attempting to duplicate what the eye sees) and making (developing an independent artifact). Gombrich's discussion isolates the differences between the processes in which the eye reads the natural scene and its representation in painting. He focuses upon the development of formal schemes — which both painters and viewers learn through experiencing art — that provide the illusion that the created artifact is a representation. The representational value of the object, in other words, depends upon its use of specific conventions that the beholder has learned to "read" as directly imitative of the real. The New Criticism believed the criticism of Archer and Shaw to be naive because the Ibsenites did not see through the literal text to the poetic. At this point, of course, we see the mimetic claims of Ibsenism as naive because they did not recognize that the conventions of realism are not approximations to *real life* but, rather, technical strategies that organize the presentation of dramatic images differently but not, necessarily, more truthfully. At this point in Ibsen studies, we should be able to return to the subject of realism as a formal issue and address, more substantially, the aesthetic processes by which an image that appears veridical operates in the theater. We should be able to do this, as well, with the skepticism of distance — the distance achieved by time and the distance achieved by our realization that both the fictive world of Ibsen's plays and the conceptions of reality held by his original audience are cultural phenomena.

Because drama depends upon the actual presence of human figures in space and time, it has always seemed the most mimetic of the arts. The basic medium of the playwright is the representation of human behavior, and speech, of course, provides the primary form of behavior imitated by the dramatist. Playwrights create images of human consciousness through speech as the actors' language reveals their perception of the scene they inhabit and other figures within that scene, and develops self-conscious images of themselves in a physical and social environment. The economy of the dramatic form, its relative brevity in relation to epic or novel, forces the playwright to create images of character that are metonymic as Lukács points out. The spectator or reader forms these significant fragments into wholes by a process of extrapolation. For example, Ibsen's oblique references to Solness's past — his exploitation of Aline's family property, his feelings of guilt for the death of the infant twins, and his voiced perception of the image of his guilt as an open wound — constitute details that the spectator unifies in an extrapolated image of the socioeconomic and psychological complexities of the character's history. Ibsen's realistic style, built from specific referential language, stimulates the spectator to process the image of character in relationship to socioeconomic situations and, as well, to theories of psychological determinism. In other words, the style — which provides the spectator with the material to use in the process of constructing whole images from metonymic fragments — determines the kind of extrapolation to be performed.

As the physical body of the actor and his behavior substitutes for the playwright's image of *character* so the physical stage and its scenographic elements substitute for the place of that fictional world. After some experience with dramatic performance, the spectator realizes, at some level of consciousness, that each production establishes its terms of representation, or type of substitutions, and will, within those terms, relate that substitute to the place for which it stands — be that scene an image of fantasy, an image of the typical or general, or an image of an actual site. Even when the body of the actor, or a part of the actor, is the only object illuminated — as in Beckett's *Not I* or *That Time* — the physical distance between actor and spectator creates an image of space that remains external to the dramatic figure even if that space functions as void. That division embodies the idea of separation between perceiving subject and object, between *here,* the space the spectator occupies, and *there,* the dramatic space that holds the figure. The significance of the dramatic space may come from the value assigned to it by the character, but it remains a tangible place that is delineated by the perception of the spectator who perceives it both as the arena in which the actor performs and the fictional scene in which the character exists. It is rare when the scene makes no reference, visually or through the spoken perception of character, to one or more of the perceptual schemes by which we conceptualize an image of place and, thereby, give it significance beyond location. Ibsen's scenic references, of course, point toward the schemes by which his original spectators perceived their own social and physical environments.

In a deliberate attempt to counter the conventions of dramatic realism, Bertolt Brecht wrote theatrical judgments of contemporary socio-political situations by dramatizing a hypothetically removed historical world. He forced his spectators to process the dramatic image and to isolate principles from the represented history that they could, in turn, apply self-consciously to the present. Brecht's mode of presentation, which points out the temporal difference and ideological similarity between the historical period depicted and the present, forces his spectators to see the performance as an analogue rather than a representation. Dramatic realism, which Brecht's form counters, does not appear to communicate through analogy or metaphor but, rather, by the establishment of a world that duplicates or substitutes, as a hypothetical equivalent, for the world of the spectator's experience. Spectators will always situate the actor / character and the scene he or she inhabits in relationship to their own perceived reality. When that relationship approaches coincidence — that is, when the sense of discrepancy between the hypothetical reality of experience and the hypothetical world of the play dissolves — dramatic realism as a theatrical phenomenon operates. The original audiences of Ibsen's realistic plays must have perceived the human, architectural, and decorative images on the stage not as analogues or metaphors that needed to be translated in order to perceive the object of representation but, rather, as theatrical substitutes for corresponding objectivities within their experience that were directly apprehensible. In that sense, the realistic style does not demand that the spectator see through the dramatic performance to some hidden, essential event that forms the true subject. The realistic style pretends that the images on stage do not constitute a highly mediated vision of reality but a presentation of raw data that the spectators process much as they assimilate the data of experience itself. As Gombrich points out, this notion of the truthfulness of representation is an illusion, but the pretense itself is a convention.

In order to break through the literal surface of Ibsen's language, dramatic criticism had to ignore the mimetic function in order to clarify the ways in which the text sets up its systems of imagery. Frequently, however, critics read Ibsen's metaphoric language as allegorical, and their analysis divorced the language from its theatrical context.[15] Ibsen's metaphoric paradigms — built of images of heights and depths, forests and seas, vocation and sacrifice — are not, as certain critics have claimed, the aesthetic representation of a meta-reality. They are, rather, the conceptual schemes with which the characters think, and Ibsen's dramatic figures act out, self-consciously, behavior that embodies these paradigms. Ibsen drew his topographical schemes from the landscape of Norway, and it is important for us to see that these spatial coordinates do not function in the realistic dramas as discrete metaphors. They function as aspects of the physical reality the characters perceive; and the playwright develops the images of their consciousness by showing the processes in which they use these spatial coordinates metaphorically. In *The Master Builder*, the off-stage tower that Solness climbs is neither symbol nor metaphor; the tower is, simply, a tower — a strange addition to a house that the text makes plausible by references to Solness's previous projects and the uniqueness of this new building that synthesizes earlier architectural forms for him. Solness and Hilde — and to a lesser degree Aline and Ragnar — use the presence and nature of the tower metaphorically. For example, Hilde and Solness appropriate the relationship of the tower and the quarry to their idiosyncratic and subjective conceptual image of height and depth so that Solness's ascent aligns with their fantasy of escape to a fictive kingdom, enacts Hilde's imperative that Solness free himself from a sickly conscience, and — paradoxically — both embodies and prohibits the eroticism of their relationship. Hilde's insistence upon the ascent as a triumph — both before and after the fall, stimulates the audience to read the positive aspects of the paradigm. Ragnar's insistence upon the reality of the fall and Solness's death in the quarry forces the audience to confront the destructive and, perhaps, suicidal aspect of Solness's act. What is present at the conclusion of *The Master Builder* is a mixture of perceptions, each of which interprets the value of the physical object of the tower and Solness's ascent. Ibsen's text establishes a scene that creates an illusion of objectivity. That illusion is conveyed by the phenomenon of individual characters voicing different perceptions of reality. Specifically, we see them interpret the value of the tower, Solness's ascent, and his fall as the behavioral fulfillment of different conceptual paradigms. Consequently, Ibsen presents Solness's death as neither triumph nor defeat but as an action perceived as both. The tower does not function as either symbol or metaphor that unifies these antithetical perceptions into an aesthetic synthesis. While the representation of reality is hardly the assembling of unmediated, unstructured material, the formal presentation attempts to obscure the aesthetic mechanisms that select and emphasize the significant details and points of focus.

As I have suggested, Ibsen's realistic style deals with two hypothetical worlds: the world of the created fiction and the spectator's *perceived* reality, the world constituted by his or her understanding. While the writer may extend or refine the spectator's perception, he works within the general scientific, historical, psychological, and sociological beliefs of the moment. What the spectator perceives as *reality* is, of course, a transitive hypothesis that is subject to the sequence of discoveries and re-mappings that mark our understanding of the natural, physical, and social sciences. Consequently, as a dramatic mode, realism as realism "holds in perfection but a little moment." The phenomenon of illusory coincidence between these two hypothetical realities may not occur when key ontological assumptions change. In 1987 we perceive Ibsen's characters as figures who are constrained by the coordinates of their, not our, moment in history. When a realistic play is revived even one generation later, the received psychological principles that the spectators apply to the dramatic characters may differ markedly from the assumptions the playwright counted upon in creating images of individual yet typical psyches. In the same light, the accepted norms of behavior, which manifest the social covenants of one generation, may seem either peculiar or quaint to succeeding generations. At the present we look at Ibsen's realistic plays as historical rather than realistic, although they are not "historical drama" in Lukács's sense of the representation of "world historical figures." We view the play as the reproduction of a historical moment, perceiving the characters of that moment as distanced, as participants in a self-contained epoch that our sense of history differentiates from the present. And, as well, when the two hypothetical realities no longer coincide, the aesthetic mechanisms of representation become more obvious. Erich Auerbach examines these issues in *Mimesis*:

> Ibsen's masterly dramatic technique, his unerring conduct of the action, and his sharp outlining of his characters — especially of some of his women — carried away the public. The impression he made was very great, especially in Germany, where the naturalistic movement of 1890 revered him as a master on an equality with Zola, where his plays were excellently produced by the best theaters, and where the remarkable renewal of the drama which took place at that time is in general linked to his name. Through the complete transformation of the social status of the bourgeoisie since 1914 and in general through the upheavals brought about by the current world crisis, his problems have lost their timeliness and we can now better see how calculated and contrived his art often is. Yet it remains to his credit that he accomplished the historic task of giving a style to the serious bourgeois drama: a problem which had been

pending since the *comedie larmoyante* of the eighteenth century and which he was the first to solve. It is his misfortune, though perhaps it is also in a small degree due to him, that the bourgeoisie has changed beyond recognition.[16]

Auerbach's comment reinforces the point I suggest immediately above: that dramatic realism sustains no half-life as realism but metamorphoses into historical drama when its details no longer refer to correspondences in the spectator's experience. We may find more lasting value in Ibsen's plays than Auerbach does, but his statement forces us to confront the fact that the social, political, and behavioral images represented in Ibsen's realistic plays do not coincide with our world but, rather, form a discrete set of phenomena, distanced by time, that can be examined and judged. We may, however, experience the plays — in text or performance — as models of a particular set of repressions imposed upon the human figures by the historical moment. Inga-Stina Ewbank reveals the potential advantages of this kind of questioning in a speculative and provocative essay on "Ibsen and the Language of Women," which, while not reprinted in the collection itself, is recommended in the Selected Bibliography.[17] Professor Ewbank documents Ibsen's exploration of the image of woman through an examination of the potentialities and limitations of the language he gives his female characters. Ewbank's discussion uses notions of language derived from socio-linguistics exercised with careful attention to the dramatic functions of Ibsen's language. This essay provides a useful foundation for a study of the differences between the language of men and the language of women in Ibsen's plays, the limitations imposed upon his male and female speakers, and the representational value of Ibsen's sparse dialogue. Ewbank finds Ibsen's language representational in the sense of its being a deliberate imitation of cultural or societal restraints.

Clearly we need to understand more fully the processes in which Ibsen explored the conflict between his character's desire for freedom and the limitations of the language his characters were forced to use. We need to clarify the methods by which Ibsen demonstrates that language is not so much the instrument of communication or the expression of the mind as it is the agency of the social, ideological, and psychological determinants that direct its grammar, its range of subjects, and the forms in which the speaker may implement his or her subjectivity.

Our evaluation and analysis of these texts can speculate about the coincidence they once established between the dramatic scene and their specific historical moment. We need to consider, once again, that Ibsen self-consciously exercised the theater's potential for establishing an aesthetic equivalent to reality — in the physical representation of place and human behavior. The fictional world established in the original performance of Ibsen's realistic plays at one point functioned as a kind of reflective substitute for the world of the spectator's experience, reflective both in the sense of mirroring and thoughtfully considering. The performance of an Ibsen play must have established a provocative and seductive representation, the apparent aesthetic substitute for the world of the spectator's reality that excited George Bernard Shaw. While we have moved beyond the literalness of Shaw's vision, we can use his comments to document the power and seductiveness of Ibsen's realistic style when that style was fresh and innovative. The Ibsen play clearly engaged the imagination by offering itself as a possible conceptual construct that would locate and identify the self in a comprehensible reality, a reality that points outward, in reference, to the world of the spectator's experience and yet is confined within the limits of the objective reality of the stage, held within the spatial and temporal limits of performance.

The most important project for the next stage of Ibsen criticism is, as I have suggested earlier, a study of the realistic style that he defined — a reexamination of the mimetic value the plays held in their own moment. Even if we identify what Kerans calls the "affective substructure," we reach that body of concepts through the particular displacements of the realistic structure, displacements that are themselves at least partially determined by historical stringencies. Ibsen criticism needs to relate the larger conceptual paradigms to the realistic style in which they display themselves.

Other issues to be addressed relate to the project of understanding the mimetic function of Ibsen's dramas within the ideological and aesthetic perspectives of the late nineteenth century. We need to consider the hero's vocational projects as historically or culturally determined images of self-realization. Each of these self-defined missions intends to formulate a satisfying and comprehensive image of reality for its hero, and we need to see the force of cultural determination in the form those projects assume: the expression of the theological problem in *Brand*, for example, or the implicit political-philosophical content of Lovburg's history of the future and Allmers's treatise on responsibility, or the confrontation of the crisis of representation itself in Rubek's sculpture. These projects have presence, in performance, only as language, and we need to continue the probing of Ibsen's language as both an instrument of self-definition and also of societal constraint. We need to continue to explore the paradigmatic triad of the male and two women, not merely as the exploration of the psychic functions of the hero or the author, but as a model of sexuality that history has imposed upon both the writing and the reading of these texts. We need to work with the ways in which the texts themselves both voice these determinations and speak against them. That is, we need to continue our formal study of the plays and infuse that examination with a more comprehensive sense of the cultural forces that inform both these conventions and the practice of dramatic representation itself.

Charles R. Lyons

Stanford University

Notes

1. The most notable exception is Erich Auerbach, *Mimesis*, trans. Willard Trask (Princeton: Princeton University Press, 1953). Originally published in German (Berne: Francke, 1946). Herbert Lindenberger explains the affinity for this critical work among those practicing Anglo-American New Criticism on the basis of Auerbach's close readings and their ability to ignore his insistence on relating these analyses to specific cultural contexts. See "The Mimetic Bias in Modern Anglo-American Criticism," *Mimesis in Contemporary Theory: An Interdisciplinary Approach*, vol. 1, ed. Mihai Spariosu (Philadelphia: Benjamins, 1984), 1–26.

2. See, for example, G. Wilson Knight, "On the Principles of Shakespeare Interpretation," *The Wheel of Fire*, 5th ed. rev. (New York: Meridian, 1957), 1–16. Originally published by Oxford University Press, 1930.

3. French Phenomenological criticism worked itself out, to a large degree, in analyses of 17th century French drama. See, for example, Georges Poulet, *Etudes sur les temps humain* (Paris: Plon, 1956); Jean Starobinski, *L'Oeil vivant* (Paris: Gallimard, 1961); Roland Barthes, *Sur Racine* (Paris: Club Editions du Livre, 1960), trans. Richard Howard, *On Racine* (New York: Hill and Wang, 1964); See also J. Hillis Miller, *The Disappearance of God* (Cambridge: Harvard University Press, 1959); and Charles R. Lyons, *Henrik Ibsen: the Divided Consciousness* (Carbondale: Southern Illinois University Press, 1972).

4. See Norman Holland, *Psychoanalysis and Shakespeare* (New York: McGraw Hill, 1966) for a conventional Freudian perspective, and Jacques Lacan, *Speech in Language and Psychoanalysis*, trans. Anthony Wilden (Baltimore: Johns Hopkins University Press, 1968) for a Neo-Freudianism influenced by structuralism.

5. See Edward W. Said's discussion of structuralism, "Abecedarium Culturae," *Beginnings* (Baltimore: Johns Hopkins University Press, 1975), 227–343.

6. Roland Barthes, "The Death of the Author," *Image – Music – Text*, trans. Stephen Heath (New York: Hill and Wang, 1975), 142–48; Jacques Derrida, *Of Grammatology*, trans. Gayatri C. Spivak (Baltimore: Johns Hopkins University Press, 1976), 99–102.

7. A. D. Nuttall, *A New Mimesis: Shakespeare and the Representation of Reality* (London: Methuen, 1984).

8. In Ibsen studies Brian Downs represents this approach well in *Ibsen: The Intellectual Background* (Cambridge: Cambridge University Press, 1948). In Shakespeare scholarship Virgil K. Whitaker's *Shakespeare's Use of Learning* (San Marino: Huntington Library, 1953) exercises this method. A more recent example of the attempt to read the work of a literary figure through an external ideological structure would be Brian Johnston's efforts to document Ibsen's sequential use of Hegel's *Phenomenology of Spirit*.

9. See Herbert Lindenberger, "Toward a New History in Literary Study," *Profession 84* (New York: MLA, 1984), 16–23.

10. Kenneth Burke, "Terministic Screens," *Language as Symbolic Action* (Berkeley: University of California Press, 1968), 44–62.

11. Edward Dowden, *Shakespere: a Critical Study of his Mind and Art*, 3rd ed. rev. (New York: Harpers, 1900); A. C. Bradley, *Shakespearean Tragedy* (London: Macmillan, 1904).

12. M. C. Bradbrook, *Ibsen the Norwegian: a Revaluation*, 2nd. ed. rev. (Hamden: Archon, 1966), 158. Original ed. published in Great Britain, 1946.

13. See Nuttall note 7.

14. E. H. Gombrich, *Art and Illusion* (New York: Pantheon, 1960).

15. Brian Johnston, "The Metaphoric Structure of *The Wild Duck*," *Contemporary*

Approaches to Ibsen, vol. 1, ed. Daniel Haakonsen (Oslo: Universitetsforlaget, 1965–66), 72–95.

16. Auerbach, *Mimesis*, p. 459.

17. Inga-Stina Ewbank, "Ibsen and the Language of Women," *Women Writing and Writing about Women*, ed. Mary Jacobus (London: Croom Helm, 1979), 114–32.

Ibsen and the Ibsenites
The Perception of Ibsen's Realism by His Contemporaries

The Technical Novelty in Ibsen's Plays

George Bernard Shaw*

It is a striking and melancholy example of the preoccupation of critics with phrases and formulas to which they have given life by taking them into the tissue of their own living minds, and which therefore seem and feel vital and important to them whilst they are to everybody else the deadest and dreariest rubbish (this is the great secret of academic dryasdust), that to this day they remain blind to a new technical factor in the art of popular stage-play making which every considerable playwright has been thrusting under their noses night after night for a whole generation. This technical factor in the play is the discussion. Formerly you had in what was called a well made play an exposition in the first act, a situation in the second, and unravelling in the third. Now you have exposition, situation, and discussion; and the discussion is the test of the playwright. The critics protest in vain. They declare that discussions are not dramatic, and that art should not be didactic. Neither the playwrights nor the public take the smallest notice of them. The discussion conquered Europe in Ibsen's Doll's House; and now the serious playwright recognizes in the discussion not only the main test of his highest powers, but also the real centre of his play's interest. Sometimes he even takes every possible step to assure the public beforehand that his play will be fitted with that newest improvement.

This was inevitable if the drama was ever again to be raised above the childish demand for fables without morals. Children have a settled arbitrary morality: therefore to them moralizing is nothing but an intolerable platitudinizing. The morality of the grown-up is also very largely a settled morality, either purely conventional and of no ethical significance, like the rule of the road or the rule that when you ask for a yard of ribbon the shopkeeper shall give you thirty-six inches and not interpret the word yard as he pleases, or else too obvious in its ethics to leave any room for discussion: for instance, that if the boots keeps you waiting too long for your shaving water you must not plunge your razor

*From *The Quintessence of Ibsenism* (London: Faber, 1913), 171–84

into his throat in your irritation, no matter how great an effort of self-control your forbearance may cost you.

Now when a play is only a story of how a villain tries to separate an honest young pair of betrothed lovers; to gain the hand of the woman by calumny; and to ruin the man by forgery, murder, false witness, and other commonplaces of the Newgate Calendar, the introduction of a discussion would clearly be ridiculous. There is nothing for sane people to discuss; and any attempt to Chadbandize on the wickedness of such crimes is at once resented as, in Milton's phrase, "moral babble."

But this sort of drama is soon exhausted by people who go often to the theatre. In twenty visits one can see every possible change rung on all the available plots and incidents out of which plays of this kind can be manufactured. The illusion of reality is soon lost: in fact it may be doubted whether any adult ever entertains it: it is only to very young children that the fairy queen is anything but an actress. But at the age when we cease to mistake the figures on the stage for *dramatis personae*, and know that they are actors and actresses, the charm of the performer begins to assert itself; and the child who would have been cruelly hurt by being told that the Fairy Queen was only Miss Smith dressed up to look like one, becomes the man who goes to the theatre expressly to see Miss Smith, and is fascinated by her skill or beauty to the point of delighting in plays which would be unendurable to him without her. Thus we get plays "written round" popular performers, and popular performers who give value to otherwise useless plays by investing them with their own attractiveness. But all these enterprises are, commercially speaking, desperately precarious. To begin with, the supply of performers whose attraction is so far independent of the play that their inclusion in the cast sometimes makes the difference between success and failure is too small to enable all our theatres, or even many of them, to depend on their actors rather than on their plays. And to finish with, no actor can make bricks entirely without straw. From Grimaldi to Sothern, Jefferson, and Henry Irving (not to mention living actors) we have had players succeeding once in a lifetime in grafting on to a play which would have perished without them some figure imagined wholly by themselves; but none of them has been able to repeat the feat, nor to save many of the plays in which he has appeared from failure. In the long run nothing can retain the interest of the play-goer after the theatre has lost its illusion for his childhood, and its glamor for his adolescence, but a constant supply of interesting plays; and this is specially true in London, where the expense and trouble of theatre-going have been raised to a point at which it is surprising that sensible people of middle age go to the theatre at all. As a matter of fact, they mostly stay at home.

Now an interesting play cannot in the nature of things mean anything but a play in which problems of conduct and character of personal importance to the audience are raised and suggestively discussed. People have a thrifty sense of taking away something from such plays: they not only have had something for their money, but they retain that something as a permanent possession. Consequently none of the commonplaces of the box office hold good of such plays. In vain does the experienced acting manager declare that people want to be amused and not preached at in the theatre; that they will not stand long speeches; that a play must not contain more than 18,000 words; that it must not begin before nine nor last beyond eleven; that there must be no politics and no religion in it; that breach of these golden rules will drive people to the variety theatres; that there must be a woman of bad character, played by a very attractive actress, in the piece; and so on and so forth. All these counsels are valid for plays in which there is nothing to discuss. They may be disregarded by the playwright who is a moralist and a debater as well as a dramatist. From him, within the inevitable limits set by the clock and by the physical endurance of the human frame, people will stand anything as soon as they are matured enough and cultivated enough to be susceptible to the appeal of his particular form of art. The difficulty at present is that mature and cultivated people do not go to the theatre, just as they do not read penny novelets; and when an attempt is made to cater for them they do not respond to it in time, partly because they have not the habit of playgoing, and partly because it takes too long for them to find out that the new theatre is not like all the other theatres. But when they do at last find their way there, the attraction is not the firing of blank cartridges at one another by actors, nor the pretence of falling down dead that ends the stage combat, nor the simulation of erotic thrills by a pair of stage lovers, nor any of the other tomfooleries called action, but the exhibition and discussion of the character and conduct of stage figures who are made to appear real by the art of the playwright and the performers.

This, then, is the extension of the old dramatic form effected by Ibsen. Up to a certain point in the last act, A Doll's House is a play that might be turned into a very ordinary French drama by the excision of a few lines, and the substitution of a sentimental happy ending for the famous last scene: indeed the very first thing the theatrical wiseacres did with it was to effect exactly this transformation, with the result that the play thus pithed had no success and attracted no notice worth mentioning. But at just that point in the last act, the heroine very unexpectedly (by the wiseacres) stops her emotional acting and says: "We must sit down and discuss all this that has been happening between us." And it was by this new technical feature: this addition of a new movement, as musicians would say, to the dramatic form, that A Doll's House conquered Europe and founded a new school of dramatic art.

Since that time the discussion has expanded far beyond the limits of the last ten minutes of an otherwise "well made" play. The disadvantage of putting the discussion at the end was not only that it came when the audience was fatigued, but that it was necessary to see the play over again, so as to follow the earlier acts in the light of the final discussion, before it became fully intelligible. The practical utility of this book is due to the fact that unless the spectator at an Ibsen play has read the pages referring to it beforehand, it is hardly possible for him to get its bearings at a first hearing if he approaches it, as most spectators still do, with conventional idealist prepossessions. Accordingly, we now have plays, including some of my own, which begin with discussion and end with action, and others in which the discussion interpenetrates the action from beginning to end. When Ibsen invaded England discussion had vanished from the stage; and women could not write plays. Within twenty years women were writing better plays than men; and these plays were passionate arguments from beginning to end. The action of such plays consists of a case to be argued. If the case is uninteresting or stale or badly conducted or obviously trumped up, the play is a bad one. If it is important and novel and convincing, or at least disturbing, the play is a good one. But anyhow the play in which there is no argument and no case no longer counts as serious drama. It may still please the child in us as Punch and Judy does; but nobody nowadays pretends to regard the well made play as anything more than a commercial product which is not in question when modern schools of serious drama are under discussion. Indeed within ten years of the production of A Doll's House in London, audiences had become so derisive of the more obvious and hackneyed features of the methods of Sardou that it became dangerous to resort to them; and playwrights who persisted in "constructing" plays in the old French manner lost ground not for lack of ideas, but because their technique was unbearably out of fashion.

In the new plays, the drama arises through a conflict of unsettled ideals rather than through vulgar attachments, rapacities, generosities, resentments, ambitions, misunderstandings, oddities and so forth as to which no moral question is raised. The conflict is not between clear right and wrong: the villain is as conscientious as the hero, if not more so: in fact, the question which makes the play interesting (when it *is* interesting) is which is the villain and which the hero. Or, to put it another way, there are no villains and no heroes. This strikes the critics mainly as a departure from dramatic art; but it is really the inevitable return to nature which ends all the merely technical fashions. Now the natural is mainly the everyday; and its climaxes must be, if not everyday, at least everylife, if they are to have any importance for the spectator. Crimes, fights, big legacies, fires, shipwrecks, battles, and thunderbolts are mistakes in a play, even when they can be effectively simulated. No doubt they may acquire dramatic interest by putting a character through the test of an emergency; but the test is likely to be too obviously theatrical, because, as the playwright cannot in the nature of things have much experience of such catastrophes, he is forced to substitute a set of conventions or conjectures for the feelings they really produce.

In short, pure accidents are not dramatic: they are only anecdotic.

They may be sensational, impressive, provocative, ruinous, curious, or a dozen other things; but they have no specifically dramatic interest. There is no drama in being knocked down or run over. The catastrophe in Hamlet would not be in the least dramatic had Polonius fallen downstairs and broken his neck, Claudius succumbed to delirium tremens, Hamlet forgotten to breathe in the intensity of his philosophic speculation, Ophelia died of Danish measles, Laertes been shot by the palace sentry, and Rosencrantz and Guildenstern drowned in the North Sea. Even as it is, the Queen, who poisons herself by accident, has an air of being polished off to get her out of the way: her death is the one dramatic failure of the piece. Bushels of good paper have been inked in vain by writers who imagined they could produce a tragedy by killing everyone in the last act accidentally. As a matter of fact no accident, however sanguinary, can produce a moment of real drama, though a difference of opinion between husband and wife as to living in town or country might be the beginning of an appalling tragedy or a capital comedy.

It may be said that everything is an accident: that Othello's character is an accident, Iago's character another accident, and the fact that they happened to come together in the Venetian service an even more accidental accident. Also that Torvald Helmer might just as likely have married Mrs. Nickleby as Nora. Granting this trifling for what it is worth, the fact remains that marriage is no more an accident than birth or death: that is, it is expected to happen to everybody. And if every man has a good deal of Torvald Helmer in him, and every woman a good deal of Nora, neither their characters nor their meeting and marrying are accidents. Othello, though entertaining, pitiful, and resonant with the thrills a master of language can produce by mere artistic sonority is certainly much more accidental than A Doll's House; but it is correspondingly less important and interesting to us. It has been kept alive, not by its manufactured misunderstandings and stolen handkerchiefs and the like, nor even by its orchestral verse, but by its exhibition and discussion of human nature, marriage, and jealousy; and it would be a prodigiously better play if it were a serious discussion of the highly interesting problem of how a simple Moorish soldier would get on with a "supersubtle" Venetian lady of fashion if he married her. As it is, the play turns on a mistake; and though a mistake can produce a murder, which is the vulgar substitute for a tragedy, it cannot produce a real tragedy in the modern sense. Reflective people are not more interested in the Chamber of Horrors than in their own homes, nor in murderers, victims, and villains than in themselves; and the moment a man has acquired sufficient reflective power to cease gaping at waxworks, he is on his way to losing interest in Othello, Desdemona, and Iago exactly to the extent to which they become interesting to the police. Cassio's weakness for drink comes much nearer home to most of us than Othello's strangling and throat cutting, or Iago's theatrical confidence trick. The proof is that Shakespear's professional colleagues, who exploited all his sensational devices, and piled up torture on murder and incest on adultery until they had far out-Heroded Herod, are now unmemorable and unplayable. Shakespear survives because he coolly treated the sensational horrors of his borrowed plots as inorganic theatrical accessories, using them simply as pretexts for dramatizing human character as it exists in the normal world. In enjoying and discussing his plays we unconsciously discount the combats and murders: commentators are never so astray (and consequently so ingenious) as when they take Hamlet seriously as a madman, Macbeth as a homicidal Highlander, and impish humorists like Richard and Iago as lurid villains of the Renascence. The plays in which these figures appear could be changed into comedies without altering a hair of their beards. Shakespear, had anyone been intelligent enough to tax him with this, would perhaps have said that most crimes are accidents that happen to people exactly like ourselves, and that Macbeth, under propitious circumstances, would have made an exemplary rector of Stratford, a real criminal being a defective monster, a human accident, useful on the stage only for minor parts such as Don Johns, second murderers, and the like. Anyhow, the fact remains that Shakespear survives by what he has in common with Ibsen, and not by what he has in common with Webster and the rest. Hamlet's surprise at finding that he "lacks gall" to behave in the idealistically conventional manner, and that no extremity of rhetoric about the duty of revenging "a dear father slain" and exterminating the "bloody bawdy villain" who murdered him seems to make any difference in their domestic relations in the palace in Elsinore, still keeps us talking about him and going to the theatre to listen to him, whilst the older Hamlets, who never had any Ibsenist hesitations, and shammed madness, and entangled the courtiers in the arras and burnt them, and stuck hard to the theatrical school of the fat boy in Pickwick ("I wants to make your flesh creep"), are as dead as John Shakespear's mutton.

We have progressed so rapidly on this point under the impulse given to the drama by Ibsen that it seems strange now to contrast him favorably with Shakespear on the ground that he avoided the old catastrophes which left the stage strewn with the dead at the end of an Elizabethan tragedy. For perhaps the most plausible reproach levelled at Ibsen by modern critics of his own school is just that survival of the old school in him which makes the death rate so high in his last acts. Do Oswald Alving, Hedvig Ekdal, Rosmer and Rebecca, Hedda Gabler, Solness, Eyolf, Borkman, Rubeck and Irene die dramatically natural deaths, or are they slaughtered in the classic and Shakespearean manner, partly because the audience expects blood for its money, partly because it is difficult to make people attend seriously to anything except by startling them with some violent calamity? It is so easy to make out a case for either view that I shall not argue the point. The post-Ibsen playwrights apparently think that Ibsen's homicides and suicides were forced. In Tchekov's Cherry Orchard, for example, where the sentimental ideals of our amiable, cultured, Schumann playing propertied class are reduced to dust and ashes by a hand not less deadly than Ibsen's because it is so much more caressing, nothing more violent happens than that the family cannot afford to keep up its old house. In Granville-Barker's plays, the campaign against our society is carried on with all Ibsen's implacability; but the one suicide (in Waste) is unhistorical; for neither Parnell nor Dilke, who were the actual cases in point of the waste which was the subject of the play, killed himself. I myself have been reproached because the characters in my plays "talk but do nothing," meaning that they do not commit felonies. As a matter of fact we have come to see that it is no true *dénouement* to cut the Gordian knot as Alexander did with a stroke of the sword. If people's souls are tied up by law and public opinion it is much more tragic to leave them to wither in these bonds than to end their misery and relieve the salutary compunction of the audience by outbreaks of violence. Judge Brack was, on the whole, right when he said that people dont do such things. If they did, the idealists would be brought to their senses very quickly indeed.

But in Ibsen's plays the catastrophe, even when it seems forced, and when the ending of the play would be more tragic without it, is never an accident; and the play never exists for its sake. His nearest to an accident is the death of little Eyolf, who falls off a pier and is drowned. But this instance only reminds us that there is one good dramatic use for an accident: it can awaken people. When England wept over the deaths of little Nell and Paul Dombey, the strong soul of Ruskin was moved to scorn: to novelists who were at a loss to make their books sell he offered the formula: When at a loss, kill a child. But Ibsen did not kill little Eyolf to manufacture pathos. The surest way to achieve a thoroughly bad performance of Little Eyolf is to conceive it as a sentimental tale of a drowned darling. Its drama lies in the awakening of Allmers and his wife to the despicable quality and detestable rancors of the life they have been idealizing as blissful and poetic. They are so sunk in their dream that the awakening can be effected only by a violent shock. And that is just the one dramatically useful thing an accident can do. It can shock. Hence the accident that befalls Eyolf.

As to the deaths in Ibsen's last acts, they are a sweeping up of the remains of dramatically finished people. Solness's fall from the tower is as obviously symbolic as Phaeton's fall from the chariot of the sun. Ibsen's dead bodies are those of the exhausted or destroyed: he does not kill Hilda, for instance, as Shakespear killed Juliet. He is ruthless enough with Hedvig and Eyolf because he wants to use their deaths to expose their parents; but if he had written Hamlet nobody would have been killed in the last act except perhaps Horatio, whose correct nullity might have provoked Fortinbras to let some of the moral sawdust out of him with his sword. For Shakespearean deaths in Ibsen you must go back to Lady Inger and the plays of his nonage, with which this book is not concerned.

The drama was born of old from the union of two desires: the desire to have a dance and the desire to hear a story. The dance became a rant: the story became a situation. When Ibsen began to make plays, the art of the dramatist had shrunk into the art of contriving a situation. And it was held that the stranger the situation, the better the play. Ibsen saw that, on the contrary, the more familiar the situation, the more interesting the play. Shakespear had put ourselves on the stage but not our situations. Our uncles seldom murder our fathers, and cannot legally marry our mothers; we do not meet witches; our kings are not as a rule stabbed and succeeded by their stabbers; and when we raise money by bills we do not promise to pay pounds of our flesh. Ibsen supplies the want left by Shakespear. He gives us not only ourselves, but ourselves in our own situations. The things that happen to his stage figures are things that happen to us. One consequence is that his plays are much more important to us than Shakespear's. Another is that they are capable both of hurting us cruelly and of filling us with excited hopes of escape from idealistic tyrannies, and with visions of intenser life in the future.

Changes in technique follow inevitably from these changes in the subject matter of the play. When a dramatic poet can give you hopes and visions, such old maxims as that stage-craft is the art of preparation become boyish, and may be left to those unfortunate playwrights who, being unable to make anything really interesting happen on the stage, have to acquire the art of continually persuading the audience that it is going to happen presently. When he can stab people to the heart by shewing them the meanness or cruelty of something they did yesterday and intend to do tomorrow, all the old tricks to catch and hold their attention become the silliest of superfluities. The play called The Murder of Gonzago, which Hamlet makes the players act before his uncle, is artlessly constructed; but it produces a greater effect on Claudius than the OEdipus of Sophocles, because it is about himself. The writer who practises the art of Ibsen therefore discards all the old tricks of preparation, catastrophe, *dénouement*, and so forth without thinking about it, just as a modern rifleman never dreams of providing himself with powder horns, percussion caps, and wads: indeed he does not know the use of them. Ibsen substituted a terrible art of sharpshooting at the audience, trapping them, fencing with them, aiming always at the sorest spot in their consciences. Never mislead an audience, was an old rule. But the new school will trick the spectator into forming a meanly false judgment, and then convict him of it in the next act, often to his grievous mortification. When you despise something you ought to take off your hat to, or admire and imitate something you ought to loathe, you cannot resist the dramatist who knows how to touch these morbid spots in you and make you see that they are morbid. The dramatist knows that as long as he is teaching and saving his audience, he is as sure of their strained attention as a dentist is, or the Angel of the Annunciation. And though he may use all the magic of art to make you forget the pain he causes you or to enhance the joy of the hope and courage he awakens, he is never occupied in the old work of manufacturing interest and expectation with materials that have neither novelty, significance, nor relevance to the experience or prospects of the spectators.

Hence a cry has arisen that the post-Ibsen play is not a play, and that its technique, not being the technique described by Aristotle, is not a technique at all. I will not enlarge on this: the fun poked at my friend Mr. A. B. Walkley in the prologue of Fanny's First Play need not be repeated here. But I may remind him that the new technique is new only on the modern stage. It has been used by preachers and orators ever since speech was invented. It is the technique of playing upon the human conscience; and it has been practised by the playwright whenever the playwright has been capable of it. Rhetoric, irony, argument, paradox, epigram, parable, the rearrangement of haphazard facts into orderly and intelligent situations: these are both the oldest and newest arts of the drama; and your plot construction and art of preparation are only the tricks of theatrical talent and the shifts of moral sterility, not the weapons of dramatic genius. In the theatre of Ibsen we are not flattered spectators killing an idle hour with an ingenious and amusing entertainment: we are "guilty creatures sitting at a play"; and the technique of pastime is no more applicable than at a murder trial.

The technical novelties of the Ibsen and post-Ibsen plays are, then: first, the introduction of the discussion and its development until it so overspreads and interpenetrates the action that it finally assimilates it, making play and discussion practically identical; and, second, as a consequence of making the spectators themselves the persons of the drama, and the incidents of their own lives its incidents, the disuse of the old stage tricks by which audiences had to be induced to take an interest in unreal people and improbable circumstances, and the substitution of a forensic technique of recrimination, disillusion, and penetration through ideals to the truth, with a free use of all the rhetorical and lyrical arts of the orator, the preacher, the pleader, and the rhapsodist.

Introduction [to *When We Dead Awaken*]

William Archer*

From *Pillars of Society to John Gabriel Borkman*, Ibsen's plays had followed each other at regular intervals of two years, save when his indignation over the abuse heaped upon *Ghosts* reduced to a single year

*Originally published in Henrik Ibsen, *John Gabriel Borkman, Part II and When We Dead Awaken* (New York: Scribner's, 1907), 353–58.

the interval between that play and *An Enemy of the People*. *John Gabriel Borkman* having appeared in 1896, its successor was expected in 1898; but Christmas came and brought no rumour of a new play. In a man now over seventy, this breach of a long-established habit seemed ominous. The new National Theatre in Christiania was opened in September of the following year; and when I then met Ibsen (for the last time) he told me that he was actually at work on a new play, which he thought of calling a "Dramatic Epilogue." "He wrote *When We Dead Awaken*," says Dr. Elias, "with such labour and such passionate agitation, so spasmodically and so feverishly, that those around him were almost alarmed. He must get on with it, he must get on! He seemed to hear the beating of dark pinions over his head. He seemed to feel the grim Visitant, who had accompanied Alfred Allmers on the mountain paths, already standing behind him with uplifted hand. His relatives are firmly convinced that he knew quite clearly that this would be his last play, that he was to write no more. And soon the blow fell."

The *Literary Remains* contain some preliminary jottings for *When We Dead Awaken*, and a rejected draft of the final scene. From the jottings it appears that the play was to have been called *The Resurrection Day*, and that Ibsen originally thought of introducing at least two characters whom he ultimately suppressed — the Physician at the Baths, "a youngish, intelligent man," and "the Tattling Lady from the capital" who "is considered immensely amusing by the patients," and is "malicious out of thoughtlessness." At the end of a rough scenario of the first act there occurs the following curious reflection: "In this country it is only the mountains which have any resonance [literally "give an echo"] not the people." In the draft of the last scene, Rubek, Irene, Ulfheim and Maia are all assembled outside Ulfheim's hut. The fragment begins thus:

> MAIA (*interrupting*). Is it not strange that we four should meet here in the middle of the wild mountains?
> RUBEK. You with an eagle-shooter, and I with — (*to Irene*) — with what shall I say?
> IRENE. With a shot eagle.
> MAIA. Shot?
> IRENE. Winged, madam.

Ulfheim unlocks the hut, and produces from it champagne and glasses, which he fills.

> ULFHEIM (*to Maia*). What shall we drink to, honoured lady?
> MAIA. Let us drink to freedom!
> (*She empties her glass at one draught.*)
> RUBEK. Yes, let us drink to freedom. (*He drinks.*)

IRENE. And to the courage which dares to use it.
(She takes a sip from her glass and pours the rest on the ground.)

After Ulfheim and Maia have departed, Rubek and Irene have a last conversation which ends thus: —

IRENE. The craving for life is dead in me. Now I have arisen, and I see that life lies a corpse. The whole of life lies on its bier — (*The clouds droop slowly down in the form of a clammy mist*). See how the shroud is drooping over us, too! But I will not die over again, Arnold! — Save me! Save me, if you can and if you will!

RUBEK. Above the mists I see the mountain peak. It stands there glittering in the sunrise. We must climb to it — through the night mists, up into the light of morning.

(The mists droop closer and closer over the scene. RUBEK *and* IRENE *descend into the mist-veil and are gradually lost to sight.)*

(The SISTER OF MERCY's *head, spying, comes in sight in a rift in the mist.)*

(High up above the sea of the mist, the peak shines in the morning sun.)

And that is the end.

When We Dead Awaken was published very shortly before Christmas 1899. Ibsen had still a year of comparative health before him. We find him, in March 1900, writing to Count Prozor: "I cannot say yet whether or not I shall write another drama; but if I continue to retain the vigour of body and mind which I at present enjoy, I do not imagine that I shall be able to keep permanently away from the old battlefields. However, if I were to make my appearance again, it would be with new weapons and in new armour." Was he hinting at the desire, which he had long ago confessed to Professor Herford, that his last work should be a drama in verse? Whatever his dream, it was not to be realised. His last letter (defending his attitude of philosophic impartiality with regard to the South African war) is dated December 9, 1900. With the dawn of the new century, the curtain descended upon the mind of the great dramatic poet of the age which had passed away.

When We Dead Awaken was acted during 1900 at most of the leading theatres in Scandinavia and Germany. In some German cities (notably in Frankfort on Main) it even attained a considerable number of representations. I cannot learn, however, that it has anywhere held the stage. It was produced in London, by the Stage Society, at the Imperial Theatre, on January 25 and 26, 1903. Mr. G. S. Titheradge played Rubek, Miss Henrietta Watson Irene, Miss Mabel Hackney Maia, and Mr. Laurence Irving Ulfheim. In New York it was acted at the Knickerbocker Theatre, the part of Irene being taken by Miss Florence Kahn, and that of Rubek by Mr. Frederick Lewis.

In the above-mentioned letter to Count Prozor, Ibsen confirmed that critic's conjecture that "the series which ends with the Epilogue really began with *The Master Builder.*" As the last confession, so to speak, of a great artist, the Epilogue will always be read with interest. It contains, moreover, many flashes of the old genius, many strokes of the old incommunicable magic. One may say with perfect sincerity that there is more fascination in the dregs of Ibsen's mind than in the "first sprightly running" of more commonplace talents. But to his sane admirers the interest of the play must always be melancholy, because it is purely pathological. To deny this is, in my opinion, to cast a slur over all the poet's previous work, and in great measure to justify the criticisms of his most violent detractors. For *When We Dead Awaken* is very like the sort of play that haunted the "anti-Ibsenite" imagination in the year 1893 or thereabouts. It is a piece of self-caricature, a series of echoes from all the earlier plays, an exaggeration of manner to the pitch of mannerism. Moreover, in his treatment of his symbolic motives, Ibsen did exactly what he had hitherto, with perfect justice, plumed himself upon never doing: he sacrificed the surface reality to the underlying meaning. Take, for instance, the history of Rubek's statue and its development into a group. In actual sculpture this development is a grotesque impossibility. In conceiving it we are deserting the domain of reality, and plunging into some fourth dimension where the properties of matter are other than those we know. This is an abandonment of the fundamental principle which Ibsen over and over again emphatically expressed — namely, that any symbolism his work might be found to contain was entirely incidental, and subordinate to the truth and consistency of his picture of life. Even when he dallied with the supernatural, as in *The Master Builder* and *Little Eyolf*, he was always careful, as I have tried to show, not to overstep decisively the boundaries of the natural. Here, on the other hand, without any suggestion of the supernatural, we are confronted with the wholly impossible, the inconceivable. How remote is this alike from his principles of art and from the consistent, unvarying practice of his better years! So great is the chasm between *John Gabriel Borkman* and *When We Dead Awaken* that one could almost suppose his mental breakdown to have preceded instead of followed the writing of the latter play. Certainly it is one of the premonitions of the coming end. It is Ibsen's *Count Robert of Paris.* To pretend to rank it with his masterpieces is to show a very imperfect sense of the nature of their mastery.

Ibsen the Poet of the Theater
The Revaluation of the Language of Ibsen's Drama

Ibsen's New Drama

James Joyce*

Twenty years have passed since Henrik Ibsen wrote *A Doll's House*, thereby almost marking an epoch in the history of drama. During those years his name has gone abroad through the length and breadth of two continents, and has provoked more discussion and criticism than that of any other living man. He has been upheld as a religious reformer, a social reformer, a Semitic lover of righteousness, and as a great dramatist. He has been rigorously denounced as a meddlesome intruder, a defective artist, an incomprehensible mystic, and, in the eloquent words of a certain English critic, "a muck-ferreting dog." Through the perplexities of such diverse criticism, the great genius of the man is day by day coming out as a hero comes out amid the earthly trials. The dissonant cries are fainter and more distant, the random praises are rising in steadier and more choral chaunt. Even to the uninterested bystander it must seem significant that the interest attached to this Norwegian has never flagged for over a quarter of a century. It may be questioned whether any man has held so firm an empire over the thinking world in modern times. Not Rousseau; not Emerson; not Carlyle; not any of those giants of whom almost all have passed out of human ken. Ibsen's power over two generations has been enhanced by his own reticence. Seldom, if at all, has he condescended to join battle with his enemies. It would appear as if the storm of fierce debate rarely broke in upon his wonderful calm. The conflicting voices have not influenced his work in the very smallest degree. His output of dramas has been regulated by the utmost order, by a clockwork routine, seldom found in the case of genius. Only once he answered his assailants after their violent attack on *Ghosts*. But from *The Wild Duck* to *John Gabriel Borkman*, his dramas have appeared almost mechanically at intervals of two years. One is apt to overlook the sustained energy which such a plan of campaign demands; but even surprise at this must give way

*From *The Critical Writings of James Joyce*, edited by Ellsworth Mason and Richard Ellmann. © 1959 by Harriet Weaver and F. Lionel Monro, as administrators c.t.a. of the Estate of James Joyce. Reprinted by permission of Viking Penguin, Inc. Originally published in the *Fortnightly Review*, n.s., 67 (1 April 1900), 575–90.

to admiration at the gradual, irresistible advance of this extraordinary man. Eleven plays, all dealing with modern life, have been published. Here is the list: *A Doll's House, Ghosts, An Enemy of the People, The Wild Duck, Rosmersholm, The Lady from the Sea, Hedda Gabler, The Master Builder, Little Eyolf, John Gabriel Borkman*, and lastly — his new drama, published at Copenhagen, December 19th, 1899 — *When We Dead Awaken*. This play is already in process of translation into almost a dozen different languages — a fact which speaks volumes for the power of its author. The drama is written in prose, and is in three acts.

To begin an account of a play of Ibsen's is surely no easy matter. The subject is, in one way, so confined, and, in another way, so vast. It is safe to predict that nine-tenths of the notices of this play will open in some such way as the following: "Arnold Rubek and his wife, Maja, have been married for four years, at the beginning of the play. Their union is, however, unhappy. Each is discontented with the other." So far as this goes, it is unimpeachable; but then it does not go very far. It does not convey even the most shadowy notion of the relations between Professor Rubek and his wife. It is a bald, clerkly version of countless, indefinable complexities. It is as though the history of a tragic life were to be written down rudely in two columns, one for the pros and the other for the cons. It is only saying what is literally true, to say that, in the three acts of the drama, there has been stated all that is essential to the drama. There is from first to last hardly a superfluous word or phrase. Therefore, the play itself expresses its own ideas as briefly and as concisely as they can be expressed in the dramatic form. It is manifest, then, that a notice cannot give an adequate notion of the drama. This is not the case with the common lot of plays, to which the fullest justice may be meted out in a very limited number of lines. They are for the most part reheated dishes — unoriginal compositions, cheerfully owlish as to heroic insight, living only in their own candid claptrap — in a word, stagey. The most perfunctory curtness is their fittest meed. But in dealing with the work of a man like Ibsen, the task set the reviewer is truly great enough to sink all his courage. All he can hope to do is to link some of the more salient points together in such a way as to suggest rather than to indicate, the intricacies of the plot. Ibsen has attained ere this to such mastery over his art that, with apparently easy dialogue, he presents his men and women passing through different soul-crises. His analytic method is thus made use of to the fullest extent, and into the comparatively short space of two days the life in life of all his characters is compressed. For instance, though we only see Solness during one night and up to the following evening, we have in reality watched with bated breath the whole course of his life up to the moment when Hilda Wangel enters his house. So in the play under consideration, when we see Professor Rubek first, he is sitting in a garden chair, reading his morning paper, but by degrees the whole scroll of his life is unrolled before us, and we have the pleasure not of hearing it read out to us, but of reading it for ourselves, piecing the various parts, and going closer to see wherever the writing on the parchment is fainter or less legible.

As I have said, when the play opens, Professor Rubek is sitting in the gardens of a hotel, eating, or rather having finished, his breakfast. In another chair, close beside him, is sitting Maja Rubek, the Professor's wife. The scene is in Norway, a popular health resort near the sea. Through the trees can be seen the town harbour, and the fjord, with steamers plying over it, as it stretches past headland and river-isle out to the sea. Rubek is a famous sculptor, of middle age, and Maja, a woman still young, whose bright eyes have just a shade of sadness in them. These two continue reading their respective papers quietly in the peace of the morning. All looks so idyllic to the careless eye. The lady breaks the silence in a weary, petulant manner by complaining of the deep peace that reigns about them. Arnold lays down his paper with mild expostulation. Then they begin to converse of this thing and that; first of the silence, then of the place and the people, of the railway stations through which they passed the previous night, with their sleepy porters and aimlessly shifting lanterns. From this they proceed to talk of the changes in the people, and of all that has grown up since they were married. Then it is but a little further to the main trouble. In speaking of their married life it speedily appears that the inner view of their relations is hardly as ideal as the outward view might lead one to expect. The depths of these two people are being slowly stirred up. The leaven of prospective drama is gradually discerned working amid the *fin-de-siècle* scene. The lady seems a difficult little person. She complains of the idle promises with which her husband had fed her aspirations.

> MAJA. You said you would take me up to a high mountain and show me all the glory of the world.
>
> RUBEK (*with a slight start*). Did I promise you that, too?

In short, there is something untrue lying at the root of their union. Meanwhile the guests of the hotel, who are taking the baths, pass out of the hotel porch on the right, chatting and laughing men and women. They are informally marshalled by the inspector of the baths. This person is an unmistakable type of the conventional official. He salutes Mr. and Mrs. Rubek, enquiring how they slept. Rubek asks him if any of the guests take their baths by night, as he has seen a white figure moving in the park during the night. Maja scouts the notion, but the inspector says that there is a strange lady, who has rented the pavilion which is to the left, and who is staying there, with one attendant — a Sister of Mercy. As they are talking, the strange lady and her companion pass slowly through the park and enter the pavilion. The incident appears to affect Rubek, and Maja's curiosity is aroused.

> MAJA (*a little hurt and jarred*). Perhaps this lady has been one of your models, Rubek? Search your memory.

RUBEK (*looks cuttingly at her*). Model?

MAJA (*with a provoking smile*). In your younger days, I mean. You are said to have had such innumerable models — long ago, of course.

RUBEK (*in the same tone*). Oh, no, little Frau Maja. I have in reality had only one single model. One and one only for everything I have done.

While this misunderstanding is finding outlet in the foregoing conversation, the inspector, all at once, takes fright at some person who is approaching. He attempts to escape into the hotel, but the high-pitched voice of the person who is approaching arrests him.

ULFHEIM's voice (*heard outside*). Stop a moment, man. Devil take it all, can't you stop? Why do you always scuttle away from me?

With these words, uttered in strident tones, the second chief actor enters on the scene. He is described as a great bear-killer, thin, tall, of uncertain age, and muscular. He is accompanied by his servant, Lars, and a couple of sporting dogs. Lars does not speak a single word in the play. Ulfheim at present dismisses him with a kick, and approaches Mr. and Mrs. Rubek. He falls into conversation with them, for Rubek is known to him as the celebrated sculptor. On sculpture this savage hunter offers some original remarks.

ULFHEIM . . . We both work in a hard material, madam — both your husband and I. He struggles with his marble blocks, I daresay; and I struggle with tense and quivering bear-sinews. And we both of us win the fight in the end — subdue and master our material. We don't give in until we have got the better of it, though it fight never so hard.

RUBEK (*deep in thought*). There's a great deal of truth in what you say.

This eccentric creature, perhaps by the force of his own eccentricity, has begun to weave a spell of enchantment about Maja. Each word that he utters tends to wrap the web of his personality still closer about her. The black dress of the Sister of Mercy causes him to grin sardonically. He speaks calmly of all his near friends, whom he has dispatched out of the world.

MAJA. And what did you do for your nearest friends?

ULFHEIM. Shot them, of course.

RUBEK (*looking at him*). Shot them?

MAJA (*moving her chair back*). Shot them dead?

ULFHEIM (*nods*). I never miss, madam.

However, it turns out that by his nearest friends he means his dogs, and the minds of his hearers are put somewhat more at ease. During their conversation the Sister of Mercy has prepared a slight repast for her mistress at one of the tables outside the pavilion. The unsustaining qualities of the food excites Ulfheim's merriment. He speaks with a lofty disparagement of such effeminate diet. He is a realist in his appetite.

> ULFHEIM (*rising*). Spoken like a woman of spirit, madam. Come with me, then! They [his dogs] swallow whole, great, thumping meat-bones—gulp them up and then gulp them down again. Oh, it's a regular treat to see them!

On such half-gruesome, half-comic invitation Maja goes out with him, leaving her husband in the company of the strange lady who enters from the pavilion. Almost simultaneously the Professor and the lady recognize each other. The lady has served Rubek as model for the central figure in his famous masterpiece, "The Resurrection Day." Having done her work for him, she had fled in an unaccountable manner, leaving no traces behind her. Rubek and she drift into familiar conversation. She asks him who is the lady who has just gone out. He answers, with some hesitation, that she is his wife. Then he asks if she is married. She replies that she is married. He asks her where her husband is at present.

> RUBEK. And where is he now?
>
> IRENE. Oh, in a churchyard somewhere or other, with a fine, handsome monument over him; and with a bullet rattling in his skull.
>
> RUBEK. Did he kill himself?
>
> IRENE. Yes, he was good enough to take that off my hands.
>
> RUBEK. Do you not lament his loss, Irene?
>
> IRENE (*not understanding*). Lament? What loss?
>
> RUBEK. Why, the loss of Herr von Satow, of course.
>
> IRENE. His name was not Satow.
>
> RUBEK. Was it not?
>
> IRENE. My second husband is called Satow. He is a Russian.
>
> RUBEK. And where is he?
>
> IRENE. Far away in the Ural Mountains. Among all his goldmines.
>
> RUBEK. So he lives there?
>
> IRENE (*shrugs her shoulders*). Lives? Lives? In reality I have killed him.
>
> RUBEK (*starts*). Killed—!
>
> IRENE. Killed him with a fine sharp dagger which I always have with me in bed—

Rubek begins to understand that there is some meaning hidden beneath these strange words. He begins to think seriously on himself, his art, and on her, passing in review the course of his life since the creation of his masterpiece, "The Resurrection Day." He sees that he has not fulfilled the promise of that work, and comes to realize that there is something lacking in his life. He asks Irene how she has lived since they last saw each other. Irene's answer to his query is of great importance, for it strikes the key note of the entire play.

> IRENE (*rises slowly from her chair and says quiveringly*). I was dead for many years. They came and bound me — lacing my arms together at my back. Then they lowered me into a grave-vault, with iron bars before the loophole. And with padded walls, so that no one on the earth above could hear the grave-shrieks.

In Irene's allusion to her position as model for the great picture, Ibsen gives further proof of his extraordinary knowledge of women. No other man could have so subtly expressed the nature of the relations between the sculptor and his model, had he even dreamt of them.

> IRENE. I exposed myself wholly and unreservedly to your gaze [*more softly*] and never once did you touch me. . . .
>
> . . . .
>
> RUBEK (*looks impressively at her*). I was an artist, Irene.
> IRENE (*darkly*). That is just it. That is just it.

Thinking deeper and deeper on himself and on his former attitude towards this woman, it strikes him yet more forcibly that there are great gulfs set between his art and his life, and that even in his art his skill and genius are far from perfect. Since Irene left him he has done nothing but paint portrait busts of townsfolk. Finally, some kind of resolution is enkindled in him, a resolution to repair his botching, for he does not altogether despair of that. There is just a reminder of the will-glorification of *Brand* in the lines that follow.

> RUBEK (*struggling with himself, uncertainly*). If we could, oh, if only we could. . . .
> IRENE. Why can we not do what we will?

In fine, the two agree in deeming their present state insufferable. It appears plain to her that Rubek lies under a heavy obligation to her, and with their recognition of this, and the entrance of Maja, fresh from the enchantment of Ulfheim, the first act closes.

> RUBEK. When did you begin to seek for me, Irene?
> IRENE (*with a touch of jesting bitterness*). From the time when I realized that I had given away to you something rather indispensable. Something one ought never to part with.
> RUBEK (*bowing his head*). Yes, that is bitterly true. You gave me three or four years of your youth.
> IRENE. More, more than that I gave you — spendthrift as I then was.

Rubek. Yes, you were prodigal, Irene. You gave me all your naked loveliness —

Irene. To gaze upon —

Rubek. And to glorify. . . .

. . . .

Irene. But you have forgotten the most precious gift.

Rubek. The most precious . . . what gift was that?

Irene. I gave you my young living soul. And that gift left me empty within — soulless [*looks at him with a fixed stare*]. It was that I died of, Arnold.

It is evident, even from this mutilated account, that the first act is a masterly one. With no perceptible effort the drama rises, with a methodic natural ease it develops. The trim garden of the nineteenth-century hotel is slowly made the scene of a gradually growing dramatic struggle. Interest has been roused in each of the characters, sufficient to carry the mind into the succeeding act. The situation is not stupidly explained, but the action has set in, and at the close the play has reached a definite stage of progression.

The second act takes place close to a sanatorium on the mountains. A cascade leaps from a rock and flows in steady stream to the right. On the bank some children are playing, laughing and shouting. The time is evening. Rubek is discovered lying on a mound to the left. Maja enters shortly, equipped for hill-climbing. Helping herself with her stick across the stream, she calls out to Rubek and approaches him. He asks how she and her companion are amusing themselves, and questions her as to their hunting. An exquisitely humorous touch enlivens their talk. Rubek asks if they intend hunting the bear near the surrounding locality. She replies with a grand superiority.

Maja. You don't suppose that bears are to be found in the naked mountains, do you?

The next topic is the uncouth Ulfheim. Maja admires him because he is so ugly — then turns abruptly to her husband saying, pensively, that he also is ugly. The accused pleads his age.

Rubek (*shrugging his shoulders*). One grows old. One grows old, Frau Maja!

This semi-serious banter leads them on to graver matters. Maja lies at length in the soft heather, and rails gently at the Professor. For the mysteries and claims of art she has a somewhat comical disregard.

Maja (*with a somewhat scornful laugh*). Yes, you are always, always an artist.

and again—

> MAJA. . . . . Your tendency is to keep yourself to yourself and—
> think your own thoughts. And, of course, I can't talk properly to you
> about your affairs. I know nothing about Art and that sort of thing.
> [*With an impatient gesture.*] And care very little either, for that matter.

She rallies him on the subject of the strange lady, and hints maliciously at the understanding between them. Rubek says that he was only an artist and that she was the source of his inspiration. He confesses that the five years of his married life have been years of intellectual famine for him. He has viewed in their true light his own feelings towards his art.

> RUBEK (*smiling*). But that was not precisely what I had in my
> mind.
> MAJA. What then?
> RUBEK (*again serious*). It was this—that all the talk about the
> artist's vocation and the artist's mission, and so forth, began to strike me
> as being very empty and hollow and meaningless at bottom.
> MAJA. Then what would you put in its place?
> RUBEK. Life, Maja.

The all-important question of their mutual happiness is touched upon, and after a brisk discussion a tacit agreement to separate is effected. When matters are in this happy condition Irene is descried coming across the heath. She is surrounded by the sportive children and stays awhile among them. Maja jumps up from the grass and goes to her, saying, enigmatically, that her husband requires assistance to "open a precious casket." Irene bows and goes towards Rubek, and Maja goes joyfully to seek her hunter. The interview which follows is certainly remarkable, even from a stagey point of view. It constitutes, practically, the substance of the second act, and is of absorbing interest. At the same time it must be added that such a scene would tax the powers of the mimes producing it. Nothing short of a complete realization of the two *rôles* would represent the complex ideas involved in the conversation. When we reflect how few artists would have either the intelligence to attempt it or the powers to execute it, we behold a pitiful revelation.

In the interview of these two people on the heath, the whole tenors of their lives are outlined with bold steady strokes. From the first exchange of introductory words each phrase tells a chapter of experiences. Irene alludes to the dark shadow of the Sister of Mercy which follows her everywhere, as the shadow of Arnold's unquiet conscience follows him. When he has half-involuntarily confessed so much, one of the great barriers between them is broken down. Their trust in each other is, to some extent, renewed, and they revert to their past acquaintance. Irene speaks openly of her feelings, of her hate for the sculptor.

IRENE (*again vehemently*). Yes, for you — for the artist who had so lightly and carelessly taken a warm-blooded body, a young human life, and worn the soul out of it — because you needed it for a work of art.

Rubek's transgression has indeed been great. Not merely has he possessed himself of her soul, but he has withheld from its rightful throne the child of her soul. By her child Irene means the statue. To her it seems that this statue is, in a very true and very real sense, born of her. Each day as she saw it grow to its full growth under the hand of the skillful moulder, her inner sense of motherhood for it, of right over it, of love towards it, had become stronger and more confirmed.

IRENE (*changing to a tone full of warmth and feeling*). But that statue in the wet, living clay, that I loved — as it rose up, a vital human creature out of these raw, shapeless masses — for that was our creation, our child. Mine and yours.

It is, in reality, because of her strong feelings that she has kept aloof from Rubek for five years. But when she hears now of what he has done to the child — her child — all her powerful nature rises up against him in resentment. Rubek, in a mental agony, endeavours to explain, while she listens like a tigress whose cub has been wrested from her by a thief.

RUBEK. I was young then — with no experience of life. The Resurrection, I thought, would be most beautifully and exquisitely figured as a young unsullied woman — with none of a life's experience — awakening to light and glory without having to put away from her anything ugly and impure.

With larger experience of life he has found it necessary to alter his ideal somewhat, he has made her child no longer a principal, but an intermediary figure. Rubek, turning towards her, sees her just about to stab him. In a fever of terror and thought he rushes into his own defence, pleading madly for the errors he has done. It seems to Irene that he is endeavouring to render his sin poetical, that he is penitent but in a luxury of dolour. The thought that she has given up herself, her whole life, at the bidding of his false art, rankles in her heart with a terrible persistence. She cries out against herself, not loudly, but in deep sorrow.

IRENE (*with apparent self-control*). I should have borne children into the world — many children — real children — not such children as are hidden away in grave-vaults. That was my vocation. I ought never to have served you — poet.

Rubek, in poetic absorption, has no reply, he is musing on the old, happy days. Their dead joys solace him. But Irene is thinking of a certain phrase of his which he had spoken unwittingly. He had declared that he owed her thanks for her assistance in his work. This has been, he had said, a truly blessed *episode* in my life. Rubek's tortured mind cannot bear any more reproaches, too many are heaped upon it already. He begins throwing flowers on the stream, as they used in those bygone days on the lake of Taunitz. He recalls to her the time when they made a boat of leaves, and yoked a white swan to it, in imitation of the boat of Lohengrin. Even here in their sport there lies a hidden meaning.

IRENE. You said I was the swan that drew your boat.

RUBEK. Did I say so? Yes, I daresay I did [*absorbed in the game*]. Just see how the sea-gulls are swimming down the stream!

IRENE (*laughing*). And all your ships have run ashore.

RUBEK (*throwing more leaves into the brook*). I have ships enough in reserve.

While they are playing aimlessly, in a kind of childish despair, Ulfheim and Maja appear across the heath. These two are going to seek adventures on the high tablelands. Maja sings out to her husband a little song which she has composed in her joyful mood. With a sardonic laugh Ulfheim bids Rubek good-night and disappears with his companion up the mountain. All at once Irene and Rubek leap to the same thought. But at that moment the gloomy figure of the Sister of Mercy is seen in the twilight, with her leaden eyes looking at them both. Irene breaks from him, but promises to meet him that night on the heath.

RUBEK. And you will come, Irene?

IRENE. Yes, certainly I will come. Wait for me here.

RUBEK (*repeats dreamily*). Summer night on the upland. With you. With you. [*His eyes meet hers.*] Oh, Irene, that might have been our life. And that we have forfeited, we two.

IRENE. We see the irretrievable only when [*breaks short off*].

RUBEK (*looks inquiringly at her*). When? . . .

IRENE. When we dead awaken.

The third act takes place on a wide plateau, high up on the hills. The ground is rent with yawning clefts. Looking to the right, one sees the range of the summits half-hidden in the moving mists. On the left stands an old, dismantled hut. It is in the early morning, when the skies are the colour of pearl. The day is beginning to break. Maja and Ulfheim come down to the plateau. Their feelings are sufficiently explained by the opening words.

MAJA (*trying to tear herself loose*). Let me go! Let me go, I say!

ULFHEIM. Come, come! are you going to bite now? You're as snappish as a wolf.

When Ulfheim will not cease his annoyances, Maja threatens to run over the crest of the neighbouring ridge. Ulfheim points out that she will dash herself to pieces. He has wisely sent Lars away after the hounds, that he may be uninterrupted. Lars, he says, may be trusted not to find the dogs too soon.

> MAJA (*looking angrily at him*). No, I daresay not.
>
> ULFHEIM (*catching at her arm*). For Lars—he knows my—my methods of sport, you see.

Maja, with enforced self-possession, tells him frankly what she thinks of him. Her uncomplimentary observations please the bear-hunter very much. Maja requires all her tact to keep him in order. When she talks of going back to the hotel, he gallantly offers to carry her on his shoulders, for which suggestion he is promptly snubbed. The two are playing as a cat and a bird play. Out of their skirmish one speech of Ulfheim's rises suddenly to arrest attention, as it throws some light on his former life.

> ULFHEIM (*with suppressed exasperation*). I once took a young girl—lifted her up from the mire of the streets, and carried her in my arms. Next my heart I carried her. So I would have borne her all through life, lest haply she should dash her foot against a stone. . . . [*With a growling laugh.*] And do you know what I got for my reward?
>
> MAJA. No. What did you get?
>
> ULFHEIM (*looks at her, smiles and nods*). I got the horns! The horns that you can see so plainly. Is not that a comical story, madam bear-murderess?

As an exchange of confidence, Maja tells him her life in summary— and chiefly her married life with Professor Rubek. As a result, these two uncertain souls feel attracted to each other, and Ulfheim states his case in the following characteristic manner:

> ULFHEIM. Should not we two tack our poor shreds of life together?

Maja, satisfied that in their vows there will be no promise on his part to show her all the splendours of the earth, or to fill her dwelling-place with art, gives a half-consent by allowing him to carry her down the slope. As they are about to go, Rubek and Irene, who have also spent the night on the heath, approach the same plateau. When Ulfheim asks Rubek if he and madame have ascended by the same pathway, Rubek answers significantly.

> RUBEK. Yes, of course [*With a glance at* MAJA]. Henceforth the strange lady and I do not intend our ways to part.

While the musketry of their wit is at work, the elements seem to feel that there is a mighty problem to be solved then and there, and that a great drama is swiftly drawing to a close. The smaller figures of Maja and Ulfheim are grown still smaller in the dawn of the tempest. Their lots are decided in comparative quiet, and we cease to take much interest in them. But the other two hold our gaze, as they stand up silently on the fjaell, engrossing central figures of boundless, human interest. On a sudden, Ulfheim raises his hand impressively towards the heights.

ULFHEIM. But don't you see that the storm is upon us? Don't you hear the blasts of wind?

RUBEK (*listening*). They sound like the prelude to the Resurrection Day.

. . . .

MAJA (*drawing* ULFHEIM *away*). Let us make haste and get down.

As he cannot take more than one person at a time, Ulfheim promises to send aid for Rubek and Irene, and, seizing Maja in his arms, clambers rapidly but warily down the path. On the desolate mountain plateau, in the growing light, the man and the woman are left together — no longer the artist and his model. And the shadow of a great change is stalking close in the morning silence. Then Irene tells Arnold that she will not go back among the men and women she has left; she will not be rescued. She tells him also, for now she may tell all, how she had been tempted to kill him in frenzy when he spoke of their connection as an episode of his life.

RUBEK (*darkly*). And why did you hold your hand?

IRENE. Because it flashed upon me with a sudden horror that you were dead already — long ago.

But, says Rubek, our love is not dead in us, it is active, fervent and strong.

IRENE. The love that belongs to the life of earth — the beautiful, miraculous life of earth — the inscrutable life of earth — that is dead in both of us.

There are, moreover, the difficulties of their former lives. Even here, at the sublimest part of his play, Ibsen is master of himself and his facts. His genius as an artist faces all, shirks nothing. At the close of *The Master Builder*, the greatest touch of all was the horrifying exclamation of one without, "O! the head is all crushed in." A lesser artist would have cast a spiritual glamour over the tragedy of Bygmester Solness. In like manner here Irene objects that she has exposed herself as a nude before the vulgar gaze, that Society has cast her out, that all is too late. But Rubek cares for such considerations no more. He flings them all to the wind and decides.

RUBEK (*throwing his arms violently around her*). Then let two of the dead — us two — for once live life to its uttermost, before we go down to our graves again.

IRENE (*with a shriek*). Arnold!

RUBEK. But not here in the half-darkness. Not here with this hideous dank shroud flapping around us!

IRENE (*carried away by passion*). No, no — up in the light and in all the glittering glory! Up to the Peak of Promise!

RUBEK. There we will hold our marriage-feast, Irene — oh! my beloved!

IRENE (*proudly*). The sun may freely look on us, Arnold.

RUBEK. All the powers of light may freely look on us — and all the powers of darkness too [*seizes her hand*] — will you then follow me, oh my grace-given bride!

IRENE (*as though transfigured*). I follow you, freely and gladly, my lord and master!

RUBEK (*drawing her along with him*). We must first pass through the mists, Irene, and then —

IRENE. Yes, through all the mists, and then right up to the summit of the tower that shines in the sunrise.

The mist-clouds close in over the scene. RUBEK *and* IRENE, *hand in hand, climb up over the snowfield to the right and soon disappear among the lower clouds. Keen storm-gusts hurtle and whistle through the air.*

The SISTER OF MERCY *appears upon the rubble-slope to the left. She stops and looks around silently and searchingly.*

MAJA *can be heard singing triumphantly far in the depths below.*

MAJA. I am free! I am free! I am free!
No more life in the prison for me!
I am free as a bird! I am free!

Suddenly a sound like thunder is heard from high up on the snowfield, which glides and whirls downwards with rushing speed. RUBEK *and* IRENE *can be dimly discerned as they are whirled along with the masses of snow and buried in them.*

THE SISTER OF MERCY (*gives a shriek, stretches out her arms towards them, and cries*), Irene! [*Stands silent a moment, then makes the sign of the cross before her in the air, and says*], Pax Vobiscum!

MAJA's *triumphant song sounds from still further down below.*

Such is the plot, in a crude and incoherent way, of this new drama. Ibsen's plays do not depend for their interest on the action, or on the incidents. Even the characters, faultlessly drawn though they be, are not the first thing in his plays. But the naked drama — either the perception of a great truth, or the opening up of a great question, or a great conflict which is almost independent of the conflicting actors, and has been and is of far-reaching importance — this is what primarily rivets our attention. Ibsen has chosen the average lives in their uncompromising truth for the groundwork of all his later plays. He has abandoned the verse form, and has never sought to embellish his work after the conventional fashion. Even when his dramatic theme reached its zenith he has not sought to trick it out in gawds or tawdriness. How easy it would have been to have written *An Enemy of the People* on a speciously loftier level — to have replaced the *bourgeois* by the legitimate hero! Critics might then have extolled as grand what they have so often condemned as banal. But the surroundings are nothing to Ibsen. The play is the thing. By the force of his genius, and the indisputable skill which he brings to all his efforts, Ibsen has, for many years, engrossed the attention of the civilized world. Many years more, however, must pass before he will enter his kingdom in jubilation, although, as he stands to-day, all has been done on his part to ensure his own worthiness to enter therein. I do not propose here to examine into every detail of dramaturgy connected with this play, but merely to outline the characterization.

In his characters Ibsen does not repeat himself. In this drama — the last of a long catalogue — he has drawn and differentiated with his customary skill. What a novel creation is Ulfheim! Surely the hand which has drawn him has not yet lost her cunning. Ulfheim is, I think, the newest character in the play. He is a kind of surprise-packet. It is as a result of his novelty that he seems to leap, at first mention, into bodily form. He is superbly wild, primitively impressive. His fierce eyes roll and glare as those of Yégof or Herne. As for Lars, we may dismiss him, for he never opens his mouth. The Sister of Mercy speaks only once in the play, but then with good effect. In silence she follows Irene like a retribution, a voiceless shadow with her own symbolic majesty.

Irene, too, is worthy of her place in the gallery of her compeers. Ibsen's knowledge of humanity is nowhere more obvious than in his portrayal of women. He amazes one by his painful introspection; he seems to know them better than they know themselves. Indeed, if one may say so of an eminently virile man, there is a curious admixture of the woman in his nature. His marvellous accuracy, his faint traces of femininity, his delicacy of swift touch, are perhaps attributable to this admixture. But that he knows women is an incontrovertible fact. He appears to have sounded them to almost unfathomable depths. Beside his portraits the psychological studies of Hardy and Turgénieff, or the exhaustive elaborations of Meredith, seem no more than sciolism. With a deft stroke, in a phrase, in a word, he does what costs them chapters, and does it better. Irene, then, has to face great comparison; but it must be acknowledged that she comes forth of it bravely. Although Ibsen's women are uniformly true, they, of course, present themselves in various lights. Thus Gina Ekdal is, before all else, a comic figure, and Hedda Gabler a tragic one — if such old-world terms may be employed without incongruity. But Irene cannot be so readily classified; the very aloofness from passion, which is not separable from her, forbids classification. She interests us strangely — magnetically, because of her inner power of character. However perfect Ibsen's former creations may be, it is questionable whether any of his women reach to the depth of soul of Irene. She holds our gaze for the sheer force of her intellectual capacity. She is, moreover, an intensely spiritual creation — in the truest and widest sense of that. At times she is liable to get beyond us, to soar above us, as she does with Rubek. It will be considered by some as a blemish that she — a woman of fine spirituality — is made an artist's model, and some may even regret that such an episode mars the harmony of the drama. I cannot altogether see the force of this contention; it seems pure irrelevancy. But whatever may be thought of the fact, there is small room for complaint as to the handling of it. Ibsen treats it, as indeed he treats all things, with large insight, artistic restraint, and sympathy. He sees it steadily and whole, as from a great height, with perfect vision and an angelic dispassionateness, with the sight of one who may look on the sun with open eyes. Ibsen is different from the clever purveyor.

Maja fulfills a certain technical function in the play, apart from her individual character. Into the sustained tension she comes as a relief. Her airy freshness is as a breath of keen air. The sense of free, almost flamboyant, life, which is her chief note, counterbalances the austerity of Irene and the dullness of Rubek. Maja has practically the same effect on this play, as Hilda Wangel has on The Master Builder. But she does not capture our sympathy so much as Nora Helmer. She is not meant to capture it.

Rubek himself is the chief figure in this drama, and, strangely enough, the most conventional. Certainly, when contrasted with his Napoleonic predecessor, John Gabriel Borkman, he is a mere shadow. It must be borne in mind, however, that Borkman is alive, actively, energetically, restlessly alive, all through the play to the end, when he dies; whereas Arnold Rubek is dead, almost hopelessly dead, until the end, when he comes to life. Notwithstanding this, he is supremely interesting, not because of himself, but because of his dramatic significance. Ibsen's drama, as I have said, is wholly independent of his characters. They may be bores, but the drama in which they live and move is invariably powerful. Not that Rubek is a bore by any means! He is infinitely more interesting in himself than Torvald Helmer or Tesman, both of whom possess certain strongly-marked characteristics. Arnold Rubek is, on the other hand, not intended to be a genius, as perhaps Eljert Lövborg is. Had he been a genius like Eljert he would have understood in a truer way the value of his life. But, as we are to suppose, the facts that he is devoted to his art and that he has attained to a degree of mastery in it — mastery of hand linked with limitation of thought — tell us that there may be lying dormant in him a capacity for greater life, which may be exercised when he, a dead man, shall have risen from among the dead.

The only character whom I have neglected is the inspector of the baths, and I hasten to do him tardy, but scant, justice. He is neither more nor less than the average inspector of baths. But he is that.

So much for the characterization, which is at all times profound and interesting. But apart from the characters in the play, there are some noteworthy points in the frequent and extensive side-issues of the line of thought. The most salient of these is what seems, at first sight, nothing more than an accidental scenic feature. I allude to the environment of the drama. One cannot but observe in Ibsen's later work a tendency to get out of closed rooms. Since *Hedda Gabler* this tendency is most marked. The last act of *The Master Builder* and the last act of *John Gabriel Borkman* take place in the open air. But in this play the three acts are *al fresco*. To give heed to such details as these in the drama may be deemed ultra-Boswellian fanaticism. As a matter of fact it is what is barely due to the work of a great artist. And this feature, which is so prominent, does not seem to me altogether without its significance.

Again, there has not been lacking the last few social dramas a fine pity for men — a note nowhere audible in the uncompromising rigour of the early eighties. Thus in the conversion of Rubek's views as to the girl-figure in his masterpiece, "The Resurrection Day," there is involved an all-embracing philosophy, a deep sympathy with the cross-purposes and contradictions of life, as they may be reconcilable with a hopeful awakening — when the manifold travail of our poor humanity may have a glorious issue. As to the drama itself, it is doubtful if any good purpose can be served by attempting to criticize it. Many things would tend to prove this. Henrik Ibsen is one of the world's great men before whom criticism can make but feeble show. Appreciation, hearkening is the only true criticism. Further, that species of criticism which calls itself dramatic criticism is a needless adjunct to his plays. When the art of a dramatist is perfect the critic is superfluous. Life is not to be criticized, but to be faced and lived. Again, if any plays demand a stage they are the plays of Ibsen. Not merely is this so because his plays have so much in common with the plays of other men that they were not written to cumber the shelves of a library, but because they are so packed with thought. At some chance expression the mind is tortured with some question, and in a flash long reaches of life are opened up in vista, yet the vision is momentary unless we stay to ponder on it. It is just to prevent excessive pondering that Ibsen requires to be acted. Finally, it is foolish to expect that a problem, which has occupied Ibsen for nearly three years, will unroll smoothly before our eyes on a first or second reading. So it is better to leave the drama to plead for itself. But this at least is clear, that in this play Ibsen has given us nearly the very best of himself. The action is neither hindered by many complexities, as in *The Pillars of Society*, nor harrowing in its simplicity, as in *Ghosts*. We have whimsicality, bordering on extravagance, in the wild Ulfheim, and subtle humour in the sly contempt which Rubek and Maja entertain for each other. But Ibsen has striven to let the drama have perfectly free action. So he has not bestowed his wonted pains on the minor characters. In many of his plays these minor characters are matchless creations. Witness Jacob Engstrand, Tönnesen, and the demonic Molvik! But in this play the minor characters are not allowed to divert our attention.

On the whole, *When We Dead Awaken* may rank with the greatest of the author's work — if, indeed, it be not the greatest. It is described as the last of the series, which began with *A Doll's House* — a grand epilogue to its ten predecessors. Than these dramas, excellent alike in dramaturgic skill, characterization, and supreme interest, the long roll of drama, ancient or modern, has few things better to show.

Joyce and Ibsen's Naturalism   Hugh Kenner*

Joyce is commonly admired for a sort of raw realism which unresolved theological preoccupations have unfortunately rendered somewhat defective. Harry Levin treats *Ulysses* as a shotgun wedding between naturalism and symbolism; Wyndham Lewis, less inhibited by academic usage, calls its heaping-up of thousands of concrete stupidities "a record diarrhoea." It would be easy to multiply instances of the assumption that Joyce took seriously the sort of *tranche-de-vie* reproduction of externals sanctioned by the French realists of the Nineteenth Century and by the cult of Ibsen at the beginning of the Twentieth. The intemperance with which the young Joyce championed Ibsen at Dublin, and his palpable imitation of Ibsenian methods in *Exiles*, have contributed to this misunderstanding; the Joyce legend has been thoroughly mixed up with the Ibsen legend, apparently with Joyce's overt endorsement.

It is not difficult to cast serious doubt on the bucolic simplification of Joyce as realist *manqué*; this involves getting Ibsen, and Joyce's relations with Ibsen, into some sort of rational perspective, a problem complicated by the absence of any critically respectable book on Ibsen in English. Such being the case, it is useful to start by indicating (though a proper demonstration must wait) what sort of respect for naturalistic conventions *Ulysses* in fact represents.

> What did the first drawer unlocked contain?
> A Vere Foster's handwriting copybook, property of Milly (Millicent) Bloom, certain pages of which bore diagram drawings marked *Papli*, which showed a large globular head with 5 hairs erect, 2 eyes in profile, the trunk full front with 3 large buttons, 1 triangular foot: 2 fading photographs of Queen Alexandra of England and of Maud Branscombe, actress and professional beauty: a Yuletide card, bearing on it a pictorial representation of a parasitic plant, the legend, *Mizpah*, the date Xmas 1892, the name of the senders, from Mr. and Mrs. M. Comerford, the versicle: *May this Yuletide bring to thee, Joy and peace and welcome glee: . . .*   (U–705)

and so on for fifty lines. It is not likely to be disputed that the function of such a passage (it is representative of the 73-page *Ithaca* episode) is comic:

*Originally published in the *Sewanee Review* 49, no. 1 (Winter 1951), 75–96, by the University of the South. Reprinted by permission of the editor.

it parodies not only Bloom's foolishly meticulous interest in the matter in which his spirit is immersed, but in its insane superabundance the methods of naturalism proper. From beginning to end *Ulysses* parodies the naturalistic novel with genial ferocity. Nor does this parody proceed from an irrelevant temperamental whim of Joyce's. He regards the naturalistic superstition as a social product coming within his diagnostician's provenance as much as any other freak of popular culture: a Bloomian product, by Blooms for Blooms. There are several indications that Bloom would like to write the sort of book many readers imagine *Ulysses* to be: a fact which should not be altogether comforting for such readers:

> Time I used to try jotting down my cuff what she said dressing. Dislike dressing together. Nicked myself shaving. Biting her nether lip, hooking the placket of her skirt. Timing her. 9.15. Did Roberts pay you yet? 9.20. What had Gretta Conroy on? 9.23. What possessed me to buy this comb? 9.24. I'm swelled after that cabbage. A speck of dust on the patent leather of her boot.   (U–69)

Such systematic false notes as the enumeration of the hairs in Milly's drawing have persuaded almost no one that a vigorous comic consciousness is everywhere present. At most, they have been taken as humorless lapses of taste. The Ibsen legend is of the same kind. William Archer makes scandalized noises at what he conceives to be the radical lapse of *When We Dead Awaken*:

> . . . He sacrificed the surface reality to the underlying meaning. Take, for instance, the history of Rubek's statue and its development into a group. In actual sculpture this development is a grotesque impossibility. In conceiving it we are deserting the domain of reality, and plunging into some fourth dimension where the properties of matter are other than those we know. . . . Here, . . . without any suggestion of the supernatural, we are confronted with the wholly impossible, the inconceivable. . . . So great is the chasm between *John Gabriel Borkman* and *When We Dead Awaken* that one could almost suppose his mental breakdown to have preceded instead of following the writing of the latter play.[1]

The analogies of What is the Exact Age of Hamlet? and How Many Children Had Lady Macbeth? will occur to the reader. It is difficult to imagine the author of *Finnegans Wake* being impressed by Archer's notions of the probable in art; and we have seen the author of *Ulysses* concealing his grin. Insofar as dramaturgy à la William Archer is the basis for Ibsen's reputation (and his reputation so based is only beginning to be shaken) Joyce was never an Ibsenite at all.

This much by way of quelling the temptation to explain Joyce's interest in Ibsen by way of "naturalism." Ibsen represented for Joyce, first and foremost, a remarkable prototype of the successful provincial artist —

one who might offer not only a paradigm of personal integrity but a set of strategies for dealing with a starved milieu and a half-baked culture. This sort of example was not to be found at the cliché-Ibsenite levels of the realistic setting and the socially unmentionable subject. Joyce must be granted sufficient acuteness to have realized that the sort of greatness he sensed in the Norwegian dramatist was incompatible with a habitual use of barren Archerese. That is why, at the age of seventeen or so, he taught himself Dano-Norwegian. Rehabilitating Ibsen, Miss M. C. Bradbrook writes: "Ibsen's prose is dramatic, which means that in balance, movement, and rhythm it is adapted for speaking; and it is literature, which means that it is built on the natural virtues of the tongue and upon Ibsen's personal idiom as he fashioned it for his needs. His writing can be understood only in terms of the Norse, with its clear, pungent but concrete vocabulary, its strong, live metaphors ("we felt our hearts *beat strongly towards* him"), its lack of reverberations or overtones."[2]

It is possible to see, without becoming involved in a far-reaching revaluation of Ibsen, that Joyce by reading him in the original could find a writer congenial to his own preoccupations with setting language significantly in action. If Ibsen wrote no *Anna Livia Plurabelle* (and Joyce, it should be remembered, was writing *English* in the densest sections of *Finnegans Wake*, exploiting to the full a sophisticated and hybrid tongue), he did do whatever a strong sensibility and tentacular roots to a vigorous popular culture could do with a sinewy if barren language: so much so that Miss Bradbrook's quotations are a satisfactory index of linguistic life, even when we come to the Norse with the help of a translation and by way of its affinities with German and Anglo-Saxon. It is, for instance, illuminating to be told apropos of a key phrase in *Rosmersholm* that "*Kinsmen* in Norwegian are *skyldfolk*, those who share a common guilt": a typical example of thematic immersion in language that defies translation. Ibsen (like Dante and Joyce, though this is not to imply equations of value) wrote in a language whose relations with popular culture were still uneasy and just becoming consolidated. Writes Miss Bradbrook, "A multiplicity of dialects were spoken in the countryside; the official language, Dano-Norwegian, had only just come into use as a spoken tongue. Ibsen was of the first generation who naturally wrote and spoke in this form." Ibsen's biographer Koht offers a still more suggestive phrase: "For the older Norwegian writers the Danish language had been much more purely a book language than it was for the new generation." That English was a book-language explains much of the vacuity of the Anglo-Irish poets from Moore and Mangan to early Yeats. It abetted the *Zeitgeist*'s drift toward private worlds. Yeats became a great poet when with Pound's help he related his use of English to the spoken idiom; as Joyce, encouraged by Ibsen and Ben Jonson, had never from the beginning failed to do. Joyce's advantage in dealing with a language that was still in process of becoming fused with an already vigorous cultural sensibility (the analogy of Shakespeare's relations with the Elizabethan word-hunger is suggestive) underlies the range and zest of his vocabulary and grammar, and the sureness with which he could spot and parody cliché. It is possible that Ibsen's ability to disentangle moral realities from pious formulae is related to the analogous freedom of his new idiom from commonplaces. Only when thought is carried on in living language can the intellect be maintained at the tips of the senses.

Joyce's unwillingness to flirt with Yeats, Lady Gregory, and the Gaelic League was probably stiffened by the example of Ibsen's experience. Ibsen in his early years had been involved in a similar campaign for a national drama and a purely Norwegian language. Imbued with a Yeatsian resolve to recall to the people "the rich imagery of the distant past" and "the forgotten tales of childhood," he wrote one popular success and a series of failures. With *Brand* he dropped the ballad-themes and came to terms with himself; and the fall of 1866 found him removing the ultra-Norwegian words for a new edition of *Love's Comedy*. He had wasted fifteen years.

The 18-year-old Joyce's essay on *Ibsen's New Drama* indicates the importance he attached to Ibsen's personal integrity. The key phrases of the opening paean, "Seldom, if at all, has he condescended to join battle with his enemies. It would appear as if the storm of fierce debate rarely broke in upon his wonderful calm. The conflicting voices have not influenced his work in the very smallest degree," are readily assimilated with the portrait of the dramatic artist, "refined out of existence, aloof, paring his fingernails." The extent to which Ibsen offered a personal example should not be underrated, and his biography — disgust with Norway, exile, early poems, middle monuments of construction and solidity accompanied by *succèss de scandale*, later symbolic experiments, denounced by fellow-travelers as madness — this career, excepting his ultimate return to homeland fame, resembles Joyce's in the most striking way; and a recent writer on Ibsen whom one need not suppose has given Joyce a thought remarks on the striking parallel between Dano-Norse and Anglo-Irish relations. This was the sector of Ibsen's appeal which the young Joyce found it easiest to focus. The letter he sent Ibsen in 1901 speaks of "what, as it seemed to me, was your highest excellence — your lofty impersonal power," with only a glance at what were later to become less kinetic and more nourishing preoccupations, "your satire, your technique and orchestral harmony." The letter goes on:

> I did not tell them (i.e. the Dubliners) what bound me closest to you. I did not say how much I could discern dimly of your life was my pride to see, how your battles inspired me — not the obvious material battles but those that were fought and won behind your forehead, how your wilful resolution to wrest the secret from life gave me heart and

how in your resolute indifference to public canons of art, friends, and
shibboleths you walked in the light of your inward heroism.

This, of course, is Stephen Dedalus talking; the decisive reorientation
that was to make possible *Dubliners* and all the later achievement was still
nearly five years off. For this reason one should be chary of supposing that
Joyce in 1901 had said all there is to say about the importance his mature
self attached to Ibsen. A Joyce who was merely Ibsen would be merely
provincial; the Norwegian at his best does not belie the clumsy iconoclasm
with which his disciples have been associated. The man who roared at a
review of *Peer Gynt*, "My book *is* poetry, and if it is not, it shall be. The
conception of poetry shall in our land, in Norway, come to adapt itself to
the book"; who at sixteen told his sister that his ambition was to attain the
utmost perfection of greatness and clarity and after that to die; and who
insisted with the vehemence of uneasiness that he did not write only for
the immediate future but for all eternity, could not help being on his
weakest as well as on his strongest side congenial to the lustful arrogance of
Stephen Dedalus, and could not have mustered the ironic detachment
from his own weakness to have written more than a caricature of *Ulysses*.
The uncompromising meddling of the Brand-like Gregers Werle in *The
Wild Duck* invites no sympathy whatever, while Brand invites too much of
the wrong kind, and is perfunctorily extinguished in a closing scene which
neither Ibsen nor any commentator has satisfactorily related to the rest of
the drama. On the Dedalian idealist Ibsen blows with alternate vehemence hot and cold; much of the teasing interest of the generic problem-
play derives simply from an inability to digest and detach himself from his
passions.

Joyce had done this digesting by 1905; the casting off of the devil
represented by Dedalus is one of his major themes, and led him on to those
vast explorations of the possibility of metaphysical self-sufficiency of
which *Exiles* is a firm preliminary statement. Now the relation of Ibsen's
earliest poems to his latest plays (which Miss Bradbrook[3] has done a great
service to emphasize) indicates how Ibsen, even in his "realistic" middle
period, was obsessed with a similar theme, the theme of the unfulfillable
vocation, what may be generalized as the moral paradox of the human
condition. It is toward a definition of this theme that the sordid particular-
ities in which he deals become numinous symbols: the crippling inherited
disease, the rotten ship, the captive wild duck. A personal conflict
centering around the particular example of the artist's vocation (Ibsen left
Norway for much the same reasons that drove Joyce from Ireland) and
particularized in many modes in some highly relevant poems and in over a
dozen plays is what gives Ibsen's work thematic coherence. This cannot be
too much insisted upon. One would have thought from the claims made by
his disciples that he conceived himself primarily as a reformer of the
middle class. Yet however he might throw his weight about in practical

politics, he always denied that, for example, *A Doll's House* was circumscribed by the feminist movement, or had any frame of reference less wide than "humanity."

Nor was Joyce ever deceived on this point. In a portion of the *Stephen Hero* manuscript that can hardly date later than 1904, the following exchange occurs:

> — Ah, if he were to examine even the basest things, said the President with a suggestion of tolerance in store, it would be different if he were to examine and then show men the way to purify themselves.
> — That is for the Salvationists, said Stephen.
> — Do you mean. . . .
> — I mean that Ibsen's account of modern society is as genuinely ironical as Newman's account of English Protestant morality and belief.
> — That may be, said the President appeased by the conjunction.
> — And as free from any missionary intention.
> The President was silent.   (SH–92).

On an earlier page is an even more unequivocal ascription of poetic rather than rhetorical virtues: a conventional Ibsenite says to Stephen,

> — That is not the teaching of Ibsen.
> — Teaching! cried Stephen.
> — The moral of *Ghosts* is just the opposite of what you say.
> — Bah! You regard the play as a scientific document.
> — *Ghosts* teaches self-repression. . . .
> — You have connected Ibsen and Eno's fruit salt forever in my mind, said Stephen.
>
> (SH–52)

The essential conflicts which are realized and elaborated in the early plays appear half-swallowed in the early poems, which in turn bear a striking relation to the final "symbolic" plays. One of them, *Et Vers*, clearly places the origin of art in experimental conflict:

> To live is to war with the troll
> In the caverns of heart and of skull.
> To write poetry — that is to hold
> Doom-session upon the soul.[4]

Joyce was saved from the Romantic disease, the uncritical obtrusion of the bleeding heart, by a Jesuit education that preserved communications with pre-Romantic ethics and rhetoric. Ibsen's insistence on doom-session rather than out-pouring has a slighter pedigree reaching merely to Hegel. The Danish poet and critic Johan Ludvig Heiberg, who introduced Hegel to Scandinavia and became the intellectual dictator and aesthetic teacher of Ibsen's generation, had proclaimed as his first aesthetic law that "the poet, instead of yielding himself to his inspiration, should through the power of the intellect make himself its master." With the help of Hegel, he had also "shown that the desire for freedom was of necessity a revolt against restraint, that it was born in strife and could live only in strife,"[5] setting the witchword "freedom" in a dramatic context that on the one hand redeemed from a doctrinaire Shavianism Ibsen's handling of contro-versial topics, and on the other hand betrayed him all too easily to a doctrinaire misreading. Here, of course, Joyce's Aristotelian heritage saved him. For Stephen Dedalus conflict is the negation of order: he is at best and at worst a contemplative.

On Hegel and Heiberg may be blamed Ibsen's lifelong inability to assess the validity of the artist's role; he worried whether the very writing of *Brand* had not constituted an evasion of the strenuous action it advocated, a worry which he cast in Kierkegaardian terms. It was through this Hegelian stage-door that Ibsen stepped into an indefensible but roughly practicable role of Byronic scorn. The contradiction inherent in that role constituted his lifelong theme.

The poem *On the Vidda* (1859–60; aetat. 32) establishes most clearly the themes of which *When We Dead Awaken* (which had special relevance for Joyce) was the final exploration. The young hero of the poem lies on the heather upland thinking of his betrothed and wishing her path may be difficult so that he can smooth it. His wish is granted more terribly than he can foresee: when she at length comes to wed another man he has not only tired of her, but has lost all taste for the level of practical action represented by her existence in the valley. He has been visited by a strange hunter "with cold eyes like mountain lakes" who has called him to a life of strenuous contemplation, and induced him to stay in the mountains all summer. An impulse to see his mother and his sweetheart has been frustrated by the snow-choked passes of winter; and the first stage of his transformation into an artist has been the recognition that the life of the valley is no longer for him. When his mother's cottage burns, "the hunter coolly points out the beauty of the fire and advises on the best way to get the view. Then he disappears and leaves the son with his blood freezing and burning, yet acknowledging after all, in spite of himself, the beauty of the scene." In the last section, watching the bridal procession of his beloved and another man wind through the trees, "he discovers that he has grieved himself free at last. *Cantat vacuus.* He curves his hand to get the perspective right . . . self-steeled he looks on at joy from above life's snow-line. The Strange Hunter reappears and tells him he is now free. . . ." The young man's final speech strikes the now-congenial Dedalus pose:

> Now I am steel-set: I follow the call
> To the height's clear radiance and glow.
> My lowland life is lived out: and high
> On the *vidda* are God and Liberty —
> Whilst wretches live fumbling below.[6]

The author of *The Holy Office* (1904) appears to have taken several gestures from this poem:

So distantly I turn to view
The shamblings of that motley crew,
Those souls that hate the strength that mine has
Steeled in the school of old Aquinas.
Where they have crouched and crawled and prayed
I stand, the self-doomed, unafraid,
Unfellowed, friendless, and alone,
Indifferent as the herring-bone,
Firm as the mountain ridges where
I flash my antlers in the air.

The interest of *The Holy Office* lies partly in its date: it indicates how, even after the scrupulously ironic and intensely felt writing of *Dubliners* was under way, the Dedalus pose remained as a habit behind which Joyce's rhetorical energy could most readily be mobilized. It bears all the marks of extremely rapid writing (a distinction, it must be insisted, not only from *Finnegans Wake* but from the simplest phrases of the *Portrait* and *Dubliners*); and its relations to violent feelings to which Joyce did not mind attaching public importance is implicit in the fact that he had it printed and mailed to all the victims mentioned in the text. When in the *Portrait* or in *Ulysses* Stephen Dedalus is shown behaving with comparable centrifugal irrelevance, careful writing and scrupulous irony invariably set him in semi-comic contrast with a wide frame of reference. The aesthete becomes himself an aesthetic object. No one doubts that Joyce knew Dedalus from the inside; it should be equally clear that the writer who "placed" him from the outside exhibits a habitual wisdom inaccessible to Dedalus himself. Joyce is not Stephen. Yet it is evident that Stephen is for his creator something more than comic; there is tragic intensity in the spectacle of the aesthete's mask becoming fused to his flesh. And this tragic necessity, which energized the scornful violence of such a production as *The Holy Office*—the necessity, for a provincial artist deprived of any respectable tradition,[7] of becoming the enemy of his society in ways incompatible with the human necessity of remaining in touch with human wisdom—corresponds to Ibsen's generic theme of the impossible vocation. Neither Joyce nor Ibsen should be said to have succumbed to this necessity, though both experienced it insofar as it was necessary. Both made art of its central antithesis: dramatized it.

The necessity for a central portion of the contemporary artist's soul being turned toward enmity for his society, and the corollary necessity of the artist's being either on the one hand an anarchic aesthete (like Dedalus or the unhappy hero of *On the Vidda*) who sacrifices all human ties to his art, or on the other hand, if not a split man, at least a man both partly of his community and partly at cross-purposes with it (like Joyce or Ibsen)— this necessity, a reflex of the disproportionate burden laid on the artist by failure of the community, makes obvious contact at several points with the cultural history of the last two centuries. In fact, the forces that pushed the Byronic aristocrat into an anti-social role of destructive action and the Shelleyan Blithe Spirit into emasculate thrill-seeking; that drove the former forward and upward into sub-human scientific activities (so that the pedigree of the tycoon and of the sleuth reaches back through Huxley and Darwin to Byron and beyond) and that drove the latter downward and outward into complacent garrulity (so that from Shelley through Tennyson to Edgar Guest the line of descent and diffusion is clear): these dichotomizing forces reach back through the Cartesian dualism of the Seventeenth Century to the breakup of mediaeval order in the Fifteenth. The split artist reflects the split man of the split community: as martyr to that split, he is like Shem the Penman "honor bound to his own cruelfiction." His plight is therefore of more than professional significance; which is the reason for the universal contemporary validity of the myth which Ibsen and Joyce (Joyce more explicitly) construct on the plight of the provincial artist. (Of course the feeble novelist writes autobiography because he has no other interests; *he* is not here in question except as a symptom.) It is no accident that Kierkegaard's "crisis theology" (a tragically barren rationalization of the plight of the sensitive in a cultural vacuum) stands behind Ibsen and Kafka alike; or that Kafka occupies for the earnest elite of today the symbolic position a previous generation had accorded to Ibsen. In Kafka the theme of the impossible vocation gets the fullest possible statement: whatever his intentions may have been, to leave his novels unfinished was the most appropriate denouement he could have contrived.

There is, then, no paradox in saying that a deeply-rooted personal conflict, which certain early productions (notably *On the Vidda* and the play *Love's Comedy*) had explicitly stated as an artist-myth, provides the underlying tension for the ironically-detailed social documentation on which Ibsen's reputation has come to be based. (In the same way, *The Holy Office* implies *Dubliners*). *Brand* marks a transition from the personal to the public statement of this tension; Ibsen by that time (1866, aetat. 38: the age by which Joyce had nearly finished *Ulysses*) was at least conceptually uneasy about the naïve heroics of *On the Vidda*. Brand as clergyman (a more general statement of the artist as communal scapegoat) makes, like the young man on the vidda, one ruthless personal sacrifice after another in a spirit of self-conscious humility of which the better-nourished wisdom of T. S. Eliot has provided in *Murder in the Cathedral* a more complex and less ambiguous statement.[8] Having demanded the supreme sacrifice of his mother, his child, his wife, and his congregation, he winds up both among the mountain-peaks of his ambition and in the Ice-Church appropriate to his nature; when finally, renouncing pride and calling on the God of Love, he melts the ice, he and his troll-lover are engulfed in the ruins.

The extent to which Ibsen's intellectual life was conducted in jejune slogans (which must strike any reader of Koht's biography, and which no amount of allowance for the naïveté of the biographer can do much to cancel) not only underlies the Byronic indigestibility of *Brand* but makes clear how serviceable a document it could be to the supple and ironic sensibility of a Joyce intent on portraying a Stephen. The five chapters of *A Portrait of the Artist as a Young Man* constitute a rewriting of the five acts of *Brand* with infinitely greater local sensitivity and within a richly nourished milieu of classical ethics. It is from Brand that many of the most humorlessly arrogant gestures of Stephen Dedalus are derived: his behavior at his mother's deathbed, his rejection of the Christianity of the clergy, his romantic positives expressed in terms of "the spell of arms and voices" and of "exultant and terrible youth," corresponding to Ibsen's "flashing eye" and his dawn above the ice-fields. If the similarities are obvious, so are the differences. Many can be enumerated; but more important are the ones that can only be illustrated, and of which only the reader's sensibility can furnish ultimate proof: differences that reflect the civilized heritage of sensibility available to the Dubliner. If Ireland was "the afterthought of Europe," it was still European; it is partly the impossibility of a revolt against the bourgeois frontier ethics of Norway becoming enfleshed in anything more concrete than stern intentions that makes *Brand*, for the English reader, so stiff and bony. Here a letter of Ibsen's to Georg Brandes (1871) provides useful evidence:

> Undermine the idea of the State, set up voluntary choice and spiritual kinship as the only determining factors for union — that is the beginning of a freedom that is worth something. Yes, my dear friend, it is imperative not to let one's self be frightened by its venerable vested rights. The State has its roots in time, it will culminate in time. Greater things than this will fall; all religions will fall. Neither moral principles nor artistic forms have any eternity ahead of them. How much are we at bottom obliged to hold fast to? Who can guarantee that two and two are not five on Jupiter?[9]

Denial of the rational and political nature of man could scarcely go further; it is startling to learn that Ibsen was accustomed to using his question about two and two as a serious argument. This envacuumed skeletal righteousness deprived of all social, political, or theological context sharply contradistinguishes itself from the sense of collective wisdom that secures Wordsworth (who denied its intellectual roots) a dignified place in the English tradition, and that for the fifty generations running from Cicero through St. Augustine to Erasmus had nourished a complex communal ideal of which Wordsworth merely furnishes the death-mask. Ibsen shatters the mask; it is by anguish rather than by consistency that his dramas are saved from ethical anarchy. The reader should have no difficulty seeing that Stephen Dedalus at his most iconoclastic prizes a fidelity to existent being much closer to the pragmatic Ibsen as a practicing dramatist (post-*Brand*) than to Ibsen's avowed anarchic idealism.

—The modern spirit is vivisective. Vivisection itself is the most modern process one can conceive. The ancient spirit accepted phenomena with a bad grace. The ancient method investigated law with the lantern of justice, morality with the lantern of revelation, art with the lantern of tradition. But all these lanterns have magical properties: they transform and disfigure. The modern method examines its territory by the light of day. Italy has added a science to civilization by putting out the lantern of justice and considering the criminal in production and in action. All modern political and religious criticism dispenses with presumptive States, and presumptive Redeemers and Churches. It examines the entire community in action and reconstructs the spectacle of redemption.[10]

This was written before 1906; and while the mature Joyce would not have defined Stephen's position in quite that way as a naïve modern-vs.-ancient dualism, yet to dispense with a priori presumptive States is very different from Ibsen's a priori positivism. Indeed, Stephen, in the spirit of the author of *Ulysses*, goes on to distinguish Aristotle from the dialectical Aristotelians:

—. . . I do not think he is the special patron of those who proclaim the usefulness of the stationary march. . . . The toy life which the Jesuits permit these docile young men to live is what I call a stationary march. The marionette life which the Jesuit himself lives as a dispenser of illumination and rectitude is another variety of the stationary march. And yet both these classes of puppets think that Aristotle has apologized for them before the eyes of the world.

The Stephen who could emancipate Aristotle from the claims of the stationary marchers is on the way to becoming the author of *Ulysses* and *Finnegans Wake*. Stephen Hero is in fact very nearly the young James Joyce. He talks a great deal of sense of which the later and better-known book contains no hint. The Stephen of *A Portrait of the Artist as a Young Man* has been carefully recast, with the aid of *Brand*, as an anarchic aesthete, destined in the company of Buck Mulligan (a variation on Peer Gynt) to come to comprehensive grief in *Ulysses*, beneath the eyes of an author who "examines the entire community in action and reconstructs the spectacle of redemption."

It is clear that the relation of Brand to his author is highly peculiar. *Brand*, as T. S. Eliot has said of *Hamlet* in a phrase which is fast becoming a critical cliché, is "full of some stuff that the writer could not drag to light, contemplate, or manipulate into art." Eliot goes on, "The supposed identity of Hamlet with his author is genuine to this point: that Hamlet's bafflement at the absence of an objective equivalent to his feelings is the prolongation of the bafflement of his creator in the face of his artistic problem." It is so: for Hamlet read Brand. Ibsen in the utter absence of a tradition couldn't even decide whether writing were worth while.[11] A valid perception of the distinction between artist and dilettante was elevated through Kierkegaard's categorical absolutism into an Either-Or conflict which energized all his plays, yet prevented him from achieving a plenary resolution of the conflicts of any of them. The surplus emotional energy thus left lying was absorbed by the generic irony of his "naturalist" convention: his passion for documentation in the prose plays prevents the emotion from becoming rhetorical, and the emotion saves the documentation from being trivial. It was Ibsen's triumph to have achieved in the problem-play an adequate personal form, as it was Joyce's to control through the manipulation of myths an even more complex personal tension, between the artist as contemporary rebel, and the man as inheritor of a massive structure of civilization. Neither Ibsen nor Joyce can be blamed for the botches of interpreters and imitators.

The plays on which Ibsen's reputation is chiefly based, from *Pillars of Society* to *The Master Builder*, depend on a number of thematic conventions and assumptions that have been from the beginning largely obscured by a complexly-motivated cloud of unknowing. The completely irrelevant valuations to which Ibsen has thus been subjected present an instructive likeness to the legend that since the first stir and rumor of *Ulysses* has enshrouded the achievement of Joyce. The "naturalist" red herring has already been mentioned. It arose in England partly from the barrenness of the Archer translations (a barrenness the product of doctrine more than illiteracy), but much more from the sequence of what we may describe as "inevitable accidents" by which Ibsen's reputation fell into the hands of muscular missionaries whose type is Bernard Shaw, and who combined utter insensitivity to the complex rhetorical modes of traditional art with a naïve determination to pull the theater, with its obvious facilities for the imitation of superficies, out of the hands of irresponsible popular entertainment and into the purlieu of the social reformer. The contemporary attempt to make the cinema an "art" form via the documentary is similar in intention. Shaw's *Quintessence of Ibsenism* is a representative document of this preconception; Archer's *The Old Drama and the New* rewrites European dramatic history in its light in an attempt to provide the problem-play, by Darwinian strategies, with a pedigree.

Of even greater importance in establishing conventional attitudes to Ibsen was the "unpleasant subject," the socially-unmentionable theme: the most celebrated example is the hereditary insanity in *Ghosts*. So thoroughly did the very defense-mechanism he was concerned to analyse frustrate Ibsen's intention, that champion and detractor alike have failed to notice that he was employing mental unbalance of venereal origin as a relevant metaphor for original sin. His biographer notes that Oswald and his illness were for a long time regarded as the center of *Ghosts*, and doctors discussed whether the case was rightly diagnosed: an attitude which the present decade has not really outgrown. Koht further shows (vol. II, p. 166) by a consideration of early drafts that it was the mother's sin rather than the father's lust that Ibsen meant the disease to transmit: and the mother's sin had a spiritual rather than a physical connection with the disease.

A couplet in *Brand*, "Blood of the children must be spilt / To atone for parents' guilt," points to the religious orientation of one of Ibsen's constant preoccupations; that his characters, like his audience, were aware of such principles only when they presented themselves in terms of corporeal pathology is one of the perceptions controlling the organization of *Ghosts*; a good example of his ironic use of naturalist conventions. The scrupulous documentation of externals masking psychological and super-natural realities to which, until the catastrophe, the protagonists are indifferent, is an elaborate aesthetic imitation of the condition of a whole society. In Joyce a similar technique transcends social preoccupations to make the ironic and unsuspected presence of supernatural significance in natural facts an image of the entire condition of man. In these terms it is easy to see that Joyce and Ibsen employed "unmentionable" themes not as Shavian Ibsenites thought with the purpose of promoting "open discussion," but because of the dramatic significance that could be extracted from the social and psychological mechanisms that insured their going unmentioned. The irony directed toward audiences and protagonists who imagine because of their grasp on external phenomena, that they are in strict control of the business of living while remaining frantically oblivious to the kinds of meaning concealed by the vaunted profusion of data, is clearly related to the resolve of the artist to pursue intelligibility at the expense of exclusion from the crowd; it is one more example of the thematic bearings of the artist-myth discussed above. Ibsen's conception of the entire drama as a presentation of dawning moral illumination, a colossal catastrophe motivated by the nemesis entrained by hidden sins, has obvious affinities with, for example, the tragedy of Oedipus that underlies *Finnegans Wake*, and that was Aristotle's showpiece of *anagnoesis* combined with *peripeteia*. The naturalist technique is plainly functional to this conception: it projects the dramatically essential un-awareness of the protagonists.

It ought to be said that for the mature artist the use of the "naturalist" convention will invariably involve and permit an irony of this kind, because of the insistent indication, beneath the superficially thorough documentation, of what is being left out. Joyce and Ibsen display this irony on inspection, though it will scarcely carry its full weight to the reader unable to realize their implications, in the charged handling of language, of what a very different convention, like the Shakespearean, would permit. Mr. Eliot's experiments with modern diction convey the ironic judgment (it cannot be called simply a sneer at the speakers) in a similar though simpler way:

> People with money from heaven knows where—
> Dividends from aeroplane shares.
> They bathe all day and they dance all night
> In the absolute *minimum* of clothes.

This reflection of supercultivated gossip is framed and "placed" by a superimposed rhythm (that of the dance-tune and of *Sweeney Agonistes*) belonging to what the speakers innocently imagine to be a very different world. And it follows, in its context, a sudden shift from the charged intensity of:

> O Sun, that was once so warm, O Light that
>   was taken for granted
>
> When I was young and strong, and sun and light
>   unsought for
> And the night unfeared and the day expected
> And clocks could be trusted, tomorrow assured
> And time would not stop in the dark!

It is a subtlety of this kind (not, by Eliot's best standards, really very subtle; but he was writing for a contemporary theater audience) that a critic like Cyril Connolly, in preferring *Sweeney Agonistes* to the rest of Eliot's output because it reflects the way people really talk, has palpably missed. Because Joyce employs this critical principle from his first published pages to his last, it is fatal for the Joycean to miss it; though it is perhaps no accident that Mr. Connolly on *Ulysses* ("Narcissus with his pool before him") sounds exactly like all the other commentators.

There was then, despite what we are told by historians of the naturalistic novel, no simple formula for the meaning of Ibsen for Joyce. It was a relation of affinity and of differentiation, of example and of caution, an interpenetration neither definitive enough to be accounted "influence," nor sufficiently alien to be disowned. Ibsen was both a catalyst and a heresiarch: a warning. He understood as did no one else in his time the burden of the dead past and the wastefulness of any attempt to give it spurious life: his "I think we are sailing with a corpse in the cargo!" is in the mode of Stephen Dedalus' apprehension of the nightmare of history from which H. C. Earwicker strains to awake. But he had never known, and could not know in the frontier vacuum of the fiords, the traditions of the European community, of richly-nourished life; and the lonely starvation of his ideal of free personal affinity in no context but that of intermingling wills inspired Joyce with a fascination which generated *Exiles* and a civilized repulsion that found its objective correlative when Leopold Bloom felt "the apathy of the stars."

Notes

1. Introduction to *When We Dead Awaken*. Ibsen, *Works*, New York, 1917, vol. 11, pp. 357–358.

2. *Ibsen the Norwegian*, p. 24.

3. *Ibsen the Norwegian*, pp. 26–35.

4. Miss Bradbrook's translation (op. cit., p. 16). It is incidentally convenient to be able to show that Joyce knew this poem (and inferentially, the rest of Ibsen's) in the Norse. The account on page 199 of *Finnegans Wake*, of HCE "hunger-striking all alone and holding doomsdag over hunselv" alludes to the last two lines, which read in Norwegian, "At digte — det er at holde / dommedag over sig selv." Ibsen the Norwegian has many analogues with HCE the Scandinavian invader, who supersedes Finnegan at Dublin in the same way that Joyce's Gargantuan novels supersede easygoing popular art, and who undergoes a nightlong introspection looking forward to the (unwritten) epilogue *When We Dead Awaken*.

5. Koht's *Ibsen*, vol. I, pp. 60–61.

6. This translation, like the substance of the outline above, is taken from Miss Bradbrook (p. 33).

7. Cf. Joyce in *The Day of the Rabblement*, 1901: ". . . The Irish Literary Theatre must now be considered the property of the rabblement of the most belated race in Europe. . . . A nation which never advanced so far as a miracle play affords no literary model to the artist. . . ."

8. Compare with the speeches of Eliot's Fourth Tempter the following:

> It is not martyrdom to toss
> In anguish on the deadly cross:
> But to have *will'd* to perish so,
> To *will* it through each bodily throe,
> To will it with still-tortured mind,
> This, only this, redeems mankind.
> —*Brand* III; in *Works*, vol. III, p. 114

9. Koht, vol. II, p. 84.

10. *Stephen Hero*, p. 186.

11. Cf. Koht, vol. II, p. 27: "Recently, while writing *Brand*, he had felt as if he were taking part in strife and action, and there had been a sense of jubilation within him. . . . Now, afterwards, it seemed to him that he had merely evaded the struggle and the call to action; it appeared to him, as he wrote in a letter, that *Brand* was 'wholly and thoroughly an aesthetic work without a trace of anything else.' " It should be remembered that "aesthetic" was, in the Kierkegaardian system, pejorative.

Ibsen's Dramatic Language as a Link between His "Realism" and His "Symbolism"

Inga-Stina Ewbank*

The title of this paper was chosen in the murky gloom of a Liverpool winter; now that I look at it in the more relentless light of a Norwegian summer, I realize that it appears not only cumbersome, but also, at one and the same time, vague and question-begging. So I had better explain just what lies behind it, and what it aims at.

*Originally published in *Contemporary Approaches to Ibsen*, vol. 1, ed. Daniel Haakonsen (Oslo: Universitetsforlaget, 1965–66), 96–123.

Ibsen's dramatic language is a problem peculiarly alive to a Scandinavian teaching Ibsen in English (and indeed as part of an English Literature syllabus). One's students have been brought up in the tradition of Shakespearean studies where they learn to see Shakespeare as a poetic dramatist: as one whose linguistic devices are essentially and inextricably part of his dramatic action, characters, symbolism and (what I must call, for lack of a better word) meaning. Inevitably, when faced with an Ibsen play, they will ask how far Ibsen's language plays a part in the creation of particular dramatic effects, or in what the play as a whole says and means. Not so very long ago, of course, they may not have thought of asking such questions. In 1936 that stern judge of literary values, *Scrutiny*, told its readers that "one of the most striking qualities of the drama of Ibsen . . . is its antiseptic, delocalized, universal flavour"—and then, going back on itself: "perhaps antiseptic is the wrong word for Ibsen, who moves in a kind of bourgeois fug," a fug of "cigar-smoke and rum punch."[1] Ten years later, the same readers were asked to contemplate what Henry James wrote in an anti-Ibsen moment: "Ibsen is ugly, common, hard, prosaic, bottomlessly bourgeois."[2] But since then we have had several distinguished studies in English of Ibsen, showing that his sphere extends beyond the cigar-smoke and rum punch, and stressing the poetic, rather than prosaic, qualities of his plays. It has, however, been the poetry of the action and the visual symbolism—in the words of Professor Fergusson's helpful distinction, the poetry *of* the theatre, rather than the poetry *in* the theatre; the poetry *under* the words, rather than *in* the words[3]—which have received most attention: as, for example, in Dr. Northam's illuminating study of *Ibsen's Dramatic Method.*[4] This is natural enough in books written for a mainly non-Norwegian-speaking audience. But, it seems to me, a gathering like this first International Ibsen Seminar may be the occasion to question the assumption made by so many people—at least in England, but I have a feeling that there is a similar situation in Norway—that the language of Ibsen's prose plays is somehow like the transparent plastic casing round some intricate piece of machinery: without it the machinery could not be contained, but in itself it has no vital function or part in the working of the machine. I should like, then, to ask the Seminar to consider for a while the possibility that Ibsen's language is vitally part of his dramatic whole. This consideration opens up a subject so vast that I can only, within the limits of this paper, scratch its surface, not probe its full depths. Nor can I claim to present a finished argument, but merely to show, through a selection of examples, what happens in various plays when Ibsen chooses certain words rather than others and combines them in certain ways rather than others.

I want to say at once that I am *not* going to speak about the nature of Ibsen's language as such, or about the nature of the Norwegian language as such; nor about the merits of different English translations. (Each of these subjects, on which I am in any case not qualified to speak, would demand at least one paper to itself.) I want to start with the plays themselves and to try to show some ways in which—it seems to me—Ibsen's language takes us under the photographic surface of realism; in which it helps us to see *through* the literal superstructure to the inner dramatic form of the play, through the physical landscape into a spiritual one. Or, to put the same aim differently, I want to see how the language places a particular (realistic) action in a wider (symbolic) context of meanings.

In Shakespearean studies, such functions of the dramatic language have been the object of much attention: from the early thirties onwards, critics have been keenly aware of the importance of language, and particularly of verbal metaphors, in the Shakespearean dramatic structure. In an essay on Ibsen and Shakespeare the late Professor Una Ellis-Fermor suggested that in Ibsen, too, at his best there is the Shakespearean evocative mode, but even she tends to play down the function of language in such evocation; and, above all, she does not want to see any such mode in the plays before *Rosmersholm*, or possibly *The Wild Duck*.[5]

And, you may say, is not that reasonable? Do we not know that Ibsen repeatedly spoke of his main purpose in writing dramatic dialogue as being to make it "completely faithful and realistic"? "The effect of the play," he writes to the first Swedish producer of *Ghosts*, apropos of the translation of the dialogue, "depends to a large extent on the audience imagining it is sitting and listening and watching something actually going on in real life."[6] Are we not then confusing the issue by comparing Ibsen to Shakespeare, who happily and deliberately used his dialogue to remind his audience of the "playness of the play"? Shakespeare's dramatic structure was very largely a verbal one: he would start, in most cases, with a given story (a narrative or an old play) and turn it into great drama by a fusion of structural mastery and verbal imagination. Ibsen, we know from his working-notes and drafts, tended to start with a theoretical problem or a "theme" (in the case of such earlier plays as *Pillars of Society* and *A Doll's House*), or with a human situation or a human being (in the later plays, such as *Hedda Gabler*); and then he would gradually shape his raw material by inventing actions, developing characters and suffusing the whole with visual symbolism. Are we not then, if we look at Ibsen in terms applicable to Shakespearean poetic drama, in danger of comparing incompatibles—or, worse, of looking for new tools, new critical games, for their own sake rather than for any new insights they may give into the work of Ibsen? The answer to these questions is, I think, both yes and no; and the implications of this apparent paradox can best be seen from an actual comparison.

Let us take, for example, the end of *Ghosts* and the end of *King Lear*. As far as plot goes, they have little in common—if only because Cordelia and Lear die while Osvald and Mrs Alving do not, at least not while the audience is watching. But they are both dramatic situations of intense human emotion, in which the play's protagonist sees his or her child destroyed by what is basically his or her own blindness to the most important values in life. In some of his language here, Shakespeare seems to be observing an almost "modern" kind of realism. Lear's famous line, "pray you, undo this button," very directly communicates the pathos of a foolish, fond old man; and in rendering by the repetition of a simple word Lear's realization that Cordelia is dead — "Thou'lt come no more, / Never, never, never, never, never" — Shakespeare is hinting at agony beyond verbal articulation. And yet he does not leave us ultimately with that agony unarticulated. The task is given to those around Lear, who through their words impart immense dimensions to the scene: "Vex not his ghost: O, let him pass; he hates him / That would upon the rack of this tough world / Stretch him out longer." Again, the bystanders not only define for us Lear's state of mind and suffering but also place the action in a wider context, seeing it as a version of Doomsday and Lear's fate as that of all mankind. "Is this the promised end?" asks one. "Or image of that horror?" asks another.

Mrs Alving has no such interpreters. She is left alone, in what the stage-direction describes as *mållos redsel* (speechless horror),[7] with the wreck of her son. That speechlessness looks like a sort of epitome of the realistic theatre's method: Mrs Alving's torment is left to the actress to realize histrionically. The inarticulateness of her last speech —

Dette bæres ikke! . . . Dette bæres ikke! Aldri! [and then as she looks for the morphine tablets] Nei; nei; nei! — Jo! Nei; nei! —	I can't bear it! . . . I can't bear it! Never! . . . No, no, no! — Yes! No, no! —

does indeed achieve the effect of "something actually going on in real life"; it reminds us that the most realistic way of all of expressing intense agony would be just a groan. Rather than showing us the poet in the theatre, this scene would seem to represent, as far as dramatic language goes, the *cul-de-sac* of the realistic theatre. At the most dramatic moments language is, as it were, by-passed as a form of communication. Not only Mrs Alving's agony but also the significance of the scene as a whole must come to us by visual means, notably through the symbol of the sun rising on the remote peaks.

What is true for the ending of *Ghosts* is, in a sense, true for much of the rest of the play. There are, of course, metaphors in the language which are of the utmost importance; but they work in a very specific way. When Osvald, in Act III, after the orphanage has burnt down, says:

All ting vil brenne. Der blir ingenting tilbake som minner om far. Jeg går også her og brenner opp,	Everything will burn. There'll be nothing left to remind people of Father. And here am I, burning down, too,

then his metaphor obviously serves to link the surface with the underlying symbolical structure: through the metaphor we see for a moment Osvald as identified with the orphanage and both as products of Captain Alving's life — and of Mrs Alving's gladless "duty" to cover up. When Mrs Alving uses the same metaphor — the central one of *gengangere* (ghosts) — both for the vision of Osvald as her husband come alive again, and also for the old opinions and conventions that are ever alive and present, then we are forcibly reminded of the tightness of the structure of meanings in the play, involving individual as well as social morality. But in neither Osvald's nor Mrs. Alving's case does the verbal image do anything which *adds* to what structure and character as such are communicating. It crystallizes and concentrates meaning, but it does not enrich the play with new meanings. It provides, as it were, the equalizing sign in a preexisting equation, much in the same way as do the metaphors in Dr Stockmann's speeches in Act IV of *An Enemy of the People*, where public health and morality are fused. Two functions of the language in *Ghosts*, then, would seem to be, first, to be as unobtrusive, transparent (or nonexistent) as possible, and, secondly, to clinch the symbolism built up by structural and visual means.

But there is another aspect which suggests that language is after all used, dynamically, to trace the "figure in the carpet." Everyone would, I think, agree that the spiritual-ethical centre of the play lies in Mrs Alving's exploration and revaluation of the past. It is noticeable that the structure and syntax of her speeches build up — not to say create — the spiritual rhythm of her growing perception. In her first major speech of retrospect — that typical Ibsen form of speech — when in Act I she tells Manders the real truth about her life with Alving, she speaks in short, simple sentences, as straightforward in construction as the truth here seems to her to be. The tense she uses is a simple past; the repetition of the verb *måtte* (had to) sets up a simple categorical mode (and one to be discovered wrong later); the keyword is a simple, causal *derfor* (therefore) . . . The scheme of the speech — he *was* such: therefore I *had* to do so-and-so — is an image of her vision of the truth at this stage. But when in Act III she realizes that her kind of choice has killed "livsgledon . . . den ustyrtelige kraft og livsfylde som var i ham" ("the joy of living . . . all that boundless energy and vitality he had"), then her speech is built on quite a new pattern. She analyzes the life offered to Captain Alving, by a series of antitheses, as if she were thinking while speaking, as if the truth were being modified while uttered:

—han måtte gå her hjemme i en halvstor by, som ingen glede hadde å by på,
men bare fornoyelse.
Måtte gå her uten å ha noe livsformål;

— having to eat his heart out here in this little provincial town; pleasures of a kind it had to offer,
but no real joy;
no chance of any proper vocation,

han hadde bare et embede.	only an official position to fill;
Ikke øyne noe arbeide som han kunne kaste seg over med hele sitt sinn; —	no sign of any kind of work he could throw himself into heart and soul —
han hadde bare forretninger.	only business.
Ikke eie en eneste kamerat som var mektig å føle hva livsglede er for noe;	He never had a single real friend capable of appreciating the joy of life and what it meant —
bare dagdrivere og svirebrodre.	nothing but a lot of lazy, drunken, hangers-on.

(I have divided the speech up, to bring out the built-in antitheses.) No longer does Mrs Alving's language establish a *simple* set of antitheses: the antitheses are complex and gather into a sort of climax in the lack of "a single real friend capable of appreciating the joy of life". Nor is the *måtte* the same as her earlier categorical "had to". For the first time she is seeing Alving's life from *his* point of view, and so the speech gives us, through the new dimension of understanding, an interaction of two minds. The very structure of her speech becomes a metaphor of her new perception. We are seeing something here which I think may be true for all Ibsen's realistic plays: that in these plays Ibsen relies most heavily on language — and the language of the plays therefore becomes most vital — *not* when he is commenting on a theme, in a large, abstract, sense (i.e. using metaphors like ghosts or polluted bath-water), but when he is dealing with the human predicament, with the human mind growing in perception, defining itself; and with human minds interacting. I shall come back to this point presently. But for the moment I want to return to the point that, in the last stage of Mrs Alving's understanding, horror makes her inarticulate, and we are back with the reliance on visual symbolism, rather than on language, for our interpretation of the situation at the end of the play.

Here I want to consider the end of *The Master Builder*, as an example of how Ibsen did, after all, arrive at verbal means of analyzing the mind of the protagonist and interpreting the action to us — means which are both like and unlike Shakespeare's. Like the end of *Ghosts*, needless to say, the end of *The Master Builder* has a realistic and a symbolical level; unlike *Ghosts* the language here mediates between the two. Solness, like Lear, has bystanders who interpret his death for us. But, unlike Lear's, his interpreters do not form a unified chorus:

RAGNAR. Forferdelig dette her. Han maktet det altså dog ikke.	RAGNAR. Terrible business. So he couldn't manage it.
HILDE (*liksom i stille, fortvilet triumf*). Men helt til toppen kom han. Og jeg hørte harper i luften. (*svinger sjalet oppad og skriker i vill inderlighet.*) Min, — min byggmester!	HILDE (*as though in a quiet, bewildered triumph*). But he got right to the top. And I heard harps in the air. (*Swings the shawl up and cries with wild intensity.*) My — my master builder!

Two things are achieved by the dialogue here. First, there is the sense of two visions counterpointed: Hilde's (which is also Solness's, for he is *her* master builder) and the others'. This counterpoint dominates the whole of the last scene, as when the gruesome realism of what the voices of the crowd have to say—

| Hele hodet er knust. — Han falt | His whole head is crushed. — He |
| like i stenbruddet— | fell straight into the quarry— |

is immediately followed by Hilde's absorption with the symbolical act of Solness, an absorption which does not admit awareness of what is happening on the realistic level:

| Nu kan jeg ikke se ham der oppe. | I can't see him up there now. |

Throughout this scene, the others *state* what they can actually see, while Hilde *hints* at her (and the master builder's) vision. Secondly, and relatedly, there is the placing of Solness in a complex symbolical context: he is both the mangled corpse at the quarry bottom and the man who got right to the top of the spire. His end, then, is both the defeat and the triumph of a human spirit. We are given the perception (which this play shares with all great tragedy) of simultaneous victory and ruin. The ambiguity of the dialogue acts as a form of submerged metaphor.

Similarly submerged metaphor is active within the individual lines. When Hilde, in her speech which accompanies the master builder's climb, arrives at the climax "For nu, nu er det fullbrakt! — " she is obviously made to echo Christ's last words on the Cross — a point unfortunately obscured by Una Ellis-Fermor's translation, which renders the line as: "For now, now it's done!"

The use of the *consummatum est* here may serve to pinpoint the difference in this handling of verbal metaphor as against the use of the ghosts or the bath-water in the earlier plays. It is a difference which, at the risk of making a pedantic distinction, I would describe as one between a more allegorical use of metaphor (in the earlier plays) and a more symbolical use (in the later plays). Vexed as the distinction is, I think it is safe to say that while allegory assumes a relatively simple and complete equivalent, a static relationship between the elements of a work of art and a set of concepts (intellectual, moral, etc.) assumed outside it, symbolism is dynamic and complex. An allegorical image tends towards an abstract concept; in a symbolical one, meanings are suggested rather than defined; they hover around, modifying each other and the work as a whole, but they are never totally paraphraseable. To return to our example: in Christopher Marlowe's *Doctor Faustus*, the protagonist, having signed his bond with the devil, exclaims "*Consummatum est!*" The effect here is one of poignant dramatic irony on the surface — Faustus closes the bargain which has lost him his soul with the very words used by Christ when he died to save that soul — but underneath it also acts as a kind of agreement between Marlowe and his audience as to how to interpret the meaning of what is going on. It acts as an allegorical signpost. Ibsen had used this echo, too, once earlier. At the end of the first Part of *Emperor and Galilean*, Julian enters, covered in blood from the sacrifice with which he has forsworn his Christian faith, to utter the one word "Fullbyrdet" ("It is fulfilled"). The irony here, too, is obvious, but unlike the case in *Doctor Faustus* it does not act as an automatic agreement between author and audience. It is not only that, where an audience in about 1590 would assume the absolutes of the Christian religion, an audience in 1873 would be in a much less certain position in regard to Christianity. It is also that, because of the position of this line in the context of a play which *balances* Emperor against Galilean, rather than resolves the antithesis between them, Ibsen's line serves to keep the two opposites — Julian and Christ — in a sustained balance. In Hilde's line — to return to it at last — the Biblical echo achieves a full symbolical, rather than allegorical, effect: Solness is seen neither as a parallel of Christ nor as a fiendish blasphemer, but the blasphemy and the triumph, the death and the victory, are the rich associations simultaneously evoked. Hilde's submerged metaphor, then, evokes meanings rather than defines them. It holds meanings in suspension, rather than clarifies and clinches them.

I have dwelt at some length on this point because I think that one can possibly measure the growing involvement of language with the total structure of Ibsen's plays by looking at how his metaphors become less allegorical and more symbolical. (Here, as always, one is of course making an artificial separation between elements of the plays; but such a separation is necessary if we are to see clearly the functions of Ibsen's dramatic language.) Because of the restricted space here, I shall limit myself to following one single image through several plays.

Ibsen repeatedly draws on an analogy between his dramatic situation or characters and Christ's temptation (Matthew, iv. 1–11 and Luke, iv. 1–13). No doubt there are undertones of such an analogy in the passage we have been looking at, from the end of *The Master Builder*: Solness on top of his spire (as on that occasion, ten years earlier, when he challenged God from the top of the Lysanger church spire) is both the Christ and the devil (but also neither) of that temptation. The first time, however, that we find it in Ibsen's plays is in Act V of *The Pretenders* where Skule meets the ghost of Bishop Nikolas, who in the shape of a Monk promises him that he will

føre deg opp på et høyt berg	lead you up to a high mountain
og vise deg all jordens herlighet.	and show you all the glories of the world.

The Biblical echoes here are almost verbatim, and the scene as a whole is clearly allegorical: it tells us in a well-defined way how to take the meaning of the situation. It is happening on the mountain-side above Nidaros, and a metaphorical landscape of temptation is briefly and somewhat awkwardly fitted into a geographical one. The next time we meet the image is in Act IV of the second Part of *Emperor and Galilean*. Here again the actual scene takes place on a mountain, high over a valley down below. But between this play and *Pretenders* lie *Brand* and *Peer Gynt*, in which Ibsen had learnt to fuse outer and inner landscape, physical and spiritual geography. And in the *Emperor and Galilean* passage the landscape, though it has a geographical pretext, is really internal, spiritual. The external scene merges into the dream which Julian, now aspiring to divine status, pretends he has had:

Se, da steg Minerva og solkongen, som hersker over jorden, ned i hans nærhet, løftet ham opp til fjellets tinde, pekte ut for ham og viste ham hele hans slekts arv. Men denne arv var jordens krets fra hav til hav, og utenfor havet.

And behold, Minerva, and the Sun-King, who rules over the earth, came down beside him, lifted him up to the summit of the mountain, and showed him all the inheritance of his family. But this inheritance was the whole globe, from ocean to ocean, and beyond the ocean.

And so these gods (like the Biblical devil) tell the youth that if he follows them, they will make him a god, like them. Julian's attitude to other humans in this scene anticipates in some ways both that of Solness and that of John Gabriel Borkman:

Den som skal herske, må kunne herske over viljene, over menneskenes sinn. I dette er det at hin Jesus av Nazaret står meg imot og gjør meg makten stridig.

He who shall rule must rule over the wills, over the minds of men. That is where Jesus of Nazareth opposes me and disputes my power.

As in both *John Gabriel Borkman* and *The Master Builder*, a challenge to the Christian God is built into the protagonist's speech. The effect in *Emperor and Galilean* of the Biblical echoes, acting as metaphor, is to parallel *and* contrast Julian with Christ. There is nothing remote or far-fetched about this, in a play which is so full of Biblical imagery and references, and the very meaning of which is contained in the title. What is interesting is that the metaphor does not simply "place" Julian as either right or wrong. Like Macrina's description of Julian later in the same Act:

Engel og slange, enet til *ett*; den frafalnes lengsel og fristerens list på en gang—

Angel and serpent in one; the apostate's yearning and the tempter's wiles combined—

it keeps the two halves of the play's central antithesis in balance.

In *John Gabriel Borkman* Ibsen uses the mountain-top image, with its half-submerged reference to Christ's temptation, to break through the surface meaning of the death-scene, into the vision of Borkman. As

Borkman leaves the house where he has sat in self-willed imprisonment, landscape is internalized:

Bare gå og gå og gå. Se om
jeg kan vinne frem til frihet
og til liv og til mennesker igjen.

Just go on and on and on. See if I
can reach freedom and life and
people again.

It is not the literal, wintry, landscape he is talking into. Nor is his vision physical: from his seat — the seat from which he and Ella used to look out over their shared vision, their "drømmeland" ("dreamland") — he now sees again the vision which drove him to his destruction. He sees

det rike jeg var like ved å
ta i besiddelse den gang jeg —
den gang jeg dode;

the kingdom I was just about to
take possession of that moment
when I — when I died;

and, in the mountains beyond, he sees

mitt dype, endeløse, uuttømmelige
rike.

my deep, unending, inexhaustible
kingdom.

The nature of the metaphor becomes clear as Ella turns to accuse him of having sacrificed her warm, human heart for those cold depths — sold it:

BORKMAN (ryster; det går liksom
koldt igjennem ham). For ri-
kets — og maktens — og ærens
skyld, — mener du?

ELLA. Ja, det mener jeg . . .
Og derfor så spår jeg deg det . . .
Du får aldri holde noe seiersinntog
i ditt kolde, mørke rike!

BORKMAN (shivering, as though a
chill went through him). For the
kingdom — and the power — and
the glory — do you mean?

ELLA. Yes, that's what I mean
. . . And therefore I prophesy this
. . . You will never march in triumph into your cold, dark kingdom!

And so the Nemesis of an "ishånd" ("a hand of ice"), significantly reinterpreted as a "malmhånd" ("a hand of metal"), seizes him and he dies. The verbal image here is of a truly symbolical nature: it grows and develops; meanings change and accumulate.

This dynamism is, I think, what above all characterizes the use of the same image in *When We Dead Awaken*. For all its dependence on parallelisms and contrasts, and for all the allegorical elements that it contains, this play does not ultimately work out as an allegory. In the case of the image of "all verdens herlighet" ("all the glories of the world") in the play we have an example of symbols with no easy or obvious equivalents, and in which meanings hover around, change and develop as the play progresses — an example, perhaps, of the kind of thing Coleridge had in mind when he spoke of the poetic imagination as combining "sameness with difference." The mountain-top image does not remain static; it is used through the mouths of all the main characters, in each case with different connotations; and finally it merges into action. *When We Dead*

Awaken is a play where the literal turns into the metaphorical without a perceptible transition, and so the physical and spiritual geography, the outer and inner landscape, intermingle and feed each other with significance. Thus Irene, departing from Rubek's literal statements about sunset and sunrise on the mountain, turns them into spiritual metaphor:

Jeg har engang sett en vidunderlig deilig soloppgang.	*I* once saw a marvellously lovely sunrise.
RUBEK. Har du? Hvor var *det?*	RUBEK. Did you? Where was *that?*
IRENE. Høyt, høyt oppe på en svimlende fjelltopp. — Du narret meg med der opp og lovet at jeg skulle få se all verdens herlighet dersom jeg bare . . . gjorde som du sa. Fulgte med deg opp i høyden. Og der falt jeg på mine kne, — og tilba deg. Og tjente deg . . . *Da* så jeg soloppgangen.	IRENE. High, high up on a dizzy mountain-top. — You beguiled me up there by promising that I should see all the glory of the world if only I . . . did as you told me — went with you up to the heights. And there I fell upon my knees, and worshipped you, and served you . . . *Then* I saw the sunrise.

The same promise of all the glories of the world had been made to Maja. She refers to it three times, but in quite a different way from Irene. "Du har kanskje tatt meg med deg opp på et nokså høyt berg, Rubek" ("You have perhaps taken me up with you to a high enough mountain, Rubek"), Maja says to Rubek in Act II, "men du har ikke vist meg all verdens herlighet" ("but you have not shown me all the glory of the world"). Here the metaphor is part of the growing awareness in both her and Rubek of what, respectively, they have lost. Like Ibsen's poem "På Viddene" ("On the Heights"), it hints at the opposition of Art and Life. In Act III Maja tells Ulfheim of Rubek's promise; and by now she sees that she has not even been taken up onto a high mountain but instead been beguiled into

et koldt, klamt bur, hvor der hverken var sol eller fri luft, . . . men bare forgylning og store, forstenede menneskespokelser rundt veggene.	a cold, clammy cage, where . . . there was neither sunlight nor fresh air, but only gilding and great petrified ghosts of people all round the walls.

Maja is using the image here to develop, in her way, an insight parallel to Rubek's awareness that he has not been able to create a true work of art since he lost Irene, and to Irene's awareness that he has really died. But she uses the image in terms of a fairy-tale: when Ulfheim promises her a castle, she turns to him to ask if he, too, is offering her all the glories of the world, as one might ask about "the princess and half the kingdom." Her metaphorical language is obviously on quite a different level of intensity from Irene's. The image which to Maja has overtones of fairy-tale, has to Irene — in her speech quoted above — strong religious overtones. "Placed" by those overtones, and by its position in the dramatic structure, it communicates the nature of Irene's experience: we know that her relationship with Rubek meant submission of her self to the Tempter-figure of Rubek, and that the false "sunrise" of that submission meant death. So, in a different sense, does the sunrise — both literal and metaphorical — which Irene and Rubek go together to meet at the end. Irene sees their way as:

opp i lyset og i all den glitrende herlighet. Opp til forjettelsens tinde!	up in the light, and in all the glittering glory! Up to the Peak of Promise!

And her last words are:

Og så helt opp til tårnets tinde, som lyser i soloppgangen.	And then right up to the summit of the tower that shines in the sunrise.

But by now the image carries the full ambiguity of the ending of *The Master Builder* (and as in that play two visions are counterpointed, as Irene and Rubek's marriage-death is accompanied by Maja's triumphant song of freedom). The peak of glory is both marriage and death, triumph and defeat, sunrise and avalanche.

When We Dead Awaken, then, shows us how in Ibsen's late plays verbal metaphors not only grow out of the very fabric of the play but also feed new meanings back into it. Metaphors as such are not the only aspect of his language which shows a more intimate and complex relation with dramatic structure, as we move from Ibsen's earlier to his later plays. We find a similar pattern if we look at what I would call his "key-words" — those words, usually varying from play to play, which within each play tend to be repeated so often that the very iteration (and often iteration at crucial points) tends to give them a symbolical quality. Often the title itself is such a keyword: *Samfundets Støtter* (*Pillars of Society*), *Gengangere* (*Ghosts*), *Et Dukkehjem* (*A Doll's House*); in other plays it is a more or less pure abstract, such as *den kompakte majoritet* ("the compact majority") in *An Enemy of the People*, or *frihet og ansvar* ("freedom and responsibility") in *The Lady from the Sea*, or indeed just *ansvar* ("responsibility") in *Little Eyolf*. These words are a feature of Ibsen's art which irritates some and can drive translators to despair; but they hold a great deal of illumination as to his use of dramatic language.

Let us look first at *Pillars of Society*. This play builds on a fairly simple irony: that those who appear as *samfundets støtter* ("pillars of society") are not, and those who appear as rebels or even criminals are in fact the true carriers of *sannhetens og frihetens ånd* ("the spirit of truth and the spirit of freedom"). This basic irony is heavily played on by the dialogue, especially in the revelation scene at the end of Act II and in the civic celebration of Bernick in Act IV. Words like "moral," "true," etc. are made to yield all the irony possible in each situation. But these words are exclamation-marks rather than agents; they act in a pretty mechanical fashion, and nothing much happens to or through their use. Their meaning is the same at the end of the play as it was at the beginning. It is interesting to compare this play with *An Enemy of the People*, where the key-words are, as it were, part of the action, interacting with the development of the central character. *An Enemy of the People* is a play in which the key-words, for all their abstract nature, have an exceptional vitality. People clash and fight in terms of abstract concepts; and in a sense the play is about what these concepts mean, i.e. about what words can hide. The structural formula is one of antithesis: each scene is a debate where thesis clashes with antithesis. Only the nature of the antithesis changes and develops, and the action of the play consists of this development — centred, of course, on the figure of Dr Stockmann. For example, the opposition between the two Stockmann brothers is articulated at the beginning of the play as "Makten" ("Might") — Peter — versus "Retten" ("Right") — Thomas. This antithesis returns at the end, but now both the protagonist and the audience have a deepened understanding of what each of those two words implies. Similarly, the implications of the key-word "sannheten" ("truth") grow richer throughout the play (as in Act IV, when Dr Stockmann speaks of "old truths" as "lies"): the key-word, while remaining semantically the same, has changed in human significance. Characteristic of *An Enemy of the People*, then, is that a few crucial words appear in a succession of contexts which endow them with a developing meaning; and this play shows the perfection of one kind of linguistic technique.

But with Ibsen, as with Eliot,

> every attempt
> Is a wholly new start, and a different kind of failure
> Because one has only learnt to get the better of words
> For the thing one no longer has to say, or the way in which
> One is no longer disposed to say it. And so each venture
> Is a new beginning, a raid on the inarticulate;

for it is true that the thing he had to say in *An Enemy of the People*, he no longer had to say in *The Wild Duck*. Not that the plays which followed were produced "with shabby equipment always deteriorating," as Eliot feels about his own poetry.[8] Nor did Ibsen so much abandon the technique he had arrived at in *An Enemy of the People* as transfer it into a different mode. *An Enemy of the People* represents the most vital use of keywords, tested *rationally* through the progress of the play. In the plays that follow, these words begin to be "proved upon the pulses." The transitional play in this respect is *The Wild Duck*, where a word like *livslognen* ("the life-lie") is so much more than an abstract concept and so much involves the whole range of human emotions and fates in the play. This kind of human life is infused into the abstract keywords of the next play, *Rosmersholm* (a play where, as in *An Enemy of the People*, the dialogue turns to a very large extent on abstract concepts). In this play, iterated words like *frigjørelse* ("emancipation") and *skyld* ("guilt") are entirely tied up with the whole complex of human experience which the play is about. The key-words are bandied back and forth and used by various characters according to their point of view. Thus Kroll can speak, in Act II, with a sneer of "en frafallen mann og en – frigjort kvinne" ("an apostate and . . . an emancipated woman") and make the words mean the very opposite of what Rosmer means by them; and yet that sneer leads eventually to Rebekka's revelation of what was the real nature of her "emancipation," and so to Rosmer's revaluation of the words themselves. In the end, all their implications have been explored, at the cost of two human lives.

All this is really another way of seeing and saying that by the time of *Rosmersholm*, Ibsen had, in a new way, become preoccupied, not so much with one single mind defining itself against its surroundings, its own past, etc., as with the interaction between minds, the effect of one mind on another. For all their difference in structure, plays like *An Enemy of the People* and *Ghosts* (with the possible exception of that speech of Mrs Alving's which I discussed above) share with *Brand* and *Peer Gynt* the basic quality of concentrating on the quest of a single individual. In *Pillars of Society* people do not interact, they merely clash: even when, as in the dialogue between Bernick and Johan Tønnesen in Act III, there is a struggle practically for life or death, it is pushed forward by plot twists, not by the modification of one mind by another. *The Wild Duck* has an idealist's quest at the centre, but here for the first time the protagonist is set in a circle of characters who profoundly interact. Such interaction is carried very much by the language of the play; and it is in this play that we first begin to see the dialogue itself forming a "figure in the carpet," an extension of the characters' personalities towards general humanity (which in no way detracts from their specific humanity).

The character in *The Wild Duck* who is fondest of using metaphorical language is Gregers Werle. He turns actual situations into metaphor, as when he tells the Ekdal family that what he really wants to be is:

en riktig urimelig flink hund; en slik en, som går til bunns efter villender når de dukker under og'biter seg fast i tang og tare nede i mudderet.	a really absurdly clever dog; the sort that goes in after wild ducks when they dive down and bite on to the weeds and tangle in the mud.

It is a metaphor which helps to define each member in the Ekdal family, for it echoes, verbatim, old Ekdal's description of how wild ducks die, it puzzles Hjalmar Ekdal, amuses Gina; and only Hedvig begins to understand that "he meant something different from what he was saying"; In *Ghosts* and in *An Enemy of the People*, those who used metaphors – Mrs Alving, Osvald, Dr Stockmann – were the ones who saw the truth most clearly. In *The Wild Duck* the cost of such clear sight is the human

issue of the play; and by a playing off of Gregers's mode of speech against
that of others, the very value of such sight is questioned. When, for the
sake of truth, Gregers Werle informs Hjalmar Ekdal of the true state of
affairs between old Werle and Gina, Ibsen makes Hjalmar's mind work as
a feeble copy of Werle's. Hjalmar uses Gregers's metaphors without having
his understanding. There is no doubt where our sympathies are meant to
lie in the following interchange:

HJALMAR.   Si meg om ikke du
hver dag, hver time, har angret på
den vev av fortielse som du, liksom en edderkopp, har spunnet
meg inn i? Svar meg på det! Har
du virkelig ikke gått her og våndet
deg i anger og nag?

HJALMAR.   Tell me this. Haven't
you — every day, every hour —
regretted this web of deceit
you've spun around me like a
spider? Answer me that! Haven't
you in fact been suffering agonies
of worry and remorse?

GINA.   Å snille Ekdal, jeg har
hatt så rundelig nok med å tenke
på huset og alt det daglige besty-
ret.

GINA. Oh, my dear Hjalmar, really I've had far too many other
things to think of, what with running the house and everything.

The language here enacts a kind of discrediting of metaphorical subtleties,
and implicitly of idealistic theories — "den ideale fordring" ("the claim of
the ideal") — as against common humanity.

In *Rosmersholm* the use of the dialogue to trace the interpenetration
of minds is still more apparent. In fact, it is at the centre of the whole play.
The play starts with prose dialogue of a precise kind, but gradually the
language shifts more and more into one of allusive, metaphorical, expression. This, of course, reflects the movement of the play, from the surface
and the present, into the depths and the past: Rosmer and Rebekka both
turn naturally to metaphor when they talk about the state of their minds.
Not only that, however, but the particular metaphors used enact the
interconnection between those minds. Thus, Rosmer's vision of his great
future task, at the beginning of Act III —

Å, hvor glad, — hvor glad jeg ville
føle meg om jeg kunne få det til å
lysne litt i all denne skumle styg-
ghet —

Oh, how happy I should feel if I
could bring a little light into all
this murky nastiness —

is expressed in the same imagery as Rebekka's analysis, near the end of the
same Act, of *her* vision when she first came to Rosmersholm:

Jeg ville at vi to skulle gå sammen
fremad i frihet. Alltid videre . . .
Men så var der jo denne skumle,
uoverstigelige mur imellem deg og
den hele, fulle frigjørelse.

I wanted us to go forward together in freedom. On and on,
ever further. But between you and
full and complete freedom was
this grim, insurmountable barrier.

. . . Jeg mener det, Rosmer, at du ikke kunne vokse deg fri uten i det lyse solskinnet. Og så gikk du her og skrantet og syknet i et slikt ekteskaps mørke.	I mean, Johannes, that you could only grow to freedom in the clear light of the sun. But there you were, wilting and sickly in the gloom of a marriage like yours.

(The English translation obscures some of the similarity between these two passages by rendering the adjective *skumle* as "murky" in Rosmer's passage and as "grim" in Rebekka's.) Truly Rosmer turns to Rebekka to say that she has never spoken thus about his marriage before: this is how *he* has been speaking of the world and his idealistic mission in it. His own great heroic vision of truth is like Rebekka's (tainted) vision of his marriage. On a level below the absolutely rational we here find the dialogue evoking the deeper meaning of what is going on, of the interaction of one vision on another, the pull and tension between two minds. Thus we are prepared for Rebekka's analysis in the last Act of how the Rosmer vision has infected *hers*, how her desire to make Rosmer free has — now that the goal might have been reached — defeated its own purpose. In contact with Rosmer as he really is, she has found him the stronger. She is now at once the "slave" under the Rosmer family spirit and "ennobled" by Rosmer's own vision. Thus her speeches interpret for us the action at the end both as a kind of hypnotizing of the will (and, as such, a re-enactment of Rebekka's "soul-murder" of Beate) and as a kind of moral retribution, in terms of the Rosmer standards. Rebekka's question and Rosmer's answer as, after their symbolical marriage, they go out to die in the mill-race, form an epitome of the interaction of minds and visions which their relationship — we now fully see — has meant:

REBEKKA . . . Er det deg som følger meg? Eller er det meg som følger deg?	REBEKKA . . . Is it you who goes with me, or I with you?
ROSMER. Det grunner vi aldri ut til bunns. . . . Vi to følger hinannen, Rebekka. Jeg deg og du meg . . . For nu er vi to *ett*.	ROSMER. That is something we shall never fathom . . . We go together, Rebecca. I go with you, you with me. . . . For now we two are one.

In *Rosmersholm* the figure in the carpet created by the dialogue *is* the play.

What this play also shows us is that Ibsen is beginning to use metaphorical language to probe depths of mind not available to ordinary rational discourse. When Rebekka reaches the heart of her experience, we are moving at levels which can only be reached by metaphor:

Der falt en sinnshvile over meg, — en stillhet som på et fugleberg under midnattssolen oppe hos oss.	A feeling of tranquillity came over me . . . a stillness like that which comes over a colony of sea-birds

on the Northern coast under the
midnight sun.

This becomes even more obvious in the next play, *The Lady from the Sea*,
where, from the very nature of the plot, Ibsen is dealing with emotions
and states of mind which demand metaphorical expression. If that play, as
I think, is less powerful than *Rosmersholm*, it may be because what was
the very centre of the action there—the power of one mind over another—
is here something which is talked about, rather than seen in action—
except for the two brief scenes between the Lady and the Stranger. But in
The Master Builder again, Hilde and Solness get nowhere in rational
dialogue (unlike Elida and Dr Wangel). It is only when they converse in
metaphors, and when he is—as it were—released by taking over her
language and her vision, that they do communicate. The same is even
more true of *When We Dead Awaken*, where all the characters communicate in this way: their minds interacting via metaphor. The whole play is
constructed as a series of duologues: Rubek–Maja, Maja–Ulfheim, Rubek
–Irene; and in each set—and even in the cross-groupings, as when Maja
and Irene in Act II have a brief interchange about "opening a casket that
has snapped to"—people interact by penetrating and taking over each
others' verbal symbols. We are at the other end of a scale here from *Pillars
of Society:* people's interrelationships are changed through language
rather than through plot-moves. The obvious example, and the core of the
play, are the scenes between Rubek and Irene, during which their
respective visions of "life," "death" and "awakening" are in interplay. But
even Maja and Ulfheim carry out their crucial dialogue in Act III, where
the deepest personal truths are brought forth, through a third-person,
fairy-tale type of speech—a technique which cannot help but remind me
of the wooing between the lovers across the brook in *The Caucasian Chalk
Circle*, and which ultimately has a similar distancing effect: i.e. we think
more of what the lovers say, and evaluate it, than of who they are. What
this indicates, I think, is that Ibsen is now moving away from characters
towards fates, from individual human beings towards universals. Yet the
strength of the play very much depends on its evocation of minds
converging and diverging. The dialogue of the characters is uniquely alive;
their minds strip each other bare as much as do those of the characters in
John Gabriel Borkman; their words mark the progress of the quest which
the play is.

It is, however, not only the interaction of minds, but also the lack of
interaction—the alienation—which Ibsen traces through his dramatic
language. We need only think of how the two different visions of Ella
Rentheim and John Gabriel Borkman are developed, side by side, to see
that this is one major way in which Ibsen dramatically realizes human
relationships. It is a type of counterpoint device which we can find in

various forms from the early plays onwards. *Emperor and Galilean* has two obvious and rather spectacular instances of counterpoint. One is the scene at the end of Part I where the completion of Julian's apostasy is counterpointed, almost literally, with the choir chanting Our Father, to press home such antitheses as:

JULIAN. Fri, fri! Mitt er riket!	JULIAN. Free, free! Mine is the kingdom!
SALLUST. . . . Og makten og æren!	SALLUST. . . . And the power and the glory!
KORET (*i kirken*). Ditt er riket og makten og æren.	CHOIR (*in the church*). Thine is the kingdom, and the power, and the glory.

The other is in Act II of Part II, where the two processions, one of Apollo worshippers in a Dionysiac frenzy and one of martyred Christian prisoners, meet; and where the Christian and pagan visions are pointedly contrasted:

Deilig å juble i solhåps-gløden! Salig å våndes i bloddåps-døden!	Lovely our joy as the sun warmly glows! Blissful our groans as the martyr-blood flows!

In *The Wild Duck* this counterpoint technique, used realistically rather than as ritual, helps to develop the visions of Relling, the realist, and Gregers Werle, the idealist — notably in the last few moments of the play:

GREGERS. Hedvig er ikke død forgjeves. Så De hvorledes sorgen frigjorde det storladne i ham [Hjalmar Ekdal]?	GREGERS. Hedvig has not died in vain. Didn't you see how grief brought out what was noblest in him [Hjalmar Ekdal]?
RELLING. Storladne blir de fleste når de står i sorg ved et lik. Men hvor lenge tror De den herligheten varer hos *ham?*	RELLING. Most people feel some nobility when they stand grieving in the presence of death. But how long do you suppose this glory will last in *his* case?
GREGERS. Skulle ikke den vare og vokse for livet!	GREGERS. Surely it will continue and flourish for the rest of his life!
RELLING. Innen tre fjerdingår er lille Hedvig ikke annet for ham enn et vakkert deklamasjonstema.	RELLING. Give him nine months and little Hedvig will be nothing more than the theme of a pretty little party piece.

And the line of Gregers's with which this "debate" is concluded — the line which epitomizes the idealist's tragedy — shows in its rhythm and diction the same counterpoint:

Hvis *De* har rett, og *jeg* har urett,	If *you* are right and *I* am wrong,
så er ikke livet verd å leve.	life will no longer be worth living.

(Unfortunately some of the pointed effect must be lost here in translation, as "urett", literally "un-right," has to be translated as simply "wrong.") Interestingly, in the second draft of *The Wild Duck*, where this whole dialogue turns on generalities much more than on the individual fates of the characters, Gregers's line is generalized and lacks the antithesis of the finished version:

Skulde det holde stik, da var	If that were so, life would
det ikke værd at leve livet.	not be worth living.

By the end of *The Master Builder*, as we have already seen, the counterpoint technique is a way of containing within one framework two visions of the same action: Hilde's vision of the triumphant hero with the music of harps around him and the bystanders' vision of the battered corpse. And with the ending of *When We Dead Awaken* the wheel has come almost full circle. The counterpointing of Maja's song of freedom with Rubek and Irene's ascent onto the fatal heights is close to the kind of ritual we saw in *Emperor and Galilean* (and it is ritualized still further by the act and words of the Sister of Mercy). One is reminded of such modern attempts at building ritual out of a realistic action as Edward Albee's in *Who's Afraid of Virginia Woolf?*, where the wife's chatter about the imaginary son is counterpointed with the husband's recital of the requiem mass.

In the middle plays the alienation of minds is, I think, more important than the interaction. There is one play in which such alienation, and its implications, are realized by means so obvious that we perhaps tend to overlook them, just as we tend to underrate the play because of the obviousness of some of its symbolism, and of the protagonist's own articulateness about it at the end. I am thinking of *A Doll's House*. For most of this play, the dialogue brings out what the action implies: that the central characters are all playing parts before each other. Rank, in his elaborately staged farewell-to-life, is an outstanding example. So is Nora's tarantella, which means one thing to her and a different thing to each of her spectators — an action-symbol which fuses, for the audience, all the various "parts" of Nora, all the different visions of her. So, supremely, is the fancy dress ball on the floor above, for which there is no plot-necessity: it functions as a telling image of human relationships. And even during this ball, Helmer tells us, he engages in a private game, imagining himself and Nora in parts other than their real identities. The central game, or part, playing is, of course, the whole marital relationship of Helmer and Nora. To him she is a bird, or a squirrel, or even "a pretty little *thing*" (all, of course, parts below *his*, in the hierarchy of creation). Until the end she goes along with him in this playing of parts. Several times we see her deliberately put on the act, most clearly at the end of Act II:

NORA (står en stund liksom for å samle seg; derpå ser hun på sitt ur). Fem. Syv timer til midnatt. Så fireogtyve timer til neste midnatt. Da er tarantellaen ute. Fireogtyve og syv? Enogtredve timer å leve i.

NORA (stands for a moment as though to collect herself, then looks at her watch). Five. Seven hours to midnight. Then twenty-four hours to the next midnight. Then the tarantella will be over. Twenty-four and seven? Thirty-one hours to live.

HELMER (i doren til hoyre). Men hvor blir så lille lerkefuglen av?

HELMER (in the doorway, right). What's happened to our little skylark?

NORA (imot ham med åpne arme). Her er lerkefuglen!

NORA (running towards him with open arms). Here she is!

(The translation obscures the fact that Nora repeats Helmer's image of the sky-lark.) Ibsen has been rebuked for failing to make the two levels of this play cohere: the level on which Nora is a "sky-lark" and the play one about dream and reality, and the level on which she turns into a pioneer for Women's Rights and the play becomes topical-social.[9] But it seems to me that the central image, sustained by the dialogue, of part-playing links the two. On each level it is a question of lost or obscured identity — for the struggle for woman's right as Nora comes to see it, and as basically it was, is not a matter of blue stockings and tying oneself to railings but of the right to an autonomous personality. Through the dialogue, the two levels meet, in the timeless theme of human relationships.

The handling of dramatic language in A Doll's House is part of the play's vitality. It is also, incidentally, part of its modernity, for it shows Ibsen doing what has been attempted in more recent times by Harold Pinter, in The Lover, and by John Osborne, in the squirrels and bears game in Look Back in Anger (and, more blatantly, in Under Plain Cover). The difference, apart from artistic merit, is of course, that where to Pinter and Osborne, the playing of games between husband and wife is a matter of making the best of a bad job, making a disintegrated life liveable and a sterile relationship come alive, in Ibsen it is, at this stage, an evil — a form of "ghosts."

And so, to conclude, we may move from the modernity of a realistic play to the modernity of a recognizedly symbolical play. At the beginning of When We Dead Awaken Rubek and Maja are making apparently ordinary, bored, small-talk. Rubek says how, as they were coming up north on the train in the night, towards the Bath Hotel where they now are, he could tell that they were approaching their own country:

RUBEK . . . . Jeg merket at det ble så lydløst ved alle de små stop-

RUBEK. . . . I noticed how silent [actually, "soundless"] it became

pestedene—. Jeg *hørte* lydløsheten
. . . og så forsto jeg at nu var vi
kommet over grensen. Nu var vi
riktig hjemme. For ved alle de små
stoppestedene holdt toget stille, —
skjønt der ingen trafikk var.

MAJA.   Hvorfor holdt det *så*
stille. Når der ingenting var?

RUBEK.   Vet ikke. Ingen reisende
steg ut, og ingen kom inn. Og
toget, det holdt stille en lang, en-
delos stund allikevel. Og ved hver
stasjon hørte jeg at der var to
banemenn som gikk på per-
rongen, — den ene hadde en lykte i
hånden, — og de talte med hinan-
nen, dempet og klangløst og intet-
sigende ut i natten.

MAJA.   Ja, du har rett i det. Der
går alltid et par menn og taler
sammen—

RUBEK.   —om ingenting.

at all the little roadside stations. I
heard the silence . . . and that
assured me that we had crossed
the frontier—that we were really
at home. For the train stopped at
all the little stations—although
there was nothing doing at all.

MAJA.   Then why did it stop—
though there was nothing to be
done?

RUBEK.   Can't say. No one got out
or in; but all the same the train
stopped a long, endless time. And
at every station I could make out
that there were two railway men
walking up and down the platform—one with a lantern in his
hand—and they said things to
each other in the night, low, and
toneless, and meaningless.

MAJA.   Yes, that is quite true.
There are always two men walking up and down, and talking—

RUBEK.—of nothing.

The dialogue is certainly realistic—for is not this just the kind of thing
husband and wife, just arrived after a journey, and with little in common,
might talk about? But through the surface realism, because of the poetic
way in which the prosaic material has been handled, we see the conversation as an image of Rubek and Maja's relationship, and ultimately as an
image of the whole play: individuals each wrapped up in silence, walking
aimlessly and talking soundlessly of nothing, in a world where the train
stops for no reason at each isolated station. It is the world of Bergman's
film *The Silence;* and, in another way, it is a world much akin to that of
Waiting for Godot. One remembers that this is the Ibsen play which
started, so he writes himself, not as a theme or a character but as a "basic
mood."[10] Had this been a play like *Pillars of Society*, the train and the
railwaymen walking along the platform would soon have cropped up as
essential props of a well-made plot. In his Dramatic Epilogue, Ibsen is not
afraid of material which appears irrelevant to the plot—not if, as here, it
has a deeper relevance as an image. The speeches here form an image
which concentrates into itself the mood and world of *When We Dead
Awaken*, just as much as the image of the horses that eat each other
realizes the world of *Macbeth.*

This passage also shows in a small scope those different aspects of
Ibsen's dramatic language which I have tried to sketch out. It shows the

use of imagery for symbolical, rather than allegorical, ends. It shows the movement from external to internal landscape; the playing on an iterated word (*lydløst*, *klangløst* — "soundless", "toneless"). It shows dialogue carried by metaphor; it shows a kind of interaction between two minds (for Maja does get involved in Rubek's vision), and yet it also shows, in Maja's initial lack of response, the counterpointing of two minds through dialogue. Altogether, it shows that there is in the work of Ibsen, poetry *in* the theatre. Though this particular form of concentrated dramatic poetry only comes at this stage in his art, it is built up of features which we can trace right through, from the so-called "realistic" plays.

Notes

1. T. R. Barnes, "Yeats, Synge, Ibsen and Strindberg," *Scrutiny*, V (1936), 260.

2. R. G. Cox, "Rehabilitating Ibsen" (Review of Brian W. Downs, *Ibsen, The Intellectual Background* and M. C. Bradbrook, *Ibsen the Norwegian*), *Scrutiny*, XIV (1947), 217.

3. Francis Fergusson, *The Idea of a Theater* (Doubleday Anchor Books, N.Y., 1953). See esp. Chap. 5: "*Ghosts* and *The Cherry Orchard*: The Theater of Modern Realism."

4. John Northam, *Ibsen's Dramatic Method: A Study of the Prose Dramas* (London, 1953).

5. Una Ellis-Fermor, "Ibsen and Shakespeare as Dramatic Artists," *Edda*, 1958, 120–35. This essay is reprinted as Chap. VIII of her posthumous book, *Shakespeare the Dramatist*, ed. Kenneth Muir (London, 1961).

6. Letter, 2 Aug. 1883, to August Lindberg. See *The Oxford Ibsen*, V, 477–8. — Cf. also the letter to Edmund Gosse, 15 Jan., 1874, on the reason why *Emperor and Galilean* was written in prose: *The Oxford Ibsen*, IV, 606.

7. In this paper, quotations in Norwegian are taken from the three-volume edition of *Henrik Ibsen: Samlede Verker*, ed. Didrik Arup Seip (Oslo, 1960). Of English translations, I have used those of J. W. McFarlane (*The Oxford Ibsen*, London, 1960–) wherever available. Quotations from *The Master Builder* and *John Gabriel Borkman* are taken from the translations of Una Ellis-Fermor (*The Master Builder and Other Plays*, Penguin Books, London, 1958); and those from *When We Dead Awaken* are taken from William Archer's translation (*The Collected Works of Henrik Ibsen*, XI, London, 1929).

8. T. S. Eliot, "East Coker", V.

9. Else Høst, "Nora", *Edda*, 1946, 13–28.

10. Letter Suzannah Ibsen, June 13, 1897. See *Ibsen: Letters and Speeches*, ed. Evert Sprinchorn (Hill and Wang Dramabooks, N.Y., 1964), 325–6.

Ibsen and Ideology
The Evaluation of Ibsen as the Voice of a Moment in History

[From "Historical Drama and
Historical Novel"]

Georg Lukács*

Dramatic necessity, the supreme persuasive force of drama depends precisely upon the inner accord (briefly analyzed above) between the character (with his dominant passion which evokes the drama) and the social-historical essence of the collision. If this connection is present, then every individual accident, as at the close of *Romeo and Juliet*, occurs in an *atmosphere of necessity*, and in and through this atmosphere its accidental character is dramatically erased. On the other hand, if this necessity, produced by the dramatic convergence of character and collision, is not present, as in the case of Hebbel's *Judith*, then however well assembled the causal motivation, its effect will be one of mere cleverness; instead of strengthening the tragic impact, it will make it appear cold.

This convergence of character and collision is the fundamental basis of drama. The more deeply thought out, the *more direct* is its effect. We used the expression "atmosphere of necessity" advisedly, wishing to describe the organic, direct nature of this connection between character and collision that is far removed from any kind of sophistication. The fate against which the hero of drama struggles comes as much "from without" as "from within." His character, so to speak, "predestines" him for the particular collision. For there is no collision which is inescapable in itself. The majority of cases in life, where a social-historical collision occurs, are not resolved in a dramatic form. Only when the collision meets with a person like Antigone, Romeo or Lear, does drama result. This is what Aristophanes' Aeschylus says when he protests agains Euripides' conception of Oedipus in the prologue to *Antigone*, namely, that Oedipus was happy at first and then became the unhappiest of mortals. He did not become this, says Aeschylus, he never ceased to be such.

It would of course be a dangerous exaggeration to take this polemical

*From *The Historical Novel* (Boston: Beacon Press, 1963), 121–26. ©1962 by Merlin Press Limited. Reprinted by permission of Beacon Press. Originally published in USSR, translated from the German in 1937. First German edition, 1955. 2d ed., 1961. Translated from 2d German ed. London: Merlin Press, 1962.

89

sally too literally, to stretch it too far. Aeschylus is protesting here, quite rightly, against the external character of Euripides' conception, whereby Oedipus's destiny becomes a "destiny" in the sense of a mechanically inescapable fate. The majority of heroes of the really great tragedies are in no way inevitably doomed simply because of their character. They are in no way, to use a modern phrase, "problematic beings." Take Antigone, Romeo, Lear, Othello, Egmont etc. Before their dramatic essence can be released they have to encounter a concrete and *definite* collision. They do not encounter just any collision which might embody, as it were by accident, an abstract-general principle of the tragic as many theorists of the eighteenth century believed.

It follows that the dramatic collision and its tragic outcome must not be conceived in an abstract pessimistic sense. Naturally, an abstract denial of the pessimistic elements in the drama given to us by the history of class society would be senseless. The horror of the conflicts in class society, the fact that for most people there is clearly no solution to them, is certainly *one* motif, and by no means an unimportant one, in the rise of drama. But it is by no means supreme. Every really great drama expresses, amid horror at the necessary downfall of the best representatives of human society, amid the apparently inescapable, mutual destruction of men, an *affirmation of life*. It is a *glorification of human greatness*. Man, in his struggle with the objectively stronger forces of the social external world, in the extreme exertion of all his powers in this unequal battle, reveals important qualities which would otherwise have remained hidden. The collision raises the dramatic hero to a new height, the possibility of which he did not suspect in himself before. The realization of this possibility produces the enthusing and uplifting qualities of drama.

This side of drama must also be specially stressed because bourgeois theories — particularly those which became dominant during the latter half of the nineteenth century — give increasing, one-sided prominence to the pessimistic aspects, while our polemic against them often simply counters this abstract and decadent pessimism scholastically with an abstract and shallow optimism.

In reality the one-sided pessimistic theory of drama is closely connected with the destruction of the specific historicism of drama, of the direct unity between man and deed, between character and collision. Schopenhauer, the founder of these theories, sums up the nature of tragedy as follows: "that the purpose of this supreme poetic achievement is the representation of the terrible side of life, that the nameless pain, the anguish of humanity, the triumph of evil, the mocking rule of chance and the irremediable fall of the just and the innocent are here paraded before us." Thereby, Schopenhauer degrades the concrete, social-historical collision to a more or less accidental *occasion* for "universal human tragedy" (of the futility of life in general). He voices philosophically a tendency which, from the middle of the last century onwards, acquires increasing prominence in drama and leads increasingly to the dissolution of dramatic form, to the disintegration of its really dramatic elements.

We have seen these disintegrating tendencies at work in the drama of so exceptionally talented a writer as Friedrich Hebbel. We saw that the very centre of dramatic unity was attacked — the unity of hero and collision. In this way dramatic expression is faced with the following dilemma: the most deeply personal and characteristic features of the main figure have no inner and organic connection with the concrete collision. These features, therefore, require on the one hand a relatively broad exposition, if they are to be at all noticeable and intelligible on the stage; on the other hand, very complicated means are necessary if a connection is to be made between the inner, psychological "problematic" of the hero and the social-historical collision. (Hebbel's Judith, for example, is a widow, who yet remained a virgin in her marriage. The complex psychology arising from this singular situation provides the bridge to her tragic deed in the play.) These tendencies have an epic effect. They are an important factor in the development which we have called the general "novelization of drama."

However, the *a posteriori* establishment of complex psychological connections between hero and social-historical collision is not sufficient for drama. In the case of nearly all talented playwrights, who fail in the vital question, this is still further supplemented by a lyrical ecstasy at the high moments, especially at the end. These ecstasies may vary very much in content. But for the most part they take the form of a lyrical-psychological insight into the necessity of the tragic downfall. This kind of subjective lyricism is an attempt to replace and restore, subsequently and artificially, the lack of objective dramatic unity. And it is clear that the more this unity is broken up by playwrights, the less naturally historical their collision and conception of character, the more their connecting general link approaches Schopenhauer's ideas, the greater will be the abyss separating subjective psychology from universality of destiny and the more indispensable the lyrical ecstasy as a substitute for the dramatic.

It is no accident that Schopenhauer himself saw in the opera *Norma* the model of tragedy. Nor that his pupil, Richard Wagner, attempted to conquer the problematic rock of modern drama by means of music. His music-drama however, is only a marginal instance in modern drama as a whole. Various able observers, most recently Thomas Mann, have clearly seen the close connection between the Wagnerian music-drama and, say, the prose drama of Ibsen.

We believe we have now given the desired concretization of the dramatic tendencies in life, listed earlier. Without claiming any historical or systematic completeness, which would only be possible in a full dramaturgy, we nevertheless believe that the specific, dramatic embodiment of these facts of life is now clear to us. They are embodied in the fully developed, plastic personality of the "world historical individual," who is portrayed in such a way that he not only finds an immediate and complete expression for his personality in the deed evoked by the collision, but also draws the general social, historical and human inferences of the collision — without losing or weakening in the least either his personality or its immediacy.

The decisive dramatic question here is whether a person can express himself immediately and completely through a deed. Epic, in all its forms, presents the growth of events, the gradual change or gradual revelation of the people taking part in them; its maximum aim is to awaken this convergence of man and deed in the work as a whole, which it portrays, therefore, *at most as a tendency*. In contrast, dramatic form requires immediate and direct proof of this coincidence at every stage of its journey.

To give a concrete historical picture of the facts of life tending towards drama, enumerated in the previous section, we should thus have to examine the social-historical conditions of the individual periods and see whether and in what way their economic structure, the nature of their class struggles etc. favoured or did not favour a genuinely dramatic realization of such facts.

If the preconditions are lacking in social life for these dramatic tendencies to launch into real drama, then they will break through in other directions. On the one hand, they will make dramatic form problematic; on the other, they will carry dramatic elements into other literary forms. Both trends are particularly visible in nineteenth century literature. Goethe and Schiller were the first to establish the reciprocal influence of epic and dramatic form as the essential characteristic of modern literature (cf. my essay on the correspondence between Goethe and Schiller, *Goethe and seine Zeit*, [*Goethe and his Age*], Berlin, 1955). Then Balzac, with special reference to Scott as the initiator, stressed the dramatic as a distinguishing mark of the new type of novel in contrast to previous types. This penetration of the dramatic element was extremely fruitful for the modern novel. Not only did it enliven the action, enrich and deepen characterization, beyond that it created an adequate form of literary reflection for the specifically modern manifestations of life in a developed bourgeois society; namely, for the tragic (and tragi-comic) dramas of life, which though dramatic in themselves, appear in an undramatic way, because they would be unintelligible and unportrayable, except by distortion, without their small, even trivial, capillary movement onwards.

These same social forces, however, could not help exerting a very dangerous influence on drama. For the greater the playwright, the more intimately bound up with the life of his time, the less inclined he will be to do violence to important manifestations of life which are closely connected with his heroes' psychology and the nature of his collisions for the sake of dramatic form. Inevitably, these tendencies added increasingly to the "novelization" of drama. Maxim Gorky, the greatest writer of our time, underlined these factors forcefully in a quite unjustly harsh criticism of many of his own plans: "I have written nearly twenty plays and they are more or less loosely connected scenes in which the plot is never sustained and the characters are insufficiently developed, vague and unconvincing. A drama must be bound by its action, strictly and throughout; only with this condition can it serve to arouse contemporary emotions."

The trends in the present disfavouring drama are sharply and accurately described here. And to show quite clearly how fundamentally right this criticism is (irrespective of its exaggerated self-criticism), let us recall the decisive scene in one of the best plays of the representative playwright of the second half of the nineteenth century—Henrik Ibsen's *Rosmersholm*. Rebecca West loves Rosmer. She wishes to remove every obstacle between them; thus, she induces his half-mad wife, Beate, to commit suicide. But her life with Rosmer awakens and clarifies her moral instincts; she now feels her deed to be an insuperable obstacle between herself and the man she loves. Now when her change brings her to explain and confess, it happens as follows:

> REBECCA (vehemently): You think then that I was cool and calcu-
> lating and self-possessed at the time! I was not the same woman then
> that I am now, as I stand here telling it all. Besides, there are two sorts
> of will in us, I believe! I wanted Beate away, by one means or another;
> but I never really believed that it would come to pass. As I felt my way
> forward, at each step I ventured, I seemed to hear something within me
> cry out: No farther! Not a step farther! And yet I could not stop. I had to
> venture to the least little bit farther. Only one hair's breadth more. And
> then one more—and always—one more.—And then it happened.—
> That is the way such things come about.

Here, with the unflinching honesty of a great writer, Ibsen declares why *Rosmersholm could not become a real drama*. Whatever could be elicited from the material by a judicious artistic intelligence, this Ibsen accomplished. But at the decisive moment we see that the actual drama, namely Rebecca West's struggle, tragic collision and conversion, is, as far as subject-matter, structure, action and psychology are concerned, really a novel, the last chapter of which Ibsen has clothed in the outward form of drama with great mastery over scene and dialogue. Despite this, however, the basis of the play is still, of course, that of a novel, full of the undramatic drama of modern bourgeois life. As drama, therefore, *Rosmersholm* is problematic and fragmentary; as a picture of the times it is authentic and true-to-life.

As with Hebbel, whom we touched on earlier, so with Ibsen here, what interests us is only their typical and symptomatic sides. The different ways in which novel and drama reflect the dramatic moments of life, and which are to be seen in Ibsen and Hebbel, take us back to a central problem of our study—the ways in which the "world-historical individual" is portrayed in drama and in the novel.

We have already discussed at length why the classics of the historical novel always represented the great figures of history as minor characters. Our present observations show afresh that drama, by its very nature, demands for them the central role. Both types of composition, however much they contrast, spring from the same feeling for genuine historicity, for real historical greatness; both endeavour to grasp in an adequate artistic form what is humanly and historically *significant* in the important figures of our development.

The very sketchy analysis of dramatic form given so far shows how the latter's aim all the time is to bring out immediately and visibly all that is significant in man and his deeds, how the prerequisites for its realization are concentrated in a plastic, self-contained unity of hero and action. But the "world-historical individual" is already marked by such a unifying tendency in reality itself.

Since drama then concentrates the decisive moments of a social-historical crisis in the collision, it must be so composed that what determines the grouping of the figures, from centre to periphery, is the degree to which they are caught up in the collision. And since the process of driving the essential moments of such a crisis towards a collision is achieved by vigorously bringing out their human and historical importance, this compositional ordering must at the same time create a dramatic hierarchy. Not in a crude and schematic sense, whereby the central figure of a play necessarily has to be the "greatest person" in every conceivable respect or from some abstract point of view. The hero of drama is superior to his surroundings rather because of his closer connection with the problems of the collision, with the given historical crisis. It is the way in which the latter is chosen and portrayed, the manner in which the hero's passion is linked with this force, which determines whether the formal significance bestowed upon the characters by the representational means of drama is charged with a content that is real and true, historical and human. But for this social content to make itself felt the formal tendencies, which provide the structure of drama, are, as we have seen, indispensable; that is, the singling out of the significant factors from the entire complex of reality, their concentration and the creation out of their connections of an image of life upon a heightened level.

[From "Marx and the Problem of Ideological Decay"]

George Lukács*

We have already shown how decisive for a writer is a correct evaluation of his characters and their conflicts, and this means the very opposite of a subjective evaluation. The great sureness shown by earlier writers in their portrayal of human beings, in the depiction of their relationships and in the development of their conflicts, is based on the way that they managed to put forward genuinely objective, socially objective standards that proceeded from a deep understanding of reality.

It goes without saying that these standards bear the marks of their time, of the social conditions in which they were discovered and deployed in literature. Like all other human knowledge, they contain a relative element. But only modern science of the era of decay, which always ignores the dialectic of the absolute and the relative, overlooks for the sake of this relative element the objective and absolute core in these correct and profound discoveries of standards for judging human beings, their actions and their destinies. Vulgar sociology coarsens this relativism and brings it to a head through a pseudo-Marxist "class analysis." In vulgar sociology, everything is presented as "class-dependent" in a mechanically fatalistic sense, and this gives rise to a completely relativistic view which puts everything on the same level. Everything is equally necessary, even the most repulsive apologetics for declining capitalism. It is an apology for apologetics.

The modern relativistic sentiment also protests against the objectivity of such standards of value from the standpoint of the complexity of life. It is said that the phenomena of life are so intricate and contradictory that the application to them of any standard must have a coarsening effect that violates their real refinements and transitional forms. This seems to clarify things at first, but it is fundamentally false. The great writers of former times understood the complexity of their characters and situations, with the contradictions and entangled transitional forms of real life, far better than the relativists of today. Don Quixote, Falstaff and Tristram Shandy's Uncle Toby are complex and contradictory characters, who get into highly complex and contradictory situations, so that the impression we get of them leads time and again from the comic to the noble and touching. But Cervantes, Shakespeare and Lawrence Sterne all knew very well precisely when, at what point, and to what extent their heroes were ridiculous or tragic, evoking affection or sympathy. And in complete contrast to the view of the modern relativists, these writers could depict the finest transitional forms transparently and clearly, with all their nuances that illuminate and enrich what is fundamental, precisely because they saw

*From *Essays in Realism* (Cambridge: MIT Press, 1981), 158–63. © 1981 by MIT Press. Reprinted by permission.

and assessed the correct meaning of every feeling and every action objectively.

This sureness of portrayal—and the flexibility and elasticity that is necessarily bound up with it—are lost as a result of the subjectivism and relativism of the decadent period. And this is where the bold, but of course far from always successful, battle of the major realists against the ideologically unfavourable conditions of the era of decay makes its appearance. This battle is exceedingly complex but, by analyzing it, it is possible to attain a correct and not merely schematic view of the relationship between world outlook and literary production, and see the possibilities and dangers of the "triumph of realism" in the era of decay in a more concrete fashion than we have so far presented them.

We can take as our example here Henrik Ibsen, certainly a major writer. In his play *The Wild Duck*, which he himself saw as a new departure in his work, he reached the very threshold of a magnificent and exemplary comedy of the self-destruction of bourgeois ideals, the exposure of the mechanism of hypocrisy and self-deception in declining capitalist society. Towards the end of the play, there is an important conversation between the representatives of two opposing standpoints: Gregers Werle, the Don Quixote of traditional bourgeois ideals, the "ideal demands," and the cynic Relling, who defends hypocrisy and self-deception as a vital necessity for people. In this dialogue, Relling refers to the fact that he had told the degenerate theology student Molvik that he was "demoniac":

> GREGERS: Isn't he demoniac, then?
> RELLING: What the devil does it mean to be demoniac? It's just a piece of nonsense I hit upon to keep the life going in him. If I hadn't done it, the poor simple creature would have collapsed years ago under his self-contempt and despair . . .
> RELLING: While I remember it, young Mr. Werle—don't use that exotic word "ideals." We have a good enough native word: "lies."
> GREGERS: Do you mean that the two things are related?
> RELLING: Yes. Like typhus and typhoid fever.
> GREGERS: Dr. Relling, I shan't give up until I have rescued Hjalmar from your clutches.
> RELLING: All the worse for him. Take the saving lie from the average man, and you take his happiness away too.
>
> [Ibsen, *Three Plays*, translated by Una Ellis-Fermor, Harmondsworth, 1950, pp. 243–4.]

This is a bold and profound exposure of capitalist philistinism in its various shadings. (And in how many would-be "demonic" modern writers are we not struck by the cynical truth of what Relling says here!) If it had been possible for Ibsen to pursue his argument to its logical conclusion, both artistically and in terms of world outlook, he would have been the greatest playwright of his time, a worthy successor to the classic writers of comic drama. What then is the barrier? Before *The Wild Duck* Ibsen had vigorously scourged the hypocrisy of bourgeois society, and time and again pointed out that the proclaimed ideals of the ascendant bourgeois class had now become hypocritical lies, no longer having anything in common with bourgeois practice. He accordingly portrayed the tragic conflicts that arose from the collision between ideal and reality. Although this problematic is somewhat too narrow to expose the deepest contradictions of bourgeois society, yet major and irresolvably tragic contradictions of love, marriage and family in bourgeois society do appear in his work, particularly in *A Doll's House* and *Ghosts*. Ibsen's literary practice here goes beyond his world outlook and the questions this raises for him. If Nora and Mrs. Alving take their ideals seriously and even tragically, it is this that becomes the pivot of the tragic conflicts in Ibsen's own eyes; in his actual portrayal, this moral seriousness is simply the occasion and stimulus. These women possess such moral vigour and consistency that their actions burst the shell of the bourgeois family, expose its deep and corroded hypocrisy, and tragically show up its social and human contradictions. Here Ibsen portrays the reality more broadly and objectively than his own world outlook would suggest.

In *The Wild Duck*, Ibsen stands on the threshold of a modern, bourgeois-philistine *Don Quixote*. Gregers Werle represents with equal conviction and hopelessness the ideals of the heroic period of bourgeois development, caught up in the midst of capitalist philistinism, just as Don Quixote honourably and hopelessly represented the ideals of a disappearing knighthood during the rise of bourgeois society. These "ideal demands" of Ibsen's directed at the degenerate petty bourgeois of capitalist society, dissolve as deeply into the realm of the ludicrous as did the knightly ideals of Don Quixote in his time. In Ibsen's case, this ridiculousness is intensified still further and becomes a really splendid comedy. What Gregers demands from genuine marriage, i.e. ruthless candour and honesty, is put into practice by his father, a deceitful old capitalist, with whom he had broken relations for that very reason, and by Mrs. Sorby, a shrewd hussy and careerist. The "ideal demand" of reciprocal truthfulness and honesty as the foundation of marriage is cynically realized by these two cunning cheats as the basis of the peaceful continuation of their former lives. The old ideals are thus not only debased by the inability to realize them, by being distorted by degenerate people into lies and hypocrisy, but Ibsen also shows how the cynical big capitalists can exploit these ideals for their own brutally egoistic ends. In this world of cynicism and hypocrisy, bourgeois idealism perishes in the same tragi-comic fashion as did the knightly ideals in the tragi-comic adventures of the knight of the sad countenance. Ibsen was very close to writing a great comedy of his time.

And yet however close, he failed to achieve this. As Marx said of the historic function of great comedy: "The gods of Greece, already tragically wounded to death in Aeschylus's *Prometheus Bound*, had to re-die a comic death in Lucian's *Dialogues*. Why this course of history? So that humanity should part with its past *cheerfully*" ["Contribution to the Critique of Hegel's Philosophy of Law. Introduction," *Collected Works*, Vol. 3, p. 179].

This was the historical task of the Falstaff comedies, and of *The Marriage of Figaro*.

This cheerful parting from the past is something that Ibsen failed to achieve. *The Wild Duck* already suffers from this. The character of Gregers Werle has neither the enchanting comedy nor the tremendous nobility of Don Quixote. And the reason for this is that Cervantes was both aware that the ideals of his hero had passed into history, and dissolved into its mists, and equally aware of the human purity, subjective honesty and heroism of Don Quixote. He recognized both these aspects correctly, and assessed them correctly too. Ibsen, on the other hand, despite his own profound and exposing criticism, clings desperately to the contents of Gregers Werle's proclamations. He seeks not only to rescue Werle's subjective purity and honesty, but the content of his attempts as well. Here Ibsen's own portrayal gives rise to the most frightful dialectical contradictions, as well as the most splendid comic situations. But he cannot altogether use these in his play, as he assesses his hero incorrectly, partly overrating him and partly underrating him, partly elevating him beyond his actual merits, and partly unjustly debasing him.

In the further course of his work, after the fading of his ideals — ideals which *The Wild Duck* still objectively presents, despite its mistakes — Ibsen subsequently sought to create heroes who met the demands raised by Gregers Werle and yet are not susceptible to Relling's criticism. In this way he got caught in a false aristocratism. He sought to create a man who would be superior to the average, a man who rose above the old contradictions, and yet — in closest connection with his inability to criticize the content and real historical situation of Gregers Werle's ideals — he was forced to portray this new man in terms of the old material, simply with artificial elevation and intensification.

Ibsen was far too realistic, consistent and fearless a writer not to understand and also portray what was mean, repulsive and even ridiculous in his new heroes, in Rosmer, Hedda Gabler and Solness. But he forces himself despite this to present them as tragic heroes who rise above the average level. The division in human standards apparent in *The Wild Duck* is accordingly continuously intensified. These characters are still more strongly both under- and overrated by their author. This undifferentiated and unelucidated juxtaposition of mutually exclusive judgments forces Ibsen to create characters who stand constantly on tiptoe so as to seem taller than they really are, whose "tragic nobility" is artificially and inorganically stretched upward by use of symbolist devices, even while their painfully produced and hence never really convincing stature is continuously subjected to bitter mockery by the writer himself.

It is no accident, then, that Ibsen's deliberate resort to symbolism commences precisely in *The Wild Duck*. This symbolism is the artistic means for reconciling at least in appearance what is in actual fact irreconcilable, for artificially concealing the contradiction that is unresolved in life, misunderstood, perceived in a distorted fashion and reproduced still most distortedly. Precisely in the case of such a major realist as Ibsen, we can see how symbolism failed to overcome the artistic contradictions of the realist attempts of the late nineteenth century, and was actually the literary expression of the fact that these writers had been unable to deal with these contradictions in human, ideological or artistic terms. They fled into symbolism and were ruined in it. For symbolism in no way offers any solution for the contradictions of this realism, but means on the contrary the perpetuation of these contradictions at an artistically lower level that is still further from grasping reality.

Ibsen's tragic transition, from a realism still combined with naturalistic elements, to a contradictory emptiness of symbolism is extraordinarily instructive for our present investigation. For it shows how little these processes are fundamentally artistic in nature. They represent in fact crises in the world outlook of the writers concerned. And the literary expression of these crises of world outlook is precisely the loss of a standard for the portrayal of human beings, their actions and destinies, of what these human beings socially and morally represent, what is the meaning of their fate in the reality of social life, and what form their relationships with other people actually take.

In Ibsen's case we still see the tragic seriousness of this crisis. Not simply on account of his great talent and literary honesty, but on account of the objective socio-historical significance of the problems with which he wrestled, and which he did not manage, in a tragic and crisis-bound way, to overcome. As the literature of the decadent era further developed, the figure of the maddened petty bourgeois comes ever more to the fore, inflating his philistinism into eccentric and isolated heroics, and capitulating before every modern superstition of a "cosmic" tragic destiny.

[From "Tolstoy and the Development of Realism"]   Georg Lukács*

Although Tolstoy continued and developed the traditions of the older realism, he always did so in his own original way and in accordance with the needs of the age, never as an epigone. He was always in step with his time, not only in content, in the characters and social problems he

*From *Studies in European Realism* (New York: Grosset & Dunlap, 1964), 130–37. © 1964 by Grosset & Dunlap, Inc. Reprinted by permission.

presented, but also in the artistic sense. Hence there are many common traits in his literary method and that of his European contemporaries. But it is interesting and important to note in connection with this community of method that artistic traits which in Europe were the symptoms of the decline of realism and contributed to the dissolution of such literary forms as the drama, the novel and the short story, regained their vitality and originality in Tolstoy's hands and served as the elements of a nascent new form which, continuing the traditions of the old great realism in a novel manner and in relation to new problems, rose to heights unsurpassed by the realist literature of any nation.

If we analyze Tolstoy's works from the angle of world literature, we must take for our starting-point the peculiarities of Tolstoy's style and his specific place in literature.

Without these peculiarities the world-wide success of Tolstoy's works cannot be understood. For one must always keep in mind that Tolstoy achieved this success as an essentially modern writer, modern in form as well as in content. From the seventies of the nineteenth century onwards his success was world-wide success in a literary world and with a reading public from whose memory the traditions of the pre-48 European literature were rapidly fading and the greater part of which even went so far as to oppose quite sharply and definitely those very traditions. (Stendhal's vogue in this period is based partly on misunderstanding, partly on falsification; it was an attempt to turn Stendhal into a precursor of subjective psychologism.) Zola, for instance, in rejecting Balzac's and Stendhal's alleged romanticism, criticized in them that they went beyond the workaday "average" of life, i.e. precisely the trait which made them great realists. And in Flaubert and especially in *Madame Bovary* he saw fulfilled all that he thought valuable in Balzac. The lesser representatives of naturalism, both writers and critics (and the adherents of trends subsequent to naturalism) show this deviation from the great traditions of realism even more unmistakably than Zola.

It is in this atmosphere that Tolstoy achieved his world-wide success. One should not underrate the enthusiasm with which his works were received by the adherents of the naturalist school and of other later literary trends. This world-wide success was not, of course, based exclusively or even in the first place on such enthusiasms. But on the other hand such enduring international success (still unabated to this day) could not have been possible had not the adherents of the various literary trends found or thought they had found important points of affinity with themselves in Tolstoy's works. The various naturalist "free stages" in Germany, France and England first performed *The Power of Darkness* imagining it to be a model naturalist play. Not long afterwards Maeterlinck, in his theoretical motivation of his "new" dramatic style, cited as his witnesses Ibsen's experiments and the same *The Power of Darkness*.

This same thing has been going on to this day. A study of this incongruous effect of Tolstoy's works will be found at the end of the present book.

2

However specific Tolstoy's influence on European literature may have been, it was not an isolated phenomenon. Tolstoy's irruption into world literature occurred simultaneously with the unprecedentedly rapid rise of Russian and Scandinavian literature to a leading position in Europe, where until then the great literary trends of the nineteenth century had had their origins in the leading western countries — Germany, England and France.

Writers of other nations very rarely achieved world-wide significance, until the seventies and eighties of the nineteenth century brought a sudden change. True, Turgenyev had become known in Germany and France before other Russian authors, but his influence cannot be compared with that of Tolstoy and Dostoyevski; besides, Turgenyev had achieved his fame precisely by those of his traits which really had some affinity with the French realism of the time. But in the case of Tolstoy and the Scandinavian writers who rose to fame at the same time (Ibsen in the first place) it was unfamiliarity of their subject and method which also played an important part. In a letter written by Engels to Paul Ernst about Ibsen, the former emphasises: "In the last twenty years Norway has experienced a literary upsurge like no other country except Russia. . . . The performance of these fellows is far superior to that of others and they leave their mark on other literatures, not least on the German."

Although we have mentioned the factor of unfamiliarity, the effect of this must not be mistaken for the decadent chase after exotic subjects which appeared in the later imperialist age. The cult of medieval mystery-plays, of negro sculpture, of the Chinese theatre, are symptoms of the complete dissolution of realism; the bourgeois writers — with the exception of a few outstanding humanists — are no longer able even to get near the real problems of life.

On the other hand the influence of Russian and Scandinavian literature begins when bourgeois realism has reached a crisis. Although naturalism had destroyed the artistic foundations of the greater realism, the greatest of the destroyers, such as Flaubert, Zola and Maupassant, still knew what great art was and in some of their works or parts of them they themselves did reach up to its level.

The same applies to their adherents and readers.

The impression made by Russian and Scandinavian literature is undoubtedly connected with the fact that the readers felt the decline of European realism and longed for a great realist contemporary art. Even Russian and Scandinavian writers of much less merit than Tolstoy still showed in their works the traces of the "great art" which was already lost in Europe; their composition and characters were forceful, the intellectual level of their problems and solutions high, their general conception bold and their attitude radical.

Even so critical a spirit as Flaubert hailed Tolstoy's *War and Peace* with loud enthusiasm, criticising only the passages in which Tolstoy's own philosophy of history is openly expressed.

"Thank you," he wrote to Turgenyev, "for sending me Tolstoy's novel. It is first-rate. What a painter and what a psychologist! . . . I feel that there are things of Shakespearean greatness in it! While I was reading it I cried out aloud in my delight . . . although the novel is long."

The same enthusiasm was evoked among the western European intelligentsia, and, at the same time, by Ibsen's plays.

Faithful to his world-view, Flaubert expressed his enthusiasm exclusively from an artistic point of view. But the effect of Russian and Scandinavian literature in Europe was, as we have already mentioned, not limited to the artistic sphere. The effect was due in the first place to the fact that these writers dealt with problems similar to those occupying the minds of the western reading public, but the problems were much more widely posed and their solutions, even though unfamiliar, much more radical. In the hands of the greater Russian and Scandinavian authors this topicality of subject stood in strange contrast with the almost classical form, which did not, however, appear academic and antiquated; on the contrary, it expressed contemporary problems in an entirely contemporary form. The purely epic character of Tolstoy's great novels — which appeared so improbable to the European reader of the time — we shall discuss later. Here we are for the time being discussing the effect on Europe of these works and not the works themselves, and it will suffice here to point out the severe structure and composition of Ibsen's plays.

At a time when the drama was increasingly disintegrating into mere milieu-painting, Ibsen built strictly concentrated dramatic plots, the qualities of which reminded the readers and audiences of the Greek and Roman dramatists (see the things written about *Ghosts* at the time). In those days, when dialogue had lost most of its dramatic tension and had degenerated into a gramophone record of everyday speech, Ibsen wrote a dialogue every sentence of which revealed new traits of the speaker's character and carried the plot a step further, a dialogue which was in a much deeper sense true to life than any mere copy of everyday conversation could ever be. Thus wide circles of the western European radical intelligentsia gained the impression that Russian and Scandinavian literature were the "classical" literature of their own time, or at least the artistic precursors of a coming classical literature.

To what extent the Ibsenian drama was problematic in the deeper sense, how imperfectly its formal perfection concealed the inner instability of Ibsen's conception of society and hence of his real dramatic form — to elucidate all this would require a special and longer analysis. Here it will be enough to say that the Ibsenian drama, however intrinsically problematic it may be, was vastly superior to the western European dramatic attempts of the time, both in dramatic concentration and in form. This superiority is so great that even other Scandinavian writers who were far more subject than Ibsen to the general European decay, were yet superior to the westerners in tension, concentration, and the avoidance of the banalities of naturalism and of the empty artifices of formal "experimentation." In Strindberg, for instance, there are definite naturalist tendencies, and he went much further than Ibsen in the dissolution of dramatic form. His conflicts and characters grow increasingly subjective and even pathological. But his first plays show a simplicity of structure, an economy of means of expression and a concentration of the dialogue which one would seek in vain among the playwrights of the German and French naturalist school.

The hope of the European literary vanguard that this Russian and Scandinavian literature marked a new dawn of European literary development was of course based on an illusion; those who harboured such hopes had no clear notion of the social causes either of the decline of their own literatures or of the strange flowering of literature in Russia and the Scandinavian countries.

Engels saw quite clearly the specific quality of this literary development and pithily characterized the main traits of its social basis. He wrote to Paul Ernst about Ibsen: "Whatever the faults of e.g. the Ibsen plays may be, they mirror for us a world small and petty-bourgeois, it is true, but nevertheless a world as far removed from the German as heaven from earth; a world in which people still have character and initiative and act on their own, even though often rather strangely from the outsider's point of view. I prefer to take a closer look at such things before I pass judgment."

Engels thus pointed out the essential reason for the success of Russian and Scandinavian literature in Europe: in an age in which force of character, initiative and independence were increasingly disappearing from the everyday life of the bourgeois world and in which honest writers could depict only the difference between the empty careerist and the stupid dupe (like Maupassant) the Russians and Scandinavians showed a world in which men struggled with fierce passion — even though with tragic or tragi-comic futility — against their degradation by capitalism. Thus the heroes of the Russian and Scandinavian writers fought the same battles as the characters in western literature and were defeated by essentially the same forces. But their struggle and their defeat were incomparably greater and more heroic than that of similar characters in western literature. If we compare Nora or Mrs. Alwing with the heroines of the domestic tragedies depicted in western European novels and plays, we can see the difference, and this difference was the basis of the great Russian and Scandinavian success and influence.

It is not difficult to uncover the social roots of this success and influence.

After the revolutions of 1848, the June rising and especially the Paris Commune, the ideology of the European bourgeoisie entered upon a period of apologetics. With the unification of Germany and of Italy, the decisive tasks of the bourgeois revolution had been accomplished for a time, so far as the great powers of western Europe were concerned. It is of course characteristic that both in Germany and in Italy these tasks were accomplished not by revolutionary, but decidedly reactionary methods. The class struggle between the bourgeoisie and the working class had visibly become the central issue in every social problem. The ideology of the bourgeoisie evolved increasingly towards the protection of capitalism against the claims of the workers as the economic conditions of the imperialist age matured at an accelerating pace, exercising a rapidly growing influence on the ideological evolution of the bourgeoisie.

This of course does not mean that all western European writers of the time were conscious or unconscious defenders or panegyrists of capitalism. On the contrary, there is no prominent writer of the time who did not oppose it, some with indignation, some with irony. But the general scope of this opposition and the opportunities of its literary expression were determined, limited and narrowed by the development of bourgeois society and the change in bourgeois ideology. All initiative, independence and heroism disappeared for a long time from the western European bourgeois world. The writers who attempted to depict the world in a spirit of opposition, could depict only the contemptible baseness of their own social surroundings and thus the reality which they mirrored drove them into the narrow triviality of naturalism. If, spurred on by their thirst for better things, they wanted to go beyond this reality, they could not find the life-material which they could have stepped up to greatness by true-to-life poetic concentration. If they attempted to depict greatness, the result was an increasingly empty, abstractly Utopian, in the worst sense romantic, picture.

In Scandinavia and Russia, capitalist development began much later than in western Europe and in them, in the seventies and eighties of the nineteenth century, bourgeois ideology had not as yet been driven to apologetics. The social conditions which favoured realism and which determined the development of European literature from Swift to Stendhal were still in existence in these countries, even though in a different form and in greatly changed circumstances.

In his analysis of Ibsen's plays Engels sharply contrasted this trait of Norwegian social evolution with the German situation in the same period.

The social basis of realism in Russia must not, however, be regarded as identical with that existing in Scandinavia. If we were concerned with the effect on western Europe of Russian and Scandinavian literature (and not with Tolstoy) we might confine ourselves to saying that both in Russia and in Scandinavia conditions were more favourable to realistic literature than in western Europe. The development of capitalism had been delayed in both, the part played by the class struggle between bourgeoisie and proletariat in the total social process was smaller and in accordance with this the general ideology of the ruling class was not yet, or less, apologetic.

But the backwardness of capitalist development had a totally different character in Norway and in Russia. Engels carefully pointed out the "normal" traits of Norwegian development. He wrote: "The country is backward because of its isolation and its natural conditions, but its general condition was always appropriate to its conditions of production and hence normal." Another point is that even the advance of capitalism was comparatively slow and gradual in the specific circumstances existing in Norway. "The Norwegian peasant was *never* a serf . . . the Norwegian petty-bourgeois is the son of a free peasant and in these circumstances he is a man in comparison with the German philistine."

All these favourable traits of Norwegian capitalist backwardness brought about the strange flowering of Norwegian literature. The favourable advance of capitalism rendered temporarily possible the development of a vigorously realist, extensive and promising literature. But with time Norway had to be aligned with the general capitalist evolution of Europe, in a way, of course, which preserved as far as possible the specific conditions governing the country's development. Norwegian literature distinctly mirrors this assimilation to the rest of Europe. The aged Ibsen himself manifested a growing uncertainty in his opposition and as a result he absorbed more and more of the decadent traits of western European literature and modes of expression (symbolism). The careers of the younger oppositional and realist writers show them increasingly succumbing to the general reactionary, anti-realist ideological and literary influences of western Europe. Even before the war the career of Arne Garborg, a highly gifted realist writer ended in religious obscuration and after the war Knut Hamsun capitulated to reactionary ideologies in literary trends and even fascism.

The capitalist backwardness of Russia was of a totally different character. The irruption of capitalism into the semi-Asiatic serfdom of Tsarism brought about widespread social unrest which lasted from the abolition of serfdom to the revolution of 1905. Lenin says that Tolstoy was the mirror of this epoch. Its specific development determined the specific traits of Tolstoy's art and with it the difference between the influence on Europe of Tolstoy on the one hand and of the Scandinavians on the other. Any realistic and concrete analysis of Tolstoy's influence on world literature must therefore be based on an analysis of that epoch. Lenin gave us such an analysis while the views on Tolstoy expressed by the Russian vulgar-sociologists reveal only that the influence exercised by the great writer was as much a mystery to them as it was to their contemporaries in Europe.

Ibsen

Peter Szondi*

The access to the problematic form of a work like *Rosmersholm* frustrates every concept of analytical technique by which Ibsen could be moved into the realm of Sophocles. Once the aesthetic connections that are used in Sophoclean analysis and discussed in letters between Goethe and Schiller are recognized, their concepts prove to be keys rather than hindrances to Ibsen's late work.

On October 2, 1797, Schiller writes to Goethe: "I have myself become very occupied these days with discovering the tragic material that derived from the art of *Oedipus Rex* and that obtained the maximum advantages for the poet. These advantages are immense. Just to mention a few: that one can ground the work with the composited action—which the tragic form resists entirely—in which the particular action is already happening and so consequently falls entirely beyond tragedy; further, that after the past events—seen as unalterable—his nature is much more fearful, and that the fear *wants something to happen*, which the mind affects entirely differently as the fear that *wants to happen*. The *Oedipus* is only, as it were, a tragic analysis. Everything is already there and it only becomes unravelled. That unravelling can happen within a simple action and within a very small period of time, when the events are yet still complicated and dependent upon circumstances. *Wie Beguenstigt das nicht den Poeten!* But I fear *Oedipus* is its own race and there is no second species. . . ."

A half-year earlier (on April 22, 1797) Goethe had written to Schiller that the exposition requires the dramatist to produce entirely too much, "because one demands of him an endless progression and I would rather take the best dramatic material where the exposition is already a part of the plot." Whereupon Schiller answered on April 25 that *Oedipus Rex* approached this ideal with surprising completeness.

The departure point of this thinking is the aprioristic form of drama. This form, in the service of so-called analytical technique, should make it possible to build up the exposition of dramatic movement and thereby utilize its episized workings, or "composited actions." Of course, these "composited actions" never come into question for the dramatic form, yet they select the material of the drama.

Others make their case with the Sophoclean *Oedipus*. The lost trilogy of Aeschylus that preceded Sophocles told the fate of the Theban king chronologically. Sophocles could dispense with this epic representation of

*Translated for this volume by Thomas Lindblade. Originally published in *Theorie des Modernen Drama* (Frankfurt am Main: Suhrkamp Verlag, 1965). © 1986 by the University of Minnesota. Reprinted by permission of the University of Minnesota Press, Minneapolis.

the widely displayed public event because for him it became less about the event itself and more exclusively about its tragic art. However, this art is not bound by details and lifts itself out of any frame of time. The tragic dialectic of sight and blindness—this peripeteia in an Aristotelian *and* Hegelian sense of one who gains self-knowledge of his excess through the eye and yet becomes blind—needed only *one* act of recognition, the anagnorisis, to become dramatic reality. The Athenian spectator knew the myth; he must not even have had to think about it. The only individual that has to learn to know is Oedipus himself—and he can only at the end, after the myth has become his life. So the exposition becomes superfluous and becomes the analysis of the action itself. The sighted and then blind Oedipus forms, as it were, the vacant middle of one whose fate the world already knows, and whose messengers gradually conquer his inner self and hence fulfill their horrible truth. But this truth does not belong to the past. The present—not the past—becomes exposed. Then Oedipus *is* his father's murderer, his mother's husband, and his children's brother. He is "the plague on the land" and must discover his past essence in order to recognize his present being. Hence the action of *Oedipus Rex*, although it in fact precedes the tragedy, is nevertheless contained in its present. With Sophocles, the analytical technique becomes demanded of the subject-matter itself, and not in hindsight from a supposed dramatic form but rather in order to show his tragic art itself in higher purity and poetry.

The difference between the Ibsenian dramatic structure and the Sophoclean leads us to the essential problem of form manifested by the historical crisis of drama itself. The fact that the analytical technique with Ibsen is not an isolated phenomenon but rather *the* construction pattern of his modern plays requires no proof; it is enough to remember the most important: *A Doll's House, Pillars of Society, Ghosts, Lady from the Sea, Rosmersholm, The Wild Duck, The Master Builder, John Gabriel Borkman, When We Dead Awaken.*

John Gabriel Borkman (1896) "plays on a winter's evening in the Rentheim estate near the capital." For the past eight years in "a large state-hall" of the house, John Gabriel Borkman, "ex-bank director," has lived in almost total isolation. The first-floor living room belongs to his wife Gunhild. They live in the same house without ever encountering one another. Gunhild's sister Ella Rentheim, owner of the manor, lives elsewhere. She appears only once a year, to talk with the administrator: Gunhild and Borkman never speak with her.

The winter's evening on which the play occurs brings us the meeting of these three who are linked together by the past and yet are so deeply estranged. In the first act, Ella and Gunhild stand face to face: "Yes—Gunhild, soon it will be eight years since the last time we saw each other." The second brings the conversation between Ella and Borkman: "It seems like an eternity since we two stood opposite each other, eye to eye, Borkman." And in the third act, John Gabriel and his wife meet each other: "The last time we stood across from each other—that was in court. When I was summoned to testify."

The conversations spring from the wish of the deathly-ill Ella to have Borkman's son—who many years ago was her foster son—once again take her name so that she will not die alone. The conversations expose the past of the three people:

Borkman loved Ella Rentheim but married her sister Gunhild. Denounced by his friend, the lawyer Hinkel, Borkman spends eight years in prison for embezzlement. When Borkman becomes free, he moves back to the state-hall of the estate that Ella—who never impugned his ability as the bank's director—obtains at the liquidation auction for him and his wife. During this time, Borkman's son is raised by Ella. The son then returns back to his mother nearly as an adult.

These are the events. But they do not report by themselves alone. More essential is what lies "behind" and "between" them: motifs (subject matter) and time.

"Have you independently undertaken it now to raise Erhard in my stead—? What are your intentions?" asks Mrs. Borkman of her sister.

"I have often wondered about it—why you spared me from essentially all that belonged to me—and only that alone?"—asks Ella of her brother-in-law.

And so the true relationships between Ella and Borkman, Borkman and his wife, and Ella and Erhard expose themselves:

Borkman renounced his beloved Ella to win the bank-career support of the lawyer Hinkel, who likewise wooed Ella. Instead of Ella, Borkman married Gunhild, without loving her. However, Hinkel became suspicious of the despairing Ella, harkened back to Borkman's influence, and avenged himself through the denunciation. Ella, whose life had perished with Borkman's unfaithfulness, loved only one person in the world: Erhard, *his* son. She raised him as her own child. However, when he became older, his mother took him back. Ella, whose deathly illness dates back to the "psychic shock" of Borkman's unfaithfulness, wants him back again for the last months of her life. But Erhard leaves his mother and his aunt for a woman he loves.

These are the motifs. On this winter's evening, they are unearthed out of the buried souls of three people into the light and clarity of the footlights. But the essential has not yet been stated. When Borkman, Gunhild, and Ella talk about the past, they do not push the isolated events or their motivations into the foreground, but rather time itself, which has become stained for them:

"I've already gotten my own satisfaction . . . satisfaction for my entire bungled life," says Mrs. Borkman.

When Ella tells her that she has heard that Gunhild and her husband live in the same house without seeing each other, Gunhild answers: "Yes—we have been obliged to, Ella. Continually—since they freed him and he was sent back to the house and to me. The entire eight years." And then Ella and Borkman meet each other:

> ER: It seems like an eternity since we two stood opposite each other, eye to eye, Borkman.
> JGB: (Darkly) Long, yes, it's long. Many horrors lie between then and now.
> ER: An entire human life lies between then and now. A failed human life.

Somewhat later: "From that time on when your image began to extinguish in me, I've lived there as if under a solar eclipse. In all those years it resisted me more and more . . . to love a living creature . . . until it finally became impossible for me." And when in the third act Mrs. Borkman tells her husband she has ruminated over his dark history more than enough, he answers: "I, too. During five endless years in the cell — and elsewhere — I had the time. And in the eight years there above I had still more time. I have taken up the entire suit again and renewed the examination — for myself. I have brought it up again countless times . . . I have gone back and forth in my room and have judged every one of my actions from every angle, twisted and turned them. I've just wandered about up there and fully squandered eight precious years of my life." In the last act, on the open space in front of the house: "It's high time that I lived again in the free and the open air . . . Nearly three years in detention, five years in jail, eight years up above in the room. . . ." But he cannot become one living in the free open air any longer. The curse of the past's prison pursues him not in life, but rather in death. And Gunhild and Ella, who on this evening lose the husband and son they both loved, reach their hands to each other — two "shadows over a dead man."

Compared to the Sophoclean *Oedipus*, the past here is not a function of the action but rather only a spur to the conjuring up of the past. The accent lies neither with Ella's fate nor with Borkman's death. A single event of the past is also not thematic: say, Borkman's renunciation of Ella or the lawyer's vengeance; no event of the past, but rather the past itself: the one that continually mentions its "long years" and its "bungled, failed life." But these phrases themselves deny the dramatic action. In a sense, the dramatic actualization can only become represented as a temporality and not as time itself. And so time in drama leaves itself to mere reportage and during its direct representation makes only a single artform possible, one which "takes up in the line of its constitutive principles." This artform is — as G. Lukács has demonstrated — the novel.

"In drama (and in epic poetry) the past does not exist or is completely present. As these forms don't recognize the lapse of time, they contain no qualitative differences of experience between the past and the present; time possesses no transmutative authority, nothing becomes strengthened or weakened in its meaning." In analysis of *Oedipus*, the past becomes the action: "That is the formal sense exhibited by Aristotle's typical scenes of exposition and recognition: something is unknown by the pragmatic heroes of the dramas, now it enters on their mental horizon, and because of the now-changed world they must behave differently, as they would have. But the supervener becomes paler through the lack of a time perspective; it is the present, fully analogous and equivalent." So a further difference becomes clear. The truth of *Oedipus Rex* is objective nature. It belongs to the world: only Oedipus lives in ignorance and his way to the truth builds the tragic action. With Ibsen, on the other hand, truth is that which is introspection. The motifs of the presently assumed resolve rest in this introspection, an introspection in which all exterior changes bury themselves and survive the traumatic working. Besides the time element, Ibsen's thematic in a topical sense also dispenses with every present-tense that drama requires. The thematic derives entirely, of course, from the interhuman relationships, but it belongs, as a reflex, only in the innermost souls of people who are estranged and isolated from each other.

That is to say, its direct dramatic representation is not possible. First of all, to achieve a higher density, the representation requires the analytical technique. Only as novelistic material, which Ibsen's thematic essentially is, can it really reach the stage. But finally, even in that form, it still remains alien and unpresentable. More often than not it becomes knotted (in both senses of the word) with a present-tense action and it remains in the past and is banished to introspection. That, in short, is Ibsen's dramatic problem of form.

Because his departure point was epic, he had to achieve every incomparable mastery of play construction. Because he achieved it, one didn't see the epic basis anymore. The twofold business of playwrights — representation and function — became for Ibsen an inexorable necessity and something in which he could not entirely succeed.

To aid representation, there are many things that by themselves cultivate estrangement. For instance, the technique of the leitmotiv. Here it does not, as elsewhere, hold fast the similarities in the changes or establish cross-connections. In Ibsen's leitmotivs, the past lives on: through its mention it becomes conjured up. So in the midstream of *Rosmersholm*, through the suicide of Beate Rosmers, the present becomes eternal. In terms of symbolic events where the past and present fall together, one thinks of the clink of glasses in the next room (*Ghosts*). And also, the motif of inheritance does not so much embody the rebirth of the antique faith as the representation of the past: the wanderlust of manor lord Alving in the illness of his son. Because the life of Mrs. Alving in the company of these people is not brought to representation except as a time frame or as a generational difference, it is only possible to hold onto time itself with the aforementioned analytical approach. And the dramatic functionalism, which otherwise has to work out the "causal-finale" structure of a uniform action, here must bridge the gap that endures between the present and the past that the representation removes. Seldom has Ibsen been able to seamlessly unify a present action with an equally-weighted conjured-up thematic. In this respect, *Rosmersholm* appears to be his masterwork. The political themes of the day and the introspection of the past, which in *Rosmersholm* is not exiled to the soul's abyss but lives on in the entire house, hardly cleave apart. Rather, they make it possible for the scene's subject matter appropriately to remain in the twilight. This is completely unified in the figure of Rector Krolls, who is the brother of the suicide-driven Mrs. Rosmers and yet also her political opponent. But here as well this unification doesn't succeed in adequately motivating the end of the past and hence in showing its urgency: the tragedy of the blind Oedipus that leads us into the palace is denied to Rosmer and Rebecca West when, bound by the dead wife, they throw themselves into the millstream.

Herein lies the immense distance that the bourgeois world lives from the true tragic downfall. Its immanent tragedy dwells not in death but rather in life itself. Of this life Rilke says (in direct reference to Ibsen) that it "was so unknowingly ingrained in us. . . . We had to retreat into ourselves so deeply that we were hardly even left with suppositions about it." And there belongs the Balzacian word: *"Nous mourrons tous incon-nus."* The work of Ibsen is entirely imbued with his particular essence. In works where he attempted to make the exposure of secret lives dramatic, he destroyed the drama. Ibsen's characters could only live by burying themselves with the consumptive "life-lie." Because he was not their *romancier* and they were not left to their own lives but rather were forced into "frank" conversation, they died. So time, which all dramas in a sense finally are, becomes the dramatist to the murder of its own creations.

Modern Problems   Brian Downs*

At a time when Brandes and his ideas began to affect Ibsen he was at a pause, a Hercules at the cross-roads. Despite all the great issues raised by *Love's Comedy*, *The Pretenders*, *Peer Gynt* and, especially, by *Brand*, these were works not merely centered in Norway topographically, but written with specifically Norwegian conditions in view. The holiday from deep problems which the author now permitted himself in writing *The League of Youth* might divert itself with abundant satire at "the local situation," but was still completely bound up with it. Henceforth a profound change was to be observed. Ibsen, it may be said, after some tarrying and much self-debate turned from being a Norwegian to being a

*Originally published in *Ibsen: The Intellectual Background* (Cambridge: Cambridge University Press, 1946) 136–69. © 1946 by Cambridge University Press. Reprinted by permission of Cambridge University Press.

European. Modern he had made himself beyond qualification or perad-venture in the last comedy, and to the Norwegian scene he remained unswervingly faithful in the dramas conceived after this date. But the themes, the situations and the personalities which came under his pen were no longer suggested to him, living in exile as he was, by purely local preoccupations and literary traditions, but by the interests of the civilised world at large and his observation of it, however much life and individual-ity might still accrue from the Norwegian guise in which he finally saw and presented the generalities.

That Brandes exerted no specious or unnatural influence upon him is attested by the nature of the great work on which Ibsen was intermittently engaged throughout most of the critical years and which had begun to engage his thoughts as far back as July 1864. *Emperor and Galilean* (*Kejser og Galilæer*, 1873), in its choice of subject and theme, shows that Ibsen's spirit, unaided, was prepared to transcend all the limits of space (as well as of time) in which so far it had kept itself confined. The problems to which it owes a great part of its formation and which in turn it was to transform for later debate had an urgency no greater for Norwegians than for anyone else, and their country is not so much as mentioned.

To begin with, it would seem, Ibsen was attracted to the Eastern Roman emperor Julian, the hero of this vast drama, by apprehending him to be, first and foremost, a rebel of almost Miltonic grandeur, since his repudiation and persecution of the religion of Christ could be little less awful than Lucifer's defiance of the first person of the Trinity. Plans for treating this subject alternated in Ibsen's mind with those for a drama on the pirate-king Magnus (or Mogens) Heinesen. But, as he absorbed himself in it and in some of the secondary sources which he consulted, its complexity and farther implications were borne in on him, — precisely those implications in fact to which a somewhat widespread interest in Julian was due at that epoch.[1]

In the middle third of the nineteenth century the Christian religion, firmly established in the statute-books and conventions of all civilised nations outside Asia, was sustaining attacks not always realised by its adherents, but of a seriousness in comparison with which the criticisms of a Bayle or a Voltaire had been mere skirmishes. Geology, biology, mathematics and philology — all the advancing sciences of the day — combined to undermine the foundations on which the Christian edifice was reared. Ibsen took little interest in the labours of Lyell, of Colenso, of Huxley or of those who represented their point of view in the North; he had very likely never heard of Bishop Wilberforce's animadversions upon evolutionary biology;[2] it is probable that the culmination of Renan's scholarship in *The Life of Jesus*[3] (like the similar efforts of Strauss and Feuerbach) left him indifferent, since he neglected the easiest possible opportunity for making the author's acquaintance.[4] We need therefore not consider the avenues of approach to the religious problem which they opened farther than to remark on the extensive interest and heated controversies which they were arousing, but proceed rather to the viewpoint which revealed that problem most clearly to Ibsen.

It is not improbable that Brandes impelled or helped him to occupy this standpoint. Brandes's campaign against stagnation, prejudice, tradition and convention axiomatically assumed their impermanence; he was far from enunciating or insisting on any eternal verities; already at the end of the 1860's he was declaiming that the world of thought had entered the constellation of relativity. There was nothing that might not be susceptible to its laws.[5] Mutability, the supersession of the old by the new were, of course, no new conceptions. Before the theory of evolution and progress had become fashionable, Hegel's philosophy of history had made great play with them on an elaborate system of successive "thesis," "antithesis" and "synthesis." The all but religious awe with which Hegel was regarded at Christiania[6] had impressed even so unconventional and unphilosophical a mind as Ibsen's; and, in so far as he ever thought philosophically,[7] he was prone to do so in Hegelian terms. The religious problem of the time accordingly presented itself to him somewhat in this guise: What if the Christian religion were not the final "synthesis" which for so long it has seemed to be (to those who systematize the course of history like this), but an "antithesis," waiting, as it were, for a later "synthesis" as it had confronted an earlier "thesis"?[8] To one formulating the problem in terms such as these, questions like the age of the patriarchs, Noah's flood, the special creation of man, the irreconcilability of the gospels, the prevalence of thaumaturges in Palestine would be ancillary, if not otiose.

Not only does Ibsen seem to have contemplated the religious problem in terms of this order, but he conceived of his hero Julian as doing so similarly. The rebel becomes something of a Hegelian — in a way the course of the action drives him into that position. Threatened, repressed and terrified by the religion which Constantine had officially established, Prince Julian turns against it with a violence equally great. He endeavours, as his less virulent antagonists have always maintained, to put back the hands of the clock. Soon, however, he discovers that this cannot be done, or cannot fruitfully be done. If the old truth (Christianity) is, as he believes, true no more, so the old beauty of paganism, represented by the intoxication of debauchees and the caperings of harlots, is no longer beautiful. Something new, a *tertium quid*, a synthesis, must supersede both.[9]

An impetus to meditate on the nature of such a synthesis was imparted to Ibsen by certain important political or semi-political events of the day. His old "Scandinavianism," discredited but not dead in his bosom, had betrayed a predilection for large polities;[10] he could not therefore remain indifferent to the creation round about him first of united Italy and then of re-united Germany. He saw the fashioning of two enormous political bastions where hitherto there had been little more than a heap of

114 Critical Essays on Henrik Ibsen

stones; at the same time the papacy, at the Vatican council (1870–1), was embarking, through the decree promulgating its infallibility, on a policy of strengthening the doctrinal and administrative structure of organised religion. The results, to Ibsen's sight, were not completely satisfactory, far from it. The new Rome was never so good as the asylum which had received him in 1864, and Bismarck's *Reich* as such repelled him, however many fine institutions and laborious citizens it might contain.[11] He saw at close quarters the most far-reaching experiment hitherto made to give to the state the functions of universal provider, in the realms not merely of order and security, but also of communications, health, even of art, education and religion. One of the first acts of the new centralised government at Berlin was to embark (1872) on what was called the *Kulturkampf* (or Civilisation-Fight) against the Roman Catholic Church. Was, Ibsen pondered, this *Reich*, this *rige*,[12] as the Danish-Norwegian equivalent is, the desired synthesis between the old military rule of the Caesars and the Christian rule of life? And, if not, what was the *tredie rige*, the third empire, to be?

The intellectual kernel of *Emperor and Galilean* lies perhaps in this dialogue:

> JULIAN: . . . Emperor and Galilean! How reconcile that contradiction?
>
> Yes, this Jesus Christ is the greatest rebel that ever lived. What was Brutus — what was Cassius compared with him? *They* murdered only the man Julius Caesar; but *he* murders all that is called Caesar and Augustus. Is peace conceivable between the Galilean and the Emperor? Is there room for the two of them together upon the earth? For he lives on the earth, Maximus, — the Galilean lives, I say, however thoroughly both Jews and Romans imagined that they had killed him; he lives in the rebellious minds of men; he lives in their scorn and defiance of all visible authority.
>
> "Render unto Caesar the things that are Caesar's, — and to God the things that are God's!" Never has mouth of man uttered a craftier saying than that. What lies behind it? . . .
>
> MAXIMUS: Both the Emperor and the Galilean shall succumb.
>
> JULIAN: Succumb — ? Both — ?
>
> MAXIMUS: Both. Whether in our times or in hundreds of years, I know not; but so it shall be when the right man comes.
>
> JULIAN: And who is the right man?
>
> MAXIMUS: He who shall swallow up both Emperor and Galilean.
>
> JULIAN: You solve the riddle by a still darker riddle.[13]

To *Emperor and Galilean* Ibsen was always disposed to look reverentially as his most important work; his regard for it may be pardoned, since perhaps more protracted and fatiguing labour went to its composition than to any other and it embodied the result of more abstract and philosophical ratiocination. "Alone I did it," he could also reflect.[14] It has not, however, so favourably impressed its readers, who have been content to repeat the last words of Maximus just quoted and hold it a reproach to Ibsen that, having embarked on so stupendous a quest, he carried it no farther. The fact is, that he tired of his theme before the end, and the progressive loss of control over character, situation and plot betrays it. In the letter to Georg Brandes of 4 April 1872,[15] which has already been quoted from, Ibsen says of the volume containing his critical friend's introductory lecture: "A more dangerous book could never fall into the hands of a breeding author." Ibsen was pregnant of *Emperor and Galilean*, and it is highly probable that *The Main Currents of Nineteenth Century Literature* produced nothing less than a miscarriage. True, the subject of *Emperor and Galilean* was important, and Ibsen had his own independent attitude towards it. It was big, perhaps too big, but, even if read in the light of the *Kulturkampf* (which it might not occur to everyone to direct upon it), it was scarcely modern; it certainly did not exhibit the modern world. Then it was, in origin, Hegelian, and, great as Hegel might be, the world lay not now with Hegel any more than with the fathers of the Christian Church; it lay with Darwin and Spencer,[16] or at least with Hartmann. In waking hours of the night Ibsen may have seen *Emperor and Galilean* respectable, remote and grandiose, but, if applicable to actual conditions, only quite indirectly. It just did live, it just did submit problems to debate. But of such half-and-half things there were to be no more.

. . . .

When, with Ibsen, we now turn away from the past, we may commence the next stage of the present enquiry by revolving the question: What lessons had Brandes's own teachers to impart to him? In the realm of pure aesthetics their influence on Ibsen must have been nil: it would be vain to seek for any echoes from Sainte-Beuve or Philarète Chasles in the technique and ideas of his plays. The aesthetic philosophy of Taine, however, by which at one time Brandes was profoundly impressed, which he carefully expounded[17] and to which he gave currency in northern Europe, raised issues that far exceeded the bounds of art. Ibsen would scarcely be touched by the famous doctrine of literature as the product of *milieu, race* and *moment*, but the wider question with which it was bound up, of determinism and the freedom of man's will, remained one of serious concern to him. That question not only tinges the whole catastrophe of *Emperor and Galilean*,[18] but is placed into the focus of the memorable spirit-raising scene (in Act III of the first Part), which ends with Julian's outcry: "I defy necessity! I will not serve it! I am free, free, free!"[19] Shortly before that, the shade of Judas Iscariot[20] had appeared and the following dialogue taken place:

> THE VOICE. But for me, whither had the chariot rolled?
> JULIAN. Whither did it roll by means of thee?

THE VOICE. Into the glory of glories.
JULIAN. Why didst thou help?
THE VOICE. Because I *willed*.
JULIAN. What didst thou will?
THE VOICE. What I must.
JULIAN. Who chose thee?
THE VOICE. The master.
JULIAN. Did the master foreknow when he chose thee?
THE VOICE. Ah, *that* is the riddle![21]

This was not the first riddle with which the occult world had answered Julian's frantic interrogations. Earlier,[22] when he had asked, "What is my mission?" the "Voice in the Light" had made reply:

To establish the empire.[23]

JULIAN. What empire?
THE VOICE. The empire.
JULIAN. And by what way?
THE VOICE. By the way of freedom.
JULIAN. Speak clearly! What is the way of freedom?
THE VOICE. The way of necessity.
JULIAN. And by what power.
THE VOICE. By *willing*.
JULIAN. What shall I will?
THE VOICE. What thou *must*.

Beyond this Ibsen himself does not go. The whole trend of his romantic upbringing—in so far as he enjoyed a literary upbringing at all—and the deep striving of his nature to liberate himself and his fellows from trammels of every kind made him unwilling to abandon the conception of free will. On the other hand he could not disown the strength of the deterministic argument or claim that the human mind was exempted from it. In a letter[24] in which he takes up Georg Brandes's discussion of the treatment of necessity in his own *Emperor and Galilean* and in Paul Heyse's novel, *Children of the World*, he observes that it amounts to very much the same thing to say "he is free—under neces-sity"—and to say "it lies in his blood." The observation suggests that, after a fashion which Taine would have approved, Ibsen admitted physiological causes of heredity and the like as mediate between ultimate necessity and individual volition. That he brooded on these causes and their bearings on tragedy is especially evident in *Ghosts*, on which an eminent classical scholar of the day[25] fastened at once as a translation into modern terms of the hereditary curse handled with such effect by the Greek dramatists when they too were confronted with the incompatibility of *Ananke*, necessity, and human responsibility.

Not only as a tragedian, but as a moralist also Ibsen continued to concern himself profoundly with questions of individual responsibility, for which the absolute necessitarian has so facile an answer. It is not without significance that the life's work of the most serious professed philosopher in any of his dramas, that of Alfred Allmers (in *Little Eyolf*), should be "On Human Responsibility."[26] Responsibility presented itself to Ibsen in two different guises. The first is the degree of obligation for the well-being of his neighbour and, to a less extent, of himself too which each individual should take upon himself, the problem which Alfred and Rita Allmers propose practically to solve by their school for the riff-raff of the waterfront and which Hedda Gabler consistently shelves with consequences more catastrophic than Dr Stockmann's ill-requited exertions on behalf of his fellow-townsmen; it is this conception of responsibility which flashes upon Ellida Wangel's mind when she realises that she has been sick through neglecting "freedom . . . under full responsibility"[27] and that she can regain her health by repairing the neglect. The second aspect of Responsibility may be defined as the degree to which everyone is the deliberate director of (and on that ground should be accountable for) his own actions, when these are the manifestation of a personality moulded by a chain of causes as old as the world. Ibsen cast this into the dramatic form in *A Doll's House*, where Nora's frivolity and even her crime are explained and palliated by her temperamental inheritance from her father and by her upbringing at his hands. (How close the two aspects stood to one another in Ibsen's mind is shown by the fact that her breeding produced in Nora a lack of responsibility in the other sense of the word, and the whole of *Ghosts* may be interpreted as a protracted examination of Responsibility in both of its guises.)

Taine imparted a shock to the settled notions of his time not only by his philosophy of necessity and his rigorous application of it to aesthetics, but also by his theory of the nature of man with which his disciples, *les naturalistes*, associated it. Man was a mammal, and a particularly powerful, ferocious and libidinous mammal at that, and, if the proper study of mankind should still be man, it should take the form of a natural history as free from moral preoccupations in its approach as in its findings. To Brandes, the admirer of Sainte-Beuve and Philarète Chasles and the predestined adorer of genius, the rigorism of Taine's aesthetics had only made a very partial and evanescent appeal; and he took up a highly ambiguous attitude towards Naturalism by so wide and, in a sense, old-fashioned an interpretation of the term as, for instance, to include Wordsworth and Shelley among its foremost professors. Neither in his plays nor elsewhere did Ibsen intrude speculations on the nature of man in zoological terms. His preoccupation with the problem of responsibility is an index of his remoteness from any wish to write "Natural History." As much as he knew of the great propagandist of this narrower Naturalism he thoroughly detested: "Zola descends to the sewer to take a bath, I do in order to scour it."[28] The timidity and chastity of his temperament kept him away from scenes of violence and passion, even though (as puritanical opponents were not slow to point out) his plays might involve concubinage, incest, homicide, fraud, self-slaughter and arson. But for such the devoted reader of the Bible, whose art followed in the line begun by Aeschylus and made illustrious by Shakespeare, had no need to incur any debt to a Zola or a Taine.

. . . .

The ferment which engendered the *Gjennembrud* or "Break-Through" in Georg Brandes's mind during the years on either side of 1870 was supplied to him from Great Britain as well as from France. For a short while, indeed, he adopted the private slogan "Read Mill and turn Anglo-Saxon." He made the acquaintance of the English thinker, visited him at Black-heath and by translating them into Danish (with prefaces by himself) gave to two capital works of his, *The Subjection of Women* and *Utilitarian-ism*,[29] a very notable circulation in the North.

When, in his educational design, Brandes attempted to infect Ibsen with his own admiration for *Utilitarianism*, he encountered a recalci-trance, however, which seems rather strange. For though, in later life, Ibsen is never reported to have mentioned Mill again in praise or disparagement, he came to assume towards many capital concerns very much the same attitude, and the imperceptible process by which this came about suggests that he was congenitally pre-disposed. In Ibsen there was, often overlaid or qualified, a deep strain, probably derived from Rous-seauistic romanticism, which made the happiness of the individual the ultimate criterion in morals — precisely the tenet of the "hedonistic calcu-lus" propounded by Jeremy Bentham, Mill's great predecessor. Just at the time that Brandes was translating *Utilitarianism* (1872) Ibsen was wres-tling in *Emperor and Galilean* with the problem of adjusting pagan hedonism to the demands of spiritual religion and the future common-wealth (*rige*), a problem that had not been very far below the surface in *Brand* and *Love's Comedy*. Though some of its manifestations were so shocking, as none could appreciate better than herself, Mrs Alving meditated profoundly whether sufficient importance were attached to *livsglaede*, the "joy of life," a problem which she at once submitted to the most animated debate in all Northern countries. The desperate striving of later heroines and heroes, of Rosmer, of Ellida Wangel, of Solness, for instance, to shake off their *trolde*, the monsters that constrict and hold them down, issuing in the radiant song of Maja — the last words of Ibsen which an audience was to hear:

> I am free! I am free! I am free!
> No more life in the prison for me!
> I am free as a bird! I am free![30]

and the main theme of the play in which she figures (*When We Dead Awaken*) raise more directly than its author ever did before the question whether, in the teeth of the demands put upon him by ethics, by art and his mission in life, a man should not first and foremost clutch at sensual delights, emancipate the flesh, as Enfantin put it.

In view of what has been said about his preoccupation with human responsibility, it is unnecessary to remark how deeply Ibsen reflected on the bearings of one person's welfare and happiness on the welfare and happiness of those with whom he has immediate contact—an aspect of hedonism to which Mill devoted particular attention, insisting that, if the happiness of a community were measurable by the aggregate happiness of the individuals comprising it (as the older utilitarians had urged), then reciprocally the happiness of the community promoted and increased also that of each constituent member.

. . . .

Several reasons may be alleged for Ibsen's dislike of Mill. The very coincidence of their views may be one of them; Ibsen, intent on independence and, therefore, on "originality" of thought, disliked the notion that Mill had already been enunciating his doctrines for a lifetime and might be adjudged his preceptor; his reverential awe for the name of Hegel may have been perturbed by one who could easily dismiss some of his Metaphysics as "nonsense"; for all his interest in his bank-balance and investments, he remembered perhaps the contempt for "utility" as a criterion of moral values which came natural to the great exponent of the Christian paradox; philosophy should have about it the sublime and the cryptic of a Delphic oracle, and it jarred on Ibsen to hear it exposed in intelligible sentences appealing to the highest common factor of human understanding: Mill, to him, was another philistine Cicero,[31] for whom his vexation and contempt had not yet been slaked.

But the most singular of Ibsen's objections to the hierarch of utilitarianism was Mill's chivalrous acknowledgment[32] that he owed many of his ideas to the gifted woman who ultimately became his wife. The ideas in question are those informing that other work on which Brandes had exercised his talents as a translator and expositor, *The Subjection of Women* (1869).

Nowhere else perhaps had dissatisfaction with the position of women in a rapidly changed and changing society been felt more acutely than in the Scandinavian countries. On the one hand, as the old literature abundantly shows, they had enjoyed the respect and comparative freedom which the Teutonic-speaking peoples were prone to accord to their women-folk, so that the energetic Lady Inger and ruthless Hjørdis of Ibsen's youthful fancy struck his audiences as nothing abhorrent in nature; their education had not been utterly neglected; and the ideas of the Romantic Age[33] had presumably tended to raise their *self*-esteem. On the other hand, the material backwardness of Norway in particular at the beginning of the nineteenth century and the corresponding rapidity with which it made up leeway during the next two generations often produced an adverse effect. Jonas Lie's faithful delineations in *The Family at Gilje*[34] show how a squire's lady (as we might call her) in a remote, but not uncharacteristic country neighbourhood during the 1840's presided in almost medieval fashion over highly varied and complicated domestic functions, so that her confinements procured her her only holidays: under her supervision the products of dairy, sheep-farm, vegetable-garden, orchard, lake, brewhouse, poultry-yard were converted into almost everything required for the consumption from January to December of her own family and the considerable retinue maintained by her husband and herself. The industrial revolution, the steamship, the new roads and railways changed all that; and someone like Fru Jaeger might, economically, become quite superfluous in the realm in which she had reigned supreme, or at any rate might have many of her functions reduced largely to their ornamental aspect.[35] Not only her environment would come to realise that, but she herself would do so too, in the enhanced leisure for reflection and reading which simultaneously accrued; and nowhere was this more apparent than in the rising middle class of the towns. What was true of the married woman was even more self-evident in the case of her unmarried daughters. Hence sprang dissatisfaction and unhappiness, as well as the mischief with which, according to the saying, Satan compensates for idleness, and concomitantly therewith a desire, evinced by the more resolute women, for entrance into other activities, the professions and the arts.

Camilla Collett had been a victim to this nascent dissatisfaction and a pioneer in diagnosing and liberating it. From biographical reasons (her unrequited passion for Welhaven), it was natural that in *The Sheriff's Daughters*, the novel that left its mark on *Love's Comedy*, she should devote her attention to the sentimental restrictions put on girls by being allowed no more than the negative choice of a spouse. But the publication of her grievance established also the valuable right of women to plead their own cause, and throughout a long life she continued to exercise it on a variety of subjects. Round about 1870 and again towards the end of the decade she came into fairly frequent personal contact with Ibsen, and the diatribes to which she gave voice undoubtedly made an impression upon him, though in talk he usually assumed an extremely conservative attitude, partly to tease her, but principally perhaps to stimulate her into stating her case in its extremest form.

In the meantime Camilla Collett received reinforcement from Mathilde Schjøtt[36] and the painter Aasta Hanstein. The former published a critique of Mill from the female point of view, *The Women-Friends' Discussion of The Subjection of Women* (1871), the latter carried on in 1874[37] an overt campaign against male arrogance, championing a Swedish noblewoman who had been unable to gain redress for the "insult"[38] inflicted by a Norwegian undergraduate, delivering feminist lectures all over the country and striding about with a riding-whip for the prevention of any such insult as had befallen her *protégée*. The campaign for extending women's rights and opportunities took shape and produced results. In 1882 they were admitted as matriculated members to Christiania university, and in 1884 a petition was presented to the *Storthing* for a bill giving married women a legal right to property and earnings.

Among the signatories of this petition was not only Bjørnson (as anyone might expect), but also Ibsen. In the main, however, this aspect of the feminist movement does not appear greatly to have concerned him, and he took no notice of it in his imaginative work.[39] Perhaps his dislike of the great utilitarian's labours may in part be due to his apparent preoccupation with status, rights, political and economical considerations. Yet fundamentally Mill and Ibsen were at one here also; Mill believed that women's disabilities elsewhere were only clung to in order to maintain their subjection in domestic life,[40] and he concentrated on the causes so that the effect would follow of itself; that ultimate effect, in his view, would before long make marriage an alliance of equals or at any rate of potential equals[41] — morally much the same thing; such a change would vastly benefit society at large, settling it on a firmer basis of justice and equal opportunity, tapping a reservoir of immense social energies, and in the benefit to society, husbands and men in general, would of course share.

An attitude analogous to this Ibsen unfeignedly discloses in the short speech which he made on 26 May 1898 at a banquet of the Norwegian Society for the Woman's Cause.[42] On the one hand, he defends himself against the ascription of feminism, but, on the other, he wishes it to be known that any aim he has had outside his art has been for mankind in general and the mankind inhabiting Norway in particular:

> I thank you for drinking my health, but I must reject the honour of having consciously worked for the woman's cause. I am not even clear what the woman's cause really is. For me it has been an affair of humanity.[43]

Later on his words are equally significant, and, though they may not have proved palatable to all his listeners, they take a positive form:

> I have always looked on it as a mission[44] to elevate the nation and give the people a higher status. Two factors come into play in this process; and it rests with the *mothers* by means of strenuous and protracted exertions to rouse a conscious sense of *culture* and *discipline*. These must be created in human beings before the people can be raised higher. It is the women who shall solve the problem of humanity. As mothers they are to do it. And only *so* can they do it.

These deliberately chosen words show that the last speech of Bernick in *Pillars of Society* is not the sentimental clap-trap that it is sometimes thought to be — "it is you women who are the pillars of society."[45] On one plane Bernick's words represent the author's conviction, though he would equally have acquiesced all his lifetime in the sentiment with which a woman then proceeds, as it were, to trump Bernick's card: "the spirits of Truth and Freedom — *these* are the Pillars of Society." The specifically feminine is very important in his view, but in the last resort it is no more than ancillary.

In the indictment against modern society of which Ibsen delivered himself in play after play, beginning with *Pillars of Society*, one of the counts was that it disregarded in its communal assumptions and institutions one half of itself and depressed the ancillary to the servile. Lona Hessel, who speaks the lines about Truth and Freedom and in whose ungainly deportment and provocative speech contemporaries were not slow to recognise Aasta Hanstein, puts the former point quite precisely: "your society is a society of bachelor-souls; you have no eyes for womanhood";[46] but, at one time intended to have equal prominence in *Pillars of Society* with the criticism of commercial morality, the feminist argument was only slightly developed there and relegated to fuller treatment in its successor, *A Doll's House*.

Among Ibsen's preliminary notes to the last-named occurs the following:

> There are two kinds of spiritual law, two kinds of conscience, one in man and another, altogether different, in woman. They do not understand each other; but in practical life the woman is judged by man's law, as though she were not a woman but a man. . . . A woman cannot be herself in the society of the present day, which is an exclusively masculine society. . . .[47]

The disagreement on which the drama of *A Doll's House* is built accordingly is not so much that between a wife and a husband as one between a woman and the society in which she lives, the society which imposes its laws upon her; Nora leaves her home and family in the last act not as a declaration of war, but in order that she may meditate in peace upon her position as a woman and member of the human community. The prominence which Ibsen gave to women in his plays is due not to any preponderating interest he may have taken in them as a sex[48] — there is no hint of this in the annals of his life — nor because, like his northern colleague Strindberg, he thought the private relations of women and men and the antagonisms to which they give rise to be of special dramatic interest, but because women afforded him specimens of humanity peculiarly trammelled by their conventional disabilities in the struggle for personal emancipation which formed his passionate preoccupation. Nora Helmer becomes the typical representative of the individual whose free development has been checked and who has been driven into courses which both society considers criminal and the individual eventually finds uncongenial. The claims of freedom and personality in general could best be vindicated in women, because in women they were most persistently denied. The word "slaves" which Mill had applied to the female half of humanity must have evoked the loudest echo in Ibsen.[49]

· · · ·

With the doctrines of John Stuart Mill, lay opinion on the continent commonly associated those of Herbert Spencer and with the latter the biological theses first formulated by Charles Darwin in *The Origin of Species* (1859).[50] In view of the currency which some of their conclusions enjoyed, Ibsen must have known about them, but there is no evidence that he studied[51] their works themselves, and philosophy and biology were naturally less congenial to him than morals.[52] It has been noted how he disdained the construction which the French *naturalistes* placed on the new evolutionism. Nevertheless, the order of speculations to which the latter gave rise had points of interest for him. His depreciation of the Norwegian national character made him (who had implied no criticism of the Vikings in *The Vikings in Helgeland* or of the Vikings' next descendants in *The Pretenders*) scrutinize the belief in an almost automatic progress which some thought that the doctrine of evolution justified. In meditating upon the hindrances to freedom and happiness, as well as on other occasions, he had to take into account hereditary disease and degeneracy. If certain strains improved and proliferated, others deteriorated and languished; a congenital disability could by itself stultify every striving after happiness and freedom.

Considerations of this kind were very prominently in the public eye of Norway during the 1870's, because of the controversy which was taking place about the proper treatment of lepers. Of all the civilised countries of Europe Norway suffered perhaps proportionately most at that date from the incidence of leprosy, which indeed seemed to be on the increase. In 1875 there were more than 2000 sufferers from the dread and incurable disease, and opinion, both among men of science and others, was sharply divided about its nature and transmission. Was it contagious and eradicable therefore by isolation, or was it a hereditary disability communicable only by parent to child? In 1873 Gerhard Armauer Hansen of Bergen discovered the leprosy-bacillus, eventually discredited the theory of hereditary transmission and inaugurated an agitation which culminated in the forcible segregation (when necessary) of sufferers, whose numbers subsequently decreased to about one-eighth.

The disease of syphilis offered some analogies to leprosy and, though it was sufficiently well appreciated that it was communicated in sexual intercourse, many of its effects could also be construed as the visitation of the sins of the fathers upon their children. It is possible that Ibsen's interest in venereal disease had been roused by Strodtmann's biography of Heine (1867–9),[53] who had been one of the idols of *Andhrimner's* staff in his early youth, and the poignant paradox of the great hedonist's complete paralysis from *tabes dorsalis* presented precisely that aspect of disease, hereditary or otherwise, which would most profoundly affect him. The first case which Ibsen presented was that of Dr Rank, the family friend of the Helmers, in *A Doll's House*, and with him, as with Heine, it is the central nervous system which is attacked. Rank himself attributes his illness entirely to paternal excesses.[54]

In *Ghosts* the illness no longer remains on the second plane, but is advanced into the forefront and is handled more comprehensively. The late Captain Alving, we are to suppose, contracted it by contagion during the cheerful promiscuity of his youth; the heir to his body bears about with him the uncontagious sequelae, which are manifested in his brain and which will reduce him to idiocy. Oswald thereby provides a clear instance of physical degeneration, and the enigmatic conclusion poses the question whether the degenerate members of the stock should not at a certain stage undergo extermination,[55] an extension of the measures which society, in its own real or supposed hygienic interests, was prepared to take against lepers.[56] In throwing up this question Ibsen also canvassed the original responsibility of society, its crime against the individual, in constraining a man like Captain Alving to a course of life so dreadfully visited.[57] After many years of anguished meditation on the subject, Mrs Alving has evidently reached the conclusion that the puritanical morality and cramped environment in which she herself had been bred, and which Pastor Manders represents as an ideal, had turned the sparkling, gay, energetic young man whom she had married into a furtive sot and profligate, capable of playing disgusting practical jokes on his own infant son; it was these things which brought the curse on the house both in that manner and by refusing to let her herself escape from it when the mischief to her husband had been done.

Ibsen used contagious disease thus as an illustration of an argument about private and public morality. He was not concerned to suggest pure physical loathsomeness or to construct any argument, as one of the *naturalistes* might have done, to exonerate a malefactor on account of impairment of his faculties through inherited or acquired disease.[58]

On the other hand, though he did not regard *belles-lettres* as a branch of natural history, he accepted what so many of his contemporaries could not bring themselves to accept from the newer biology, man's unprivileged position in the evolutionary process. He nowhere hints at any belief in a special creation, with special prerogatives and special obligations of a supernatural order. Not even a clergyman or pedagogue ever in his plays calls to mind that God created man in his own image.[59] The calm manner in which Mrs Alving and the horrified fury with which great sections of the public contemplated the possibility, even the desirability, of an incestuous union between Oswald and Regina — which no one would have condemned in the case of domestic animals — betrays the distance by which Ibsen had outstripped most of his co-evals in the acceptance of the new science. He not only drew his own conclusions from it, but interested himself in some of its details. In *The Wild Duck* Hjalmar Ekdal is convinced of Hedvig's bastardy on the evidence of the defective eyesight which she shares with Werle senior. Ellida Wangel's sick love of the sea (in *The Lady from the Sea*) receives a curious illumination from some observations[60] by Ibsen to the effect that the evolutionary process went astray in removing the higher animals on to dry land, so that they carry about with them an unsatisfied yearning for the element to which they belonged — a notion apparently suggested[61] by Ernest Haeckel's demonstration that the fishes stand in the direct evolutionary line leading down to man.

. . . .

Many of the ideas and tenets of Ibsen which have received consideration in this and earlier chapters, profoundly shocking the orthodox among his contemporaries, were not infrequently lumped together as "pessimism": such were his notions of torpedoing the Ark; the implied denial of a special creation and the acceptance of man's position in the long and incompleted evolutionary process, with no suggestion of any supernatural privileges such as are promised by the Christian faith; the prominence which he gave in his speculations on heredity to degeneration and the inheritance of undesirable characteristics; the delineations of the weakness of the individual and of the actions of a society which is created to promote and protect, but in effect thwarts and crushes the individual; the defeat of human effort and aspiration, which in a high degree all tragedy-writing involves. The question naturally presents itself whether Ibsen's speculation was directly affected by the consciously pessimistic thinkers in which the nineteenth century abounded.

Here Georg Brandes may be acquitted of immediate responsibility and, as far as the evidence reaches, of indirect responsibility too. His strenuous, reforming nature might, for professional purposes, acquaint itself with doctrines that, in the main, are inimical to effort, and his study of Shakespeare shows how sympathetic a knowledge he possessed of the springs of tragedy. But round about 1870 it is most unlikely that he preached pessimism or would have acted as Ibsen's director of studies in that department of philosophy. Indeed, it will be remembered that the gravamen of his charge against *Brand*, and a capital reason for diverting his friend to another order of artistic creation, was precisely the enmity to life which that play might inculcate and the stimulus it might give to Christian pessimism already so powerfully furthered by Kierkegaard.

Romantic pessimism, as it is called, was of course familiar to Ibsen, since he grew up with it, and there is reason to believe that, speaking relatively, he cherished a high regard for its chief exponent, Byron,[62] in whom Brandes's brilliant study (in the fourth volume of *Main Currents of Nineteenth Century Literature*) roused a renewed interest; and on *Adam Homo*, an outstanding successor to *Don Juan*, he drew, as has been seen,

heavily. But there is probably no more specific influence here. Schopenhauer, with his "English" style and manner, his contempt of women
and yearning for Nirvana, would seem less of a kindred spirit.

What Ibsen learned about Eduard von Hartmann (whose *Philosophy
of the Unconscious* appeared in 1869) may well have been more congenial
to him. The saturnine paradox in which Hartmann's pessimism can be
summed up—that this is the best of all possible worlds, but that it is a
damned bad one—was of the sort to enchant him. The greater part
Hartmann allotted to the intellect and his recognition of biological
evolutionism as part of the cosmic process would appeal to him; and
Hartmann's belief that we all, singly and collectively, strive perpetually
after happiness, which is unattainable, seems to be paraphrased in a note
of Ibsen's to the effect that man in his more natural aspirations shows
himself a megalomaniac. But closest of all, perhaps, Ibsen may later have
felt himself drawn to the Prussian pessimist by the large allowance which
the latter made for the operation of unconscious will and unconscious
thought—the powers that actuated an Ellida Wangel and a Hedda Gabler,
and in which, seemingly, Solness and Borkman and the Rat-Wife of *Little
Eyolf* believed. None the less, it would be an abuse of the term to write
Ibsen down a disciple of Hartmann.

. . . .

The first of Brandes's famous problems to which Ibsen applied
himself, when the long fermentation set up by his leaven was beginning to
settle, was not of so vast a scope as those just sketched. Self-knowledge had
kept even step with knowledge of the outside world, and after the
unsatisfactory immensities of *Emperor and Galilean* (1873) Ibsen clearly
felt he should attempt a less ambitious task and execute it more perfectly.
In *Pillars of Society* (*Samfundets Støtter*, 1877) he submitted to debate
certain problems of commercial morality. This may be thought the
stranger as Ibsen betrayed very little interest in the great issues of
economics and sociology which, at that time, were as prominent in the
public eye as any others. What John Stuart Mill had written on these
topics he very likely had not so much as heard of; he paid no heed to Karl
Marx; the struggles of free traders and protectionists in the new Germany
in which he lived left him completely cold. His hatred of peasants
rendered him indifferent to the plight of the poor, while he could scarcely
cherish much sympathy for those who were supposed to exploit them. The
"social question" *par excellence*, as it came to be called, hardly obtrudes
itself into any of his plays, and when it does so, as, for instance, in the
scheme of social welfare which Alfred and Rita Allmers propose to
inaugurate at the end of *Little Eyolf*, it is unaccompanied by zeal or
conviction.

Nevertheless, Ibsen had good reasons for undertaking a theme bordering on economics. As often happens after a major war, the seventies (until

near the end) were a period of great commercial activity, and Ibsen was in a particularly favourable position for observing it, in Germany, where gigantic projects and gigantic failures characterised the so-called Founders' Years.[63] But on a smaller scale, as Ibsen's visit to Norway in 1874 would show him, similar things were happening at home, and they were of a kind to be familiar with a peculiar vividness to the sections of the public from which theatre audiences were then drawn. Farthermore, these audiences had, with Balzac's *Mercadet*, some of the plays of Augier and, especially, with Bjørnson's *Bankruptcy* before them, become accustomed to the dramatic presentation of situations in which an economic element preponderated.

Ibsen chose the narrower field of *Pillars of Society* with an equal tact. The 1870's witnessed an energetic effort to extend the exiguous Norwegian railway system, and Bernick's double piece of sharp practice, first in ruining the project of a railway line which would have competed with his own coasting vessels and then in privily buying up land through which a less dangerous inland line would run, was a transaction that could probably have been nearly paralleled more than once.[64] To this matter Ibsen joined the more melodramatic theme of the *Indian Girl*, sent out in the same unseaworthy condition as the "coffin-ships" against which Samuel Plimsoll was just then (1875) successfully declaiming in the British House of Commons. Plimsoll's labours for the inspection and codification of sea-going vessels[65] were followed with great interest in the wealthy and extensive[66] shipping circles which Norway had fostered in the course of the nineteenth century,[67] while the artisan Aune's protest against the use of machinery faintly echoes perhaps a certain uneasiness felt by more opulent members of these circles at the threatened supersession of the wooden sailing-ship, which Norway could produce cheaply, by the new-fangled iron steamer, which it had neither the materials and skill to build nor the coal to work on.

Ibsen's cunning lent in this way a considerable actuality to the complicated transactions unfolded in *Pillars of Society*. But, as has been seen, they remained essentially subordinate in his interest and dramatic scheme, which, in accordance with his invariable rule, turn upon the moral problems thrown up by the chances and changes of the phenomenal world problems of freedom, guilt and responsibility.

Notes

1. Recent studies had been D. F. Strauss's *Der Romantiker auf dem Thron der Cäsaren* (1847), A. de Broglie's *L'Eglise et l'Empire au IVe siècle* (1859), E. Lamé's *Julien l'Apostat* (1861); there were plays by Hauch (1866) and Molitor (1867).

2. Which were echoed by a Northern bishop, D. G. Monrad.

3. 1863.

4. It must really be a unique circumstance that, not at mutual enmity, two of the

foremost spirits of the age should on two occasions be beneath the same roof (at Bergen in 1856 and apparently for some time in 1881 at Sorrento) without making one another's acquaintance.

5. Cf. Dr Stockmann's belief that "a normally-constituted truth lives — let us say — as a rule, seventeen or eighteen years; at the outside twenty" (IV, p. 338; Archer, VIII, p. 135).

6. It was the same at Copenhagen, when Georg Brandes's adherence to the French and British thinkers caused a correspondingly disturbing scandal; that it was the same at Upsala Strindberg's reminiscences attest.

7. At any rate until after the completion of *Emperor and Galilean*. To Hoffory he wrote (*Breve*, II, p. 169) that this was the first work he wrote under the influence of German intellectual life; "and the only," Gosse adds (*Ibsen*, 1907, p. 141).

8. A "scheme" like this and the actual subject-matter would have been very congenial to Hebbel; there is, however, no indication that Ibsen had recourse to him for any of the inspiration of *Emperor and Galilean*.

9. Julian's master Maximus formulates the matter thus: "First that empire which was founded on the tree of knowledge; then that which was founded on the tree of the cross. . . . The third is the empire of the great mystery; that empire which shall be founded on the tree of knowledge and the tree of the cross together, because it hates and loves them both . . ." (III, p. 184; Archer, V, p. 114). This passage gives the clue for the underlying confusion of Ibsen's argument: the "second empire" is always, clearly, the Kingdom of Christ; but that against which it was set up, the "first empire," is things as divergent as the dispensation of the Old Testament, a rationalistic universe, Bismarck's *Reich* and the cult of Aphrodite and Dionysos.

10. As the individual might the more easily lose himself in one, he believed it perhaps to afford a better guarantee for his independence than a small community.

11. I paraphrase some lines (VI, p. 385) from his verse "Balloon-Letter to a Swedish Lady" of December 1870, when the trend of events had become clear to him in his observation-post at Dresden: calling to mind his recent experiences in Egypt, he says: "Once again a King is God on his throne, once again the individual melts away in a swarm which bustles, yearns, worries, builds, broods, ponders all around and underneath us. Once again the pyramid is raised as the product of the whole age. Once again every vein swells, once again blood and tears flow in order that the world may see the King-God's mausoleum great. This is the caravan of the present day, with its Hathor, with its Horus and, for parliament, its chorus swearing blind oaths of fealty. What monuments rise along the level path of victory! What power in the onrush of the people! How Egyptian, the way all and each fit their little stone in its place in the fabric of the whole! How faultless is the plan and how accurate the calculation! Yes, in truth, it is great, great, so that the world stands and gapes: yet there trembles a 'but' in the gape's open void."

12. No quite satisfactory English equivalent of this key-word exists since *rige* means *kingdom* or *empire* without any monarchical implications.

13. III, pp. 334 f.; Archer, V, pp. 369 ff.

14. He deliberately left Hauch's drama, *Julian the Apostate* (1866), unread, so that his conception should not be affected.

15. *Breve*, I, p. 249.

16. The Norwegian scholar J. E. W. Sars was just making a major application of Spencer's theory of development with differentiation in his *Udsigt over den Norske Historie*, of which the first volume appeared in 1873.

17. In *Present Day French Aesthetics* (*Den Franske Æstetik i vore Dage*, 1870).

18. Which no doubt accounts for Ibsen's writing to Brandes (*Breve*, I, p. 234) that over the work he had become a "fatalist."

19. III, p. 188; Archer, V, p. 123.

20. The significance of Judas is also treated in a short poem by Ibsen (*Efterladte Skrifter*, I, p. 211), of which the second half runs: "We know that, lulled in a torpor of conscience, he went straight and gave the Redeemer the kiss. Then both heaven and hell were advantaged. But what if Judas now hadn't *wanted?*"

21. III, p. 186; Archer, V, p. 119.

22. III, p. 183; Archer, V, p. 112.

23. *Riget.*

24. *Kinder der Welt.*

25. Schjøtt, P. O., in the first number of *Nyt Tidsskrift.*

26. "Det Menneskelige Ansvar" (VI, p. 102; Archer, XI, p. 33). I take it that *Ansvar* and *ansvarlig* in Dano-Norwegian correspond exactly to "responsibility" and "responsible."

27. V, p. 289; Archer, IX, p. 349 (*The Lady from the Sea*). Compare Ellida's outburst just before: "Responsibility! This transforms everything." The interfusion of free will and determinism in Ibsen's philosophy is well illustrated by Ellida's sudden exercise of volition and her remark on it: "do you not understand that the transformation came, that it *had* to come — when I could choose in freedom" (V, p. 287; Archer, IX, p. 345).

28. *Cit.* Koht, II, p. 199.

29. *Kvindernes Underkuelse* (1869) and *Moral Grundet paa Lykke- eller Nytteprincipet* (1872); the literal re-translation of the latter title might be noted, "Ethics based on the Principle of Happiness or Utility."

30. VI, p. 295; Archer, XI, p. 456.

31. *Breve*, I, p. 276.

32. Which, with bitter irony, Ibsen declares himself quite prepared to accept (*Breve*, I, p. 277).

33. Tinged with misconceptions of the Middle Ages and their "chivalry."

34. *Familien paa Gilje* (1883).

35. Even her inalienable functions as a mother were threatened and restricted by practical malthusianism (after the birth of her only child, Fru Ibsen declared that there would be no more) and by the extensive employment of wet nurses and children's governesses, against which many moralists declaimed.

36. Daughter of Bernhard Duncker, lawyer, benefactor to Ibsen and model for Berent, the representative of society in Bjørnson's *Bankruptcy.*

37. Just about the time that Ibsen was in Norway on a short visit.

38. No doubt the same vulgar euphemism in Norwegian as in English.

39. It is true that Asta Allmers and Petra Stockmann are professional teachers; Martha Bernick works in a school as a form of "charity."

40. *Subjection of Women* (1869), p. 91.

41. *Subjection of Women* (1869), p. 89.

42. "Ved Norsk Kvindesagsforenings Fest," printed in Centenary Edition, XV (1930), pp. 717 f.

43. "For mig har det staaet som en Menneskesag."

44. The phrase ("for mig har det altid staaet som en Opgave at løfte Landet . . .") has a slightly ambiguous meaning, for Ibsen carefully refrains from saying that he looked on it as *his mission.*

45. IV, p. 104; Archer, VI, p. 409.

46. IV, p. 103; Archer, VI, p. 408.

47. *Efterladte Skrifter*, II, p. 327; Archer, XII, p. 91.

48. One may infer from the contrast between Rebecca West and Rosmer, between

Alfred Allmers and his two women, perhaps also between Hilda Wangel and Solness, that he thought women more strongly endowed with the dramatic virtue of energy.

49. When at the end of his career Ibsen considered the cases where the individual was at issue with himself rather than with society, his examples are chiefly men, and John Gabriel Borkman, Rubek, Alfred Allmers, even Halvard Solness, are brought into conjunction with comparatively uncomplicated women, for whom the living of a happy life depends on simpler conditions. It may be observed that in his analysis of one woman, possibly two women who are their own worst enemies, Hedda Gabler (and Ellida Wangel), Ibsen played with an idea to which he did not commit himself, namely that the psycho-pathological concomitants of pregnancy were responsible for their extravagant acts and outlook.

50. It is probable that Ibsen read in *The Origin of Species* and *The Descent of Man*; since 1872 and 1875 respectively those two books were accessible to readers of Danish in the translation of Jens Peter Jacobsen, who enjoyed (in Ibsen's eyes) the combined advantage of being a scientist by education, a friend of Brandes and an original author. Jacobsen and Ibsen were in Rome in the winter of 1878–9 and discussed science together (Centenary Edition, VIII, p. 261). Darwin had the good fortune to be introduced into Norway by the thorough and understanding study of his theories which P. C. Asbjørnsen contributed to the magazine *Budstikken* for February and March 1861.

51. The remark which Darwin makes on wild ducks in captivity in *The Variation of Animals and Plants under Domestication* (II, 1868, p. 278) may have come to his direct notice and contributed something to *The Wild Duck*.

52. It is significant that Fru Alving, in *Ghosts*, ranks the inheritance of ideas *pari passu* with physical inheritance (IV, p. 228; Archer, VII, p. 225).

53. Cf. in particular II, p. 529. Perhaps a guiding influence was exerted also by Ibsen's exact contemporary, Mrs Josephine Butler, whose campaign against the supervision of prostitutes was begun in 1869, and attracted much notice outside Great Britain.

54. "My poor innocent spine must do penance for my father's wild oats" (IV, p. 151; Archer, VII, p. 81).

55. It is not clear whether Ibsen believed that Oswald was capable of communicating his disease; Regina evidently holds this error.

56. Oddly enough, the playwright Dumas (the younger) had advocated the elimination of moral degenerates by private initiative in *Claud's Wife* (1873), which caused a great stir.

57. The analogy to his indictment of society in the case of Consul Bernick (IV, p. 67; Archer, VI, p. 354) will be apparent.

58. It is possible to argue, as Strindberg does, that Ibsen meant to acquit Nora Helmer of forgery, on the grounds that she had inherited her father's irresponsibility.

59. Brand comes nearest to doing so (II, p. 232; Archer, III, p. 26). A sad figure is cut by all parsons and accredited teachers in Ibsen's plays after *Emperor and Galilean*: Adjunkt Rørlund, Manders, Molvik, Kroll, Tesman.

60. E.g. the sentiment which Ibsen wrote in Count I. Milewski's album: "The development of the human race took the wrong turn from the start. Our dear fellow-men ought to have evolved themselves into maritime creatures" (Centenary Edition, XV, p. 381).

61. Cf. Centenary Edition, XV, p. 36.

62. Cf. *Breve*, I, p. 245, where he urges a Norwegian translation.

63. *Gründerjahre*; the term has reference to the founders (many self-appointed) of the new German empire.

64. Certain details of Bernick, his activities and his sister were taken from a Grimstad magnate, Smith-Peterson, who died in 1872 (Centenary Edition, VIII, p. 25).

65. The Merchant Shipping Act was passed in 1876.

66. It is reported (Due, C., *Erindringer fra Henrik Ibsens Ungdomsaar*, 1909, p. 15)

that in Ibsen's youth at Grimstad the very servant-girls used to put their savings into shares of ships and cargoes.

67. The commissioning of badly repaired ships was brought up at the annual meeting of the Norwegian Marine Assurance Company "Veritas" in 1874 and 1875 (Centenary Edition, VIII, p. 21).

Ibsen and the Structure of the Mind

Kindermord and Will in *Little Eyolf*

James E. Kerans*

Underlying this most secretive play,[1] and indeed all of Ibsen's drama, is a myth of the will. The primary features of this myth have long been familiar to us: what remains is to draw the lines between them, to reveal their constellation. Such an undertaking is appropriate less to an essay than to a book, where there is room for intricate proofs and qualifications; here we must choose rather to proceed by the clearest assertions possible in such matters and by limiting ourselves to one feature and to its place in the whole composition. That feature is the *Kindermord*[2] motif.

Kindermord is vaguely discernible in Ibsen's early work, but beginning with *Brand* (1865) it unmistakably finds its place in the larger imaginative order of the play, and in every subsequent play it is fundamental to the dramatic action. It is subject to so extraordinary a range of disguise that one cannot but believe that it is forced into his fictive structures by some irresistible imaginative energy, whether creative or compelled. It appears now in the dramatic present of a play, now in its narrative past, now figured through a statue or manuscript, now plainly presented as a child, now done abruptly, now in two separate stages, now displaced as the "childlessness" of Beata in *Rosmersholm*, now as the child that Oswald is in terror of becoming in *Ghosts*, and so on. Always it preserves certain characteristics in itself and in its relation to the destiny of the hero, and it is these characteristics which are to concern us. *Little Eyolf* seems a plausible choice for a paradigm in this study, since it is the one play that takes its title from the child who is to die, and the one most dominated by that event: indeed, we might say that the whole drama consists in the accommodation and transcendence of a *Kindermord*.

The time may well come when we discover that the narrative past of Ibsen's later plays is not simply a body of information cleverly worked in to the conversational stream as a sort of painless exposition, but is rather there to motivate the very process of reflection and revelation which seems

*Reprinted by permission of Toby Kerans from *Modern Drama: Essays in Criticism*, edited by Travis Bogard and William I. Oliver (New York: Oxford University Press, 1965), 192–208.

to be its by-product. Ibsen would then appear to be interested primarily in the process of recognition, a chemist fascinated more by the transformation of a plate by acids and light than by the faces and backgrounds emerging into the illusory stability of a photograph. However, that is a formal study which must await another occasion. Here we shall be dealing with the events and people of the play as they appear during the extended crisis of their lives which, so to speak, caught Ibsen's imagination, and as they seem to have lived before that crisis. From this point of view, *Little Eyolf* is a relatively economical play, and the past of its characters is conveniently spare.

Both the hero and the moral action involving him derive from the same source: The Allmers family. We learn of this family that it is strikingly — even ominously — ingrown. They all look alike, their names always begin with vowels, they are all poor, they are so turned in upon each other that when Alfred and Asta are orphaned there is evidently no outside source of help or care for them. Even before Asta is born her sex and destiny and personal qualities have been determined by what the family expects and has provided for. That she disappoints them by being a girl (and illegitimate, not an Allmers at all, as we find later) is only one of the ways in which she intrudes into the solidarity of the family an element of the strange and estranging. It is interesting that Ibsen first concerns himself with Alfred Allmers at that point in his life at which he is to be provided with a "Little Eyolf." He comes into existence as the boy-who-is-to-have-a-younger-brother-as-companion, and the play is to trace the transformation of the Alfred / Eyolf relationship[3] from this family fantasy through to the spiritual relationship evoked in the concluding passage.

Despite the persecution of Asta and her mother incurred by Asta's sex and origin, and the ten years difference in age, she is very close to Allmers, and when the parents die the two are drawn even closer, made even more conscious of their need to find protection from the dangers of the "outside world" both in the harmony and peace of their brotherly closeness, and also in cultivating a sense of the value of "human responsibility" in general. From this need derive Asta's attempts to live the role of "Little Eyolf" by caring for Alfred and even by dressing as a boy at home, though the pathos of the impersonation is obvious; and from the same need comes Allmers's work on his book dealing with "Human Responsibility." During the time when Allmers is a student he develops his interest in the book, and he realizes that he must find some way to care for Asta financially. His poverty stands in his way on both counts, and he solves the problem by marrying Rita — perhaps for her beauty, but more, as he himself admits, for her wealth, her "gold and green forests." Shortly after their marriage they have a son, Eyolf; and while Eyolf is still an infant he suffers the first, the figurative *Kindermord* in a complex event which should be described with some care.

One day, while Allmers was watching Eyolf as he slept on a table (that is, with his eyes closed),[4] Rita lured Allmers away to make love. While they were together, Allmers told Rita in detail of his relationship to Asta — except for the fact that Asta was illegitimate, which Allmers himself did not know. At the climax of their love-making, Allmers called out the name "Eyolf," meaning, of course, Asta, whom he used to call by that name. While Allmers and Rita were together Eyolf fell from the table, and the result was the injury which has disabled him from full participation in life, and which is symbolized by his crutch. From this event there are two main consequences. The first is the sexual estrangement of Rita and Allmers. Allmers cannot overcome the sense of guilt with which he subsequently associates his sexual relation to Rita, and he rejects her (the motives here are complex, but we must defer treating them at present). Rita, on the other hand, recognizes in Eyolf the source of Allmers's sense of guilt, and she rejects Eyolf. Her rejection is so noticeable, in fact, and so effective, that it prompts Asta to step in and take upon herself the emotional care of Eyolf. To these two consequences may be added the shift in the nature of Allmers's concern with the book on human responsibility. The book now absorbs all his attention — not only that which he withdraws from Rita, but that which he would have bestowed upon Eyolf. He cannot bring himself to "see" Eyolf's crutch, which is as much as to say that he cannot, in life, accept precisely the human responsibility he is attempting to write about, and the result is that the book drags on, as crippled — almost exactly, we might hazard — as his son. We may also infer that during the nine-year period of these false relationships Allmers falls back upon Asta as his primary orientation, leaving undeveloped whatever chance his marriage offered him of breaking out of the charmed circle of his family — or what he believes to be left of his family — in the figure of Asta.

Shortly before the action of the play begins, Allmers makes a hiking trip to the mountains, alone. He does this partly out of frustration with his "work" and partly because a doctor advises it for his health. While there he has an encounter with death, in the form of a mysterious "companion," and while we must return in greater detail to this encounter, we may say here that it results in Allmers's decision to "renounce" his book, his work, and to return to his home to put the rest of his life at the service of Eyolf, attempting thereby to enable Eyolf to bring the family destiny to the peak of achievement he had once hoped to attain himself. He returns by foot for the most part, taking the train for the last stage of his trip — a detail which will recur in our treatment.

While Allmers is away, three other developments transpire. Asta had been given by Allmers, on his departure, the task of going through her mother's papers. This she has done, with the result that she discovers the real story of her birth and of her actual relationship to Allmers. Rita, meanwhile, has succumbed to Eyolf's entreaties and bought him a child's uniform, which he is wearing during his only scene in the play. Two other characters make their appearance bringing with them evidence of their activity during this interim. One is Borghejm, an engineer who has been building a road nearby, that is now finished so that he is about to go on to another assignment "up north." His stay in the neighborhood has resulted in his love for Asta, whom he hopes to marry, and whom he has come to the Allmers home to see on the morning the play opens. The second is the Rat-virgin, a witch of sorts, though she is also known as a werewolf. Her task has been to rid the neighboring islands of rats, which she does by luring them into the water with the aid of a "little black dog," her traveling companion, Mopsemand. Exhausted though she is by this task, which has taken her all night (Borghejm, Ibsen stresses, is *not* exhausted), she appears on the morning of the First Act to ask if there is "anything she can do." It may be observed here that these are the only two characters who never meet.

Once the play is under way it is almost impossible to differentiate "events" from the flux and entanglements of recall and regret, which are the real substance of the play. In a sense there is only one event: the drowning of Eyolf. Everything else draws for significance and animation upon this weird actuality that provides a model for the several variations we encounter elsewhere in the play—and, in fact, in Ibsen's drama generally. Reduced to a chronicle, what happens is as follows. Just at that point in the first act at which Eyolf is being made to feel most keenly the discrepancy between his uniform and its implicit pretenses on the one hand, and his crutch, his damaged body and disqualified life on the other, and just as we see Allmers at his most pained and angry—the Rat-virgin arrives and asks if there is anything "gnawing" in the house which she could rid them of. As though to make sure of her prey, she shows Eyolf her horrible but fascinating black dog, and after a flurry of openly sinister *double entendres* she withdraws. During the passage directly following, Ibsen has Rita leave the room, transparently as a way of clearing the stage and counterpointing two statements of the major theme of the play. One statement is the exit of Eyolf, who "steals" out of the room, obviously following the Rat-virgin to his death. The other statement is the apparently innocent exchange in which Allmers notices Asta's briefcase and asks if she has been studying her mother's letters. Asta evades the issue. It is not until later that we learn what the letters contain: the death of Eyolf.

The logic of this episode is not particularly obscure to a reader, but like much in Ibsen's later work it asks a great deal of the concentration and recall of an audience. To spell it out: Asta's destiny, as determined by the Allmers family, was to be a "little Eyolf" to Alfred, a companion. She failed on two counts: first in being a girl, and second in being illegitimate. By renouncing her femininity, as she does by such means as dressing as a boy, acting as a companion to her "nephew," rejecting the proposals of Borghejm, or being, as the confidently feminine Rita somewhat condescendingly says, "clever," she can compensate in part for this error. But the illegitimacy was, so to speak, a "fatal" mistake, for which there is no correction. What is so "wrong" about her, clearly, is that she is sexually eligible for Allmers: as a girl she is not his brother, as illegitimate she is not his sister. The Eyolf in her — the young-brotherly, "constant" companion — has been killed.

One of the thematic currents of the play is the conflict between what Allmers calls "the law of change" and the demand, associated with Allmers's double, Borghejm, that there be "something which does not come to an end." We may put off for the present our treatment of the ironies concealed in Borghejm's position, and glance at the "law of change." Allmers invariably invokes this "law" as a way of accounting for the vagaries of sexual attraction or disinterest. On the other hand, "a brother's and sister's love . . . is the only [relation] that's not subject to the law of change," as he says (LE, p. 264). "Eyolf" is a creation exempt from the law of change; more specifically, Eyolf is the name or sign of non-sexual relationships, and when a relationship becomes sexual, or is threatened with sexuality, then Eyolf, as the symbol of that relationship, "goes," and that going is dramatized as *Kindermord*. As we shall see, notions such as non-sexual relationships, or even brother / sister relationships are too vague to account for the peculiar complexities and force of the death of Eyolf or of *Kindermord* in general — they merely screen the fundamental relation of the son to the mother; but at least we are now in a position to see why the image of Eyolf stealing off to his death is an appropriate accompaniment to the conversation about the letters that disclose the real relationship of Asta and Allmers. The relation of the Rat-virgin to Asta, to motherhood, and to sexuality remains to be demonstrated, but in her anecdote about marking "her man" and conjuring him down to the bottom of the sea, and in her compelling lure of Eyolf, we see ample sign of her lethal power, and a hint at least of its sexual content.

What is interesting about the overlap of these two dramatic "statements," from a formal point of view, is that no one could possibly understand the connection at the time it appears on the stage. Properly played, Eyolf's exit must indicate what it is — a surrender to death, to the Rat-virgin's lure. There are roughly two kinds of response to the complex episode of which this is a part. One is to think of the death of Eyolf as screened by the conversation about the letters, thus contributing to our sense, which gathers as the play proceeds, that one of the main determinants of Eyolf's death is his parents' neglect of him. (A small but suggestive detail supports this reading: when the Rat-virgin leaves, Eyolf says, "softly but triumphantly," to Asta, "Just think, Auntie! I've seen the Rat-virgin too!" (*LE*, p. 226.) It is his last line in the play — but no one answers him.) The other is to take the death of Eyolf as a datum coloring the whole scene. By this reading we are given one "certainty," one clear event or image to guide us through the slow and uncertain process of understanding the far more complex relationships for whose elaborate structure this death is the model and complement. This juxtaposition, then, marks a great advance in the definition of Allmers's relation to Asta, and hence to his own nature and destiny. The scene does not yield its effect (unless we suppose that the ominousness of the overlap *is* the full effect Ibsen wanted at that moment) until the significance of the letters, of Asta herself, and so on, begin to come clear.

Immediately after this exchange (Eyolf has by now gone off), there follows its counterpart. Rita returns, still horrified by the atmosphere of death left by the Rat-virgin. This atmosphere colors the talk of Allmers's "transformation," which, we later learn, was in fact determined by association with death as a compelling power which had, also, its aspect of "companionability." Allmers's symbolic death and transformation in the mountains thus draws for point and clarification upon the immediately present dramatic event of Eyolf's being lured by the Rat-virgin. As was the case with the previous scene, the audience has no way of seeing the connection between the compelling power of the Rat-virgin with its odor of death and the death Allmers met in the mountains; and the "precious," "lovely," and above all, "gentle" characteristics of the "companion" fig-ures—Mopsemand, Death, and Asta—have yet to emerge and to make their connections with the destructive forces at work upon Allmers. Not until very nearly the end of the play can we "see," but when we do, it is, by the light of the clearly projected, theatrical simplicity of this basic event, the luring of Eyolf into the sea.

The drowning itself, while hazy, is simple. Eyolf seems to have followed the Rat-virgin to the end of the wharf, stared out after her, become dizzy, and fallen. The boys on the beach, "all of whom could swim," simply watched, and when they came to the end of the wharf they looked down into the clear water and saw Eyolf's open eyes looking up at them. Then "something" came and drew him away. Each of these elements finds its place in the reflective passages to be treated later, so we may defer any explications for the moment.

The remainder of the play is a series of conversations in the course of which the destinies of the four leading characters are sorted out and clarified. Allmers, after brooding over the sea and his vague sense of responsibility for Eyolf's death, feels drawn by identification with his son into following him down into the sea physically as well as psychically, and is prevented by Asta's entreaties and his own "earthbound" nature, as well as by the animation supplied by a quarrel with Rita. His drift toward leaving Rita to return to Asta and their "constant" life together is blocked by Asta's disclosure of their real relationship. Asta, after forever rendering up her "Eyolf" nature in the gesture of giving Allmers the water-lilies at the end of the second act, prepares the way for her decision to take Borghejm with her as she leaves. Borghejm, after insisting that Asta, if she is to come with him, must commit herself to him unqualifiedly, the expression of which would be her going with him on the train, unaccountably changes his mind and leaves with her on the "steamer." Allmers and Rita are thus left alone to settle the terms of their life. There is insufficient space to track this process in detail, so our approach must be reductive, and while a play as complex as *Little Eyolf* admits of several possibilities, our concern with the problem of *Kindermord* and will leads us to choose as our fundamental question, What causes the death of Eyolf? and to expect of our answer that it shall clarify in some degree every important relationship in the play.

There is first the question of the "lure." The number of forms taken by this figure is extraordinary. The "charms" of the Rat-virgin, which call to mind the many "bewitching" women in Ibsen's dramas; the compelling power of Mopsemand, of the mountains, of death; the "evil eye" that Allmers accuses Rita of having; the seduction of Allmers by Rita at the time of the first "fall" of Eyolf; Rita's decision to bring up from the shore all the "poor" boys mistreated by their fathers and to put them in Eyolf's place; the undertow which draws Eyolf's body out to sea; the "attractive" power of the little Eyolf in Asta, which is what brings Rita and Allmers together, and eventually draws even the "engineer" Borghejm unexpectedly after her — and there are many others. The perils and decisiveness of these lures are suggested by their association with death or marriage, and their thematic coherence is in turn suggested by the relation of death and marriage as the fundamental alternates open to Allmers. After Eyolf's death, Allmers plans to go back to the mountains, to the "stars," the locale of his companion, death, but finally chooses to remain with Rita in at least a form of marriage. Two generalizations emerge from this welter. One is that, whatever the source of the "draw," it always works upon a male figure; the other is that it seems to fall into three modes, "earth," "sea," and "stars." These are Allmers's terms, but they are given scenic and metaphoric support throughout the play.

By earth is vaguely meant worldly happiness, and it is figured in Rita's "gold and green forests," which is to say the marital satisfaction held out to Allmers by Rita herself and by the home that is the setting of the first act. Allmers's homecoming is a return to earth after his venture into the realm of the stars — of solitude, renunciation, and death, where, as we later learn, it is impossible to live (*LE*, p. 277). It seems also a return to "champagne" and to the sexuality for which that is so obvious a symbol. But Rita's draw upon Allmers is weakened — neutralized, almost — by the guilt which blocks their sexual life, and which seems as strong at the end of the play as ever. His earthly nature is thus unstable, because incapable of fulfillment, and this instability, expressed in various ways, is most vividly projected by his behavior at the end of each act. He rushes in fear out of the "house" and down to the fjord at the end of the first act, goes reluctantly back up at the end of the second, and can promise Rita no relief from the strain and duty of earthbound life, at the end of the play, except that of "looking up" toward the stars.

While Rita may have no very secure power over Allmers at the crucial level of earthly life — the sexual — she can still exercise her influence as a mother in the sense of caring for a child, and she proposes, as she says, to take all the boys on the shore with her up to the house, where she can care for them in place of Eyolf and — significantly — of Allmers himself. Because, as we learn, she proposes to do this only after Allmers shall have left her. In this gesture she reveals the essential motherliness of her nature — and her kinship with Aline Solness, Helen Alving, and certain others of Ibsen's mother-figures. It is interesting, to say the least of it, that Allmers is ready to stay with her, when he learns this, even though he has rejected her sexually.

There is nothing strange about the place in Ibsen's mythology of what Allmers calls "earth": we meet it elsewhere as the "joy of life" or Brand's home in the valley, and so on — though it is not recognized generally, if at all, that the reason the hero's place on this "earth" is so unstable is that its "foundation," a sexually harmonious marriage, is upset by the guilt and dread attending unconscious incest with the mother. It is pertinent to this hypothesis that when Rita suggests to Allmers that he had shared her passion in the early days of their "love," he corrects her and describes his feelings as "dread" (LE, p. 261).

The sea is the dominant element of Act II. Allmers's coming down to the shore to brood upon Eyolf's death is the scenic parallel to the drowning itself, and as this meditation deepens into a form of identification with his "son," nearly leading him to suicide, we are prompted to examine the force that draws both hero and child into its figurative element.

What emerges first is its regressive nature. Like Hedvig Ekdal and Ellida Wangel before him, Eyolf faces a crisis — his entry into a world of diminished prospects, in which the awareness of time (of the "law of change," for example), of his own lameness — symbol, clearly, for many forms of inadequacy — of adult expectations, such as Allmers's loading upon him the burden of fulfilling the destiny of the family, all co-operate to expose him as the "wounded little soldier" he really is. He yields to the calm of the sea, to its appearance of soothing constancy; but, like Asta, it is not what it appears to be, and its undertow side, the lethal, vindictive sexuality of the Rat-virgin, is the reality that shocks him into open-eyed death, as had his fall nine years ago. Not for nothing has Ibsen unobtrusively made Asta and the Rat-virgin two sides of the same coin. Each comes and goes by sea, carrying a "little black bag" in which is concealed the death of Eyolf, and while this one association must carry the persuasion of several others, it at least underlines their relation to the sea.

In summary, then, the sea is the temptation of regression, of constancy in one's childish nature, but to commit oneself to that element is to discover too late the incestuous threat concealed beneath the benign surface. In an earlier draft, Ibsen compressed this logic into a scene that is perhaps too clear for the dramatic development he wanted: Eyolf runs out to greet Asta at one point, and instead encounters the Rat-virgin. Allmers's peril is that he will do the same thing, and precisely this accounts for Asta's strange and near-frantic warnings to Allmers not to brood or to approach the fjord, as well as for her decision to tell Allmers "now" about the letters, rather than to wait until some evening when they could talk quietly about them. Allmers survives the danger, but at the price of his own Eyolf nature, and when he has left behind him the earth and the sea he has only the consolation of the stars to look forward to.

The "high crag" of the third act swings us from the fjord, with its atmosphere throbbing with regressive longing, into the vertical "mood." From here we look down upon the "poor boys" on the shore, out over the fjord as the "steamer" withdraws with Borghejm, and up to the "stars" for the restorative vision of the "spirits" of those who have gone. The flag is raised in token, evidently, of the ethical content of some mysterious victory. What has happened? Asta's disclosure, of course; but beyond that is the matter of Allmers's "transformation."

While in the mountains, Allmers came to a lake. There being no way across it, he went around, lost his way, and met with a "traveling companion," death, in the form of his peaceful acceptance of his own death. He walked all day and night with death, and was lifted to the "heights of resolution," after which he came out on the other side of the lake and went directly home to put his life at the service of Eyolf.

What is disturbing about this apparently noble and serene action is, first, its inversion of the drowning. Sinking into the depths becomes a climb along the dizzy precipices; being lost in the timeless constancy of childhood becomes being lost in the spacial wilderness of solitude and a premature acceptance of death (Allmers insists that, like all his family, he will not live long); one action kills Eyolf, the other is to give him life and fulfillment. The other disturbing element is that just as the sea had its "peaceful," Asta surface, and its destructive, Rat-virgin depths, so the death Allmers met as the incarnation of the mountains and solitude and stars had also its "horrifying" side: "My companion came and took [Eyolf]. And then there *was* horror in him" (*LE*, p. 278). What Allmers does not seem to realize is that the *Kindermord* in which his "companion" was involved took place not in the fjord but on the heights, when he renounced his will and his work, which was the embodiment, however failing, of that will. To account fully for this hypothesis we shall have to wait for demonstration that "Eyolf" is in some way identified with Allmers's will. Meanwhile, we might draw attention to a sinister and oblique coincidence. There are two people in the play who offer a prospect, a lure to Eyolf: the Rat-virgin — and Allmers. What the Rat-virgin offers we have seen. Allmers offers Eyolf the task of doing what he himself has been unable to do. Each hides his offer under a riddling phrase, too odd to be inadvertent. When the Rat-virgin sees that Eyolf is "staring fixedly" at Mopsemand, despite his horror, she says, with satisfaction, "Oh, it'll come.

It'll come, all right" (*LE*, p. 224). Then she shuts the bag. Earlier, when Allmers had hinted that "someone" would come to do his work better, Eyolf had become very curious (*LE*, p. 219):

EYOLF: Whoever will that be? Oh, do tell us!

ALLMERS: Give him time. He'll come all right and declare himself.

EYOLF: And what will you do then?

ALLMERS: Then I will go to the hills again . . . up on the heights and the great waste lands.

(Asta and the Rat-virgin go back across their element, the water, but to what other destination we never know.) A moment later, when Eyolf is enthusiastically asking to accompany his father "up to the hills," soon, Asta (so the stage directions say) "changes the subject": i.e., shuts the bag.

There is yet another dissonance in the notion that Allmers's renunciation under the stars is the sign of his arrival at some ethical stability. He returns, he says, "to Eyolf." Not to his marriage. And, in fact, neither his return nor Eyolf's death involves any resumption of his marriage in the essential sense. What decides him to stay with Rita is the possibility of finding meaning in life through aid to the anonymous "boys" or substitute Eyolfs whom Rita is to bring up from the shore. Rita has renounced her marriage in the "earthly" sense of harmonious sexuality — she has become a de-sexualized, "ethical" mother, and in this venture Allmers will join her. It is then that he raises the flag to the top. Behind the lure of the stars lies the renunciation not only of will, but of vitality, leaving only selfless dedication and duty. How do we explain this poverty of alternatives?

The pattern of earth, sea, and sky, together with the forms of "lure" concealed in each, yields itself to a common-sense examination of the phenomenal surface of the play. Beneath this pattern lies another, for the detection of which we need the reductive and hermeneutic techniques proper to psychoanalytic theory. This is the pattern we have called the myth of the will.

Briefly stated, this myth dramatizes certain typical crises in the mother / son relationship. The first crisis is the *Kindermord* itself. While still an infant, the child's dependence upon the mother for nourishment, warmth, protection, and love is felt not as helplessness, but as security. When this relationship is disturbed by the introduction of a sexual element — which ultimately forces sexual rivalry with the father — the child "feels" that either he must submit to the castration / death that is the penalty for this relationship, or he must give it up. He has no choice but to give it up and withdraw, but he blames his withdrawal upon his mother as well as upon himself or his father, and this withdrawal, this break in the secure relationship to the mother, is dramatized as *Kindermord*. The element in the mother that gives rise to the threat of castration or death is converted in the child's imagination to the frightening, destructive woman whose (fascinating) aim is to drive him to an unequal struggle with the father and thus to death. However, the sexual drive that first attached itself to the mother cannot simply be discarded — it must find an object. For the object to satisfy the unconscious drive toward the mother, it must be radically identical with the mother, but for the drive to be expressible or tolerable at all to the psychic constitution of the child or hero, the object must not be recognizable as a version of the mother — hence the substitute takes the form of a mirror-image or inversion of the original mother, and the relationship between them is now expressed not in the form of sexuality, but as shared participation in the hero's "act of will." If this "will" were not dynamic, not subject, as are all things organic, to the "law of change," this secondary or substitute relationship might persist indefinitely — might, that is, be "constant." But it is threatened from two sides. First and most simply, it strives for ever more complete satisfaction, and thus ultimately discloses its frightening and lethal nature, thus forcing a recapitulation of the first "*Kindermord*" or withdrawal of the secondary mother, or both. Second, this relationship with the "mother," through a displacement of sexuality upon will, is crippled, like Eyolf, by a "fall." The fall is that complex moment at which the encouragement of the original mother, her care, was cut off, leaving the child (or hero) hungry, a hunger that ultimately expresses itself in the need for assurance in the form of absolute love, for which the typical words in Ibsen are "sacrifice," "proof," "all," and the like. Thus the hero's will is weakened, and the "ideal project," which is the particularization of that will, is doomed. A simpler way to put this second threat to a continuing or "constant" relationship is that the hero uses up his store of energizing love. When this happens, the hero abandons his "project" — in Allmers's case it is the book on "human responsibility" that he and Asta have been concerned with, but which Rita, of course, quite understandably resents — which is very apt to be tantamount to renouncing not only the "will" or vitality for which the project was the specific mode of expression, but life, with which sexuality is roughly identical, and the result is suicide, as with Rosmer, or an equivalent, such as Allmers's return to the mountains, which he equates with death.

Since we are not concerned here with all the complexities of the myth of the will, but primarily with the *Kindermord* element, we may forego an extended treatment of the myth and outline the relation of the *Kindermord* to the later stages of the hero's development.

The first step is to state the relation of the child to the hero. In a word, they are identical. True, as characters in a drama they are distinct, but as elements in a psychic composition they are only superficially differentiable. The *Kindermord* is really an event in the life of the hero, and that is why every play from *Brand* on contains such an event. If the first *Kindermord* involves only the crippling or disabling of the "child" (Hedvig's approaching blindness, in *The Wild Duck*, the spoiled statue of *When We Dead Awaken*, or the manuscript to be reconstructed from "notes" in *Hedda Gabler* are examples, as well as Eyolf, of course), the hero may play out his project indecisively and unsatisfyingly. But the second *Kindermord*, which more often than not takes place after an interval of about ten years (Eyolf is nine), brings this period of false or inadequate involvement in the project to a close with the abandonment of the project and, not infrequently, of life itself.

Two axioms are essential to this argument: that the hero and child are radically identical; and that the project or act of will through which the hero and the secondary mother are so firmly bound to each other is an inheritance from the tie between the child and the primary mother. This inheritance is already weakened by the fear that forces it into disguise and crippled by its first encounter with sexuality, and it stands always under the threat of the re-emergence of that sexuality. Would this not account for the puzzling truth that Ibsen's heroes are almost invariably sexually estranged from their wives, who inherit, typically, the "providing" characteristics of the primary mother, and yet they cannot, on the other hand, execute their "act of will" with the secondary mother? The second relationship merely recapitulates the first. Cut off, thus, from "earth" and its alternate, what is there to do but "renounce"?

There are no satisfactory tests for the truth of these propositions, but in the view underlying much of our reasoning so far — roughly that of psychoanalytic theory — the affective substructure of an imaginative work may be dealt with as a mimesis of certain forces (by no means all) at work in the imagination of the writer. We then recognize that the figures in Ibsen's drama are not ethically self-determining, nor even in every respect distinct as parts of a composition, but that they are, at a lower level, barely mobilized out of an interior drama whose balance of forces governs the disposition of material at the subtlest verbal and characterological level. A small but startling sign of the self-contained quality of Ibsen's dramatic relationships — in this case, of the radical identity of hero and child — consists in the fact, which may have struck a reader familiar with Ibsen, that the children involved in the *Kindermord* are never singled out of a family. The whole generation dies, whether that generation consists of one child, as is usual, or two, as in *The Master Builder*, or three, as are threatened with the figurative death from Nora's lie in *A Doll's House*. What is even more striking is that it is taken for granted, always, that there are to be no more children. Even in *The Lady from the Sea*, where the prospect would seem clear, the idea is never even mentioned. The reason for this is plain; the child is primarily a function of the psychic past of the hero, and not just another member of the dramatis personae. That the same is true of many of Ibsen's dramatic categories would require separate demonstration, but in the interest of underlining our position thus far, we could at least assert that such is the case, and that the organizing scheme for those categories is the same myth of the will a small feature of which we have been examining.

Full treatment of the problem of will in Ibsen's imaginative work would have to deal with the sociological and philosophical determinants on Ibsen's rational conception of will, the more immediate influences of men like Mill, Kierkegaard, and Hegel, and much more. For two reasons our concern has been only with the structural and psychological determinants. First, we accept as one of the primary tests of value in any essay in dramatic criticism the question, "How does it interest anyone who is to produce or perform in the play?" This question of form and motivation calls for most patient study. Second, and more pertinent to the larger question of response to the plays, is our dissatisfaction with the current attitudes toward Ibsen. Here, as usual, psychoanalytically oriented criticism acts best as a corrective and complicating influence. Criticism of Ibsen badly needs an alternate to the sterile conflict between those who reject symbolic exegesis, preferring to think of Ibsen as a spokesman for permanent, explicit values, such as the striving for freedom, and those who call for a new approach, one that supposes that Ibsen has outlived his age and now qualifies for a bland archtypal reduction or for treatment as a "psychologist" — by which is usually meant that the critic will show that Ibsen saw deeply into the secrets of the human heart, or, worse, will "psychoanalyze" this or that character on the basis of some plausibly revealed syndrome.

The implicit recommendation of our approach is that there is an affective substructure in Ibsen's drama, which influences the development of image, gesture, and crisis, as well as the "behavior" of "characters." However we may speculate upon the determinants of that structure, the first task is to detect and illuminate it — a task, simply, for accurate observation and formal criticism. Anyone who has compared his response to an Ibsen play well performed to the critical raptures about idealism, transcendence, noble sacrifice, wise resignation, and the like must be puzzled at the disparity. That Allmers, or Rosmer, or Solness, or Ibsen himself might talk such language ought not to blind us to the concealed maneuvers that drive toward disastrous cancellations of will, toward despair and death, through which friction is set up against the more assertive and, to be sure, far more interesting maneuvers of the upper or conscious levels of the plays or their attendant responses. In calling attention to and, hopefully, articulating some of the content of the "lower" order we may not be dignifying Ibsen, but we may call it a gain if we are encouraging a more complex response or increased understanding by acknowledging that there is still much more that he can "make us see."

Notes

1. Henrik Ibsen, *Lille Eyolf, Samlede Verker*, Oslo, Gyldendal Norsk, Forlag, 1935, Vol. XII, 175 ff.

For the reader's convenience all quotations below are from Henrik Ibsen, *The Master Builder and Other Plays*, trans. Una Ellis-Fermor, Penguin, 1958, hereafter referred to as *LE*. Where necessary I have occasionally restored a literal reading from the Norwegian.

2. The term seems preferable, because of its familiarity in critical usage, to the English "child-murder." Either term overstates, as we shall see, the violence or the quality of responsibility involved. "Child-death," on the other hand, is too tame.

3. Note the similarity of the names: it may be pertinent to observe that the drowning of Eyolf is prefigured in a very early draft of *Rosmersholm*, in which Rosmer's son, "little Alfred," is drowned in a lake with his mother.

4. This detail is later inverted into the picture of Eyolf lying dead under the clear water and looking up with his eyes "wide open," having "awakened." The conditions of this awakening cast a darker look over what critics have called Ibsen's transcendental sense of the term in his last play.

Recapitulation   Charles R. Lyons*

The essential unity of Ibsen's work is obvious. The same general actions occur again and again from *Brand* to *When We Dead Awaken*, and the repetition of the central metaphors is insistent. However, the general dramatic structures which hold the basic drama are very different. Even within the three expansive dramas, *Brand*, *Peer Gynt*, and *Emperor and Galilean*, Ibsen seems to make a conscious effort toward projecting a greater sense of realism. In *Emperor and Galilean* he abandons verse for prose with the deliberate aim of creating a more plausible and realistic work. The influences working upon Ibsen which would lead him into a more realistic form are complex, but certain major pressures are obvious. The insistence in the late nineteenth century upon phenomenal cause, the interest in the relationship between environment and character, the increasing emphasis upon the concept of the universe as man-centered and not God-centered certainly focused the work of literature upon man and the specific environment which contained his experience and which participated in determining it. One of the features which marks the difference between Ibsen's earlier, more expansive dramas and the more controlled and focused plays of the period of *A Doll's House* through *Rosmersholm* is a greater attention to the human and natural environment in which his basic drama takes place.

The pressure to respond to his own keen sense of the malicious self-interest in his contemporary society is clear even in *Brand*. The characteri-

*Originally published in *Henrik Ibsen: The Divided Consciousness* (Carbondale: Southern Illinois University Press, 1972), 173–89.

zation of such figures as the Dean and the Mayor in this play shows that Ibsen's attention was directed at least partially toward exposing the hypocrisies, the exploitations, and the apathies which offended him in his own experience. That satiric voice answers a demand within Ibsen for topical relevance. However, the major function of these characters, indeed all the characters in *Brand*, is to define what the Brand consciousness is. Their energy is directed toward their own self-interest, and they consistently sacrifice the integrity of their individual vocations to provide themselves more comfort, sensual pleasure, and reputation. Actually, we know little else about them; they exist merely to provide the antithesis of Brand's concept of an integral, self-determining will — a will which is also self-directed, but self-directed in order to become committed to an absolute, not for immediate phenomenal satisfaction.

In *Brand, Peer Gynt,* and *Emperor and Galilean* the relationship between the protagonist and the other characters is more expressionistic than realistic; that is, the characters are clarifications of the movements within the hero's own consciousness. In these plays Ibsen presents a hero who is confronted with a series of characters who are embodiments of choices which he must make. The dramas proceed in a series of episodes which test the integrity of the hero. However, the dialectic between good and evil is not absolute; the hero is in a state of anxiety because the relationship between good and evil seems to shift. The transforming images of Agnes, The Woman in Green, Helena, and Makrina are examples of that flux. Each, for a particular moment, embodies a value for the hero toward which he moves; then each is transformed into a source of restriction, pain, and guilt. These figures serve the single purpose of revealing the way in which the hero's consciousness operates, and the only development or complexity which they have as characters derives from the fact that the hero's image of them changes. They are projections of an ambivalence in the consciousness of the hero.

In the development of the more realistic plays, the primary experience of the hero stays the same, but the way in which his experience is projected through the peripheral or functional characters is extremely different. For example: both Brand and Rosmer attempt to free themselves from a guilt which they see as a familial inheritance; both of them see the conventional Christian church as hypocritical and voice their own desire for innocence in a mission in which they are the agent of a universal emancipation and ennoblement; both of them are tempted by sexuality, and both deny their wives, seeing sexuality as a restriction of their vocation; both of them become disillusioned; and both die in a suicidal act (although Brand's ascent to the known danger of the Ice Church is less deliberately suicidal). Each, as well, dies with a female figure who functions in some way as an image of his own guilt. And yet, the similarity between the temperaments of Brand and Rosmer is minimal. Brand is aggressive, dominating, and cruel in his indifference to the suffering of others, and Rosmer is passive, gentle, and ineffective. However, in Ibsen's exploration of the limits of power which the self holds, the emphasis clearly shifts from *Brand* to *Rosmersholm*. Brand's idealism is not the manifestation of his ability to declare himself free from the temptations of phenomenal experience but, on the contrary, is an unconscious evasion of such experience; his movement toward the Ice Church is not a positive act but an escape from all which is represented by the abyss. The sense of the movement as an escape is subtle, however, and perhaps, not even a part of Ibsen's own conscious scheme. In *Rosmersholm* the superficial pose of heroism is deliberately abandoned; there is no sense of the consciousness being free. Rosmer is clearly the victim of conflicting pressures—the demands of sexuality and the need to see the self free from those demands in an ordered vision of reality which would halt the processes of experience. The sacrifice which Brand's concept of identity demands is painful for him, but he sees that pain as part of his identity as he enacts a ritual of martyrdom which would allow him to transcend the phenomenal reality of his experience. However, the complexity of reality comes down upon him, literally and figuratively, in the Ice Church; and he is forced to confront the fact that the tension between the mythical and the phenomenal is not a simple dialectic in which it is possible to affirm the one and deny the other. Rosmer is less an aggressive and confident hero, less a hero in the conventional sense, because the reality in which he moves is more clearly complex, equivocal, and confusing.

The threatening complexity of that reality is presented by Ibsen primarily in the greater density of the characters which define the conflict for the hero. Agnes has a minimal inner life; Rebekka has a past and a present, an external and inner experience as complex as Rosmer's. However, she is not a co-hero as some critics suggest. She has a complex reality which is disclosed to Rosmer; and that disclosure is the primary event in his experience. Rebekka is for Rosmer what Agnes is for Brand—the object of his lust. That object undergoes a transformation as it moves from an image of innocence to an image of guilt, a confirmation of the sexuality (and the incompleteness, irrationality, and mortality) of the hero. However, as an aspect of the total consciousness represented by the play, Rebekka does far more than Agnes. In the more simple structure of *Brand*, Agnes changes as an image within Brand's consciousness. In *Rosmersholm*, the disclosure of Rebekka's character is an actual event which occurs to Rosmer, to us, and—to an interesting degree—to Rebekka herself. Her recognition of the truth of her identity, which comes to her through Kroll, is a realization that she is guilty of incest and that she, too, has inherited a guilt which finds its source in her family. Rebekka is not merely a projection of Rosmer's movement from the hope of innocence to disillusionment; she is an individual entity within the play who suffers an analogous experience and can, therefore, function more complexly as the principal object with which his consciousness deals. Rebekka then becomes not merely the illusion of innocence being transformed into guilt but an embodiment of the process. The secondary characters in these plays are not merely aspects of the protagonist's consciousness but are themselves processes of consciousness.

Hedvig's suicide signals an event within Hjalmar's psyche in a death which is somewhat analogous to the death of Alf in *Brand*. Alf's death is clearly the manifestation of Brand's renunciation. Alf is the temptation to attach himself to a human relationship which would diffuse his will. He is also the embodiment of guilt which needs to be sacrificed in order to expiate that guilt. His death is an event which happens to Brand and to Agnes — principally to Brand, although Agnes's renunciation anticipates and parallels her husband's. Hedvig's death also happens to her. It fulfills the same function as Alf's death as an event in the hero's consciousness. It is a confirmation of Hjalmar's failure, the destruction of that which affirms his identity; it is the answer to his own renunciation of Hedvig and, at the same time, the proof of her love. The sacrifice of the actual Hedvig allows him to preserve the illusion of her, an illusion which could not have been maintained in reality. However, Hevdig's action is also her own movement from a damaged and painful reality into an illusion; it is the extremity of the commitment to an aggressive, illusionary, and mythical vision of reality.

The demand of realism is to create a body of characters whose behavior is plausible in terms of acceptable notions of what people will do in given circumstances. The given circumstances must include an environment which is described in detail and appears to be related to those places which we ourselves experience. Primarily, however, the processes of action must give the illusion of being determined by the particular relationships of the characters. That is, there must be a clear and conceivable chain of events seen in a cause and effect sequence. Working on the basis of the Scribean *pièce-bien-faite*, Ibsen contained his essential drama within a sequence of events, interlocking and complex, but clearly evident. The apparent or external cause of the action in Ibsen's realistic plays is the accidental meeting at a particular point in time of a series of individual movements which are related but at the same time independent. Without the coincidence of family, school, and social revolt against Kroll's authority, he would not have intruded into the world of Rosmer and Rebekka and initiated the series of revelations and private disclosures that intrusion caused in *Rosmersholm*. If Hedda's return had not coincided with Eilert's reentry into society and if Tessman had not found the manuscript and so on, that particular action would not have resolved in the same way in *Hedda Gabler*.

However, any awareness of Ibsen's central drama makes it possible to see that the events and their peculiar resolution are inevitable within Ibsen's vision of consciousness. The creation of a project which puts experience, past, present, and future into some kind of comprehensible form—Eilert's history of mankind—is only an illusion of reality, not an understanding of reality itself, and that illusion is vulnerable to phenomenal experience and is destroyed by it. The only means of gaining a sense of form which is free from dissolution or change is to create some sense of form out of death. The suicides of Hedvig, Rosmer, Rebekka, Eilert, and Hedda are inevitable as the manifestation of a particular strategy of consciousness; to fix the self within a comprehensible vision of reality is to remove the self from the flux of phenomenal experience—to die and escape consciousness and the phenomena which feed it. These deaths are the consequence of that basic premise. However, the demands of the realistic form make it necessary for Ibsen to give those actions a plausibility within the specifically realistic world of the play.

Fulfilling the demand of realism to create more plausible, individually motivated characters, Ibsen worked to give more density to the imaginations of those characters in strong relation to his hero. I have already discussed the ways in which that character who provides an erotic object for the hero is developed with greater complexity in *Rosmersholm* than in *Brand*, but the increased sense of characterization in the realistic works accomplishes even more than that extra resonance. In the more realistic plays, Ibsen created worlds in which a series of characters enacted the basic drama, each in his individual experience. For example, in *The Wild Duck*, Hjalmar suffers the loss of his illusory vision of reality, a loss which the exposure and death of his "child" Hedvig embodies. However, the falsity of his image of Hjalmar is exposed to Gregers and functions as a dissolving illusion; Hjalmar's sudden renunciation of Hedvig destroys her created image of him which she seeks to regain. In *Rosmersholm*, both Rebekka and Rosmer function as images of illusion for each other; Rosmer suffers the transformation of the concept of the innocent Rebekka, and Rebekka is unable to accommodate the movement of Rosmer from innocent into erotic and makes her own renunciation. The primary focus remains on the consciousness of Rosmer, but a paradigmatic structure is also at work. In *The Master Builder*, Hilde is Solness's object of tempting innocence seen simultaneously as a bird of prey hunting him down. Their final relationship is a focused ambivalence: he fulfills her demand and falls; she inspires and kills. But each functions for the other. In *When We Dead Awaken*, the antithesis of the mythical and the phenomenal is very clear; and the movement toward the mythical voices itself in the desire for innocence, the desire to awake into some kind of transformed experience. Both Rubek and Irene seek each other as objects of desire, and yet they function for each other as embodiments of guilt. The ambivalent movement in the consciousness of each is to seek and destroy the object of love, and the resolution contains that ambiguity as they lead each other to their death in the form of marriage.

In his more realistic plays Ibsen compressed the metaphoric structure of his private vision within a concentrated and highly formal structure.

This structure has been considered classic in its unwavering focus and clear movement. The more open forms in which he worked — the dramatic-epic poem of *Brand*, the pseudo-folk drama of *Peer Gynt*, the history play of *Emperor and Galilean* — certainly had a set of conventions in which Ibsen moved. The conventions of these more open and episodic forms, however, are less restrictive. Consequently, the basic drama is able to range more freely among its images and lacks the intensification which that drama achieved when it was compressed into a more controlled structure.

One of the conventions of realistic literature is the closely developed representation of environment. Realism is one of the responses to the scientific conception of the environment as a determinant of experience, and in drama that emphasis was answered in an increased attention to the scene. This attention resulted both in a structural emphasis upon conditions determining character and a more natural physical environment in the stage setting itself. In Ibsen's case one of the results of his exploration of realism is his exclusive use of naturalistic interiors from *Pillars of Society* to *The Master Builder*.

The contained space of the rooms in which Ibsen's realistic dramas take place becomes a limited area in which each major object assumes importance — these rooms and the figures they hold become the phenomenal field in which the basic drama of consciousness voices itself. The spatial metaphor which is a kind of metaphysical landscape is displaced into the rooms, objects, and imaginative conceptions of those who inhabit them. The process of displacing this basic metaphoric structure is one of concealing its content in order to make its presence plausible. The process of transporting the image of the sea into the realistic environment of *The Wild Duck* demonstrates how that displacement adds layers of meaning and resonance to the basic metaphor. In the first place, Ibsen's use of the images of the sea and the forest are related — the darkness and density of the forest, the sense of it as wilderness, is close to his imaginative concept of the sea as dark, uncontrollable energy, irrationality. Also, both the sea and the forest are associated with a sense of primitive eroticism in his imagination, as we have seen. In *The Wild Duck*, these images meet in the strangeness of the created forest in the garret, that place which Hedvig sees as "the bottom of the sea." The place is a sanctuary for the Ekdals which is obviously analogous to the mythical heights which Brand and Julian use as sanctuary, but here that movement is seen as the consequence of damaging experience working upon powerless men. The garret is an escape from the threats and demands of reality. Most significantly it is a created place, a synthetic environment which attempts to re-create the past. The density of Ibsen's characterization of Hedvig allows him to use her childlike fantasy to identify the place as "the bottom of the sea," seeing the garret as being like the tangled weeds growing on the bottom of the sea floor which held the real wild duck when it dove down to the bottom of the sea. The place is, then, related to death — the objective of the duck's suicidal dive. The withered trees, the rabbits and doves which substitute for the wild and free bears and eagles, the images of death and the hourglass in the book of engravings, references to the world of the Flying Dutchman — all work together to project a concept of this created environment, which is the mythical strategy of this play, as regressive, illusory, synthetic, restrictive, and self-destructive. The metaphor moves from its original promise as a place of comfort and protection into the threatening, self-destructive place of Hedvig's suicide. Also, this creation of an artificial place, a personally constructed forest and sea, shows more clearly than ever before in Ibsen's plays that the act of creating and using a myth is an attempt to encompass the phenomenal without being subject to it. The substance of the garret is the material which is an unthreatening substitute for phenomena seen as dangerous. The compression and concentration of the concealed images of the forest and the sea as they meet in the garret reveals the complexity of their content much more fully than in the less developed use of them earlier.

The Ekdal's use of this created place illustrates a basic method in Ibsen's use of metaphor. The scenic detail of the garret is not a projection of the hero's consciousness in any simple sense. It is not the relatively unambiguous transformation of the tree into the skeleton of Kaiser's expressionistic *From Morn to Midnight*. The complexity of the garret as a metaphor comes from the fact that it is not the projection of a state of consciousness but rather a process of consciousness. The metaphoric structure is the field of consciousness itself as it gropes for an understanding of its own function, exploring these images to see what they can do to provide a sense of form which can contain the processes of thought. The distinction between seeing these metaphors as projections of process rather than embodiments of condition may be small, but it is extremely significant in an understanding of Ibsen's use of verbal and visual imagery. This distinction explains why fixed interpretations of Ibsen's metaphoric structure are not satisfying.

The rhetorical process in which the basic images transform themselves into their opposites also explains the basic ambiguity in Ibsen's use of realism. If Ibsen's middle plays are to be seen as realistic, they must be interpreted as representations of an actual social and natural environment. Ibsen, of course, represented reality as unattainable in the shifting processes of mythical and phenomenological thinking. But he did work within a form which pretended and, perhaps, intended to be realistic; and it is necessary to think more about that ambiguous choice of form. As a base, I would like to begin with the definition of realism which I find most satisfactory, Georg Lukács's statement from *Studies in European Realism*:

> The central category and criterion of realist literature is the type, a particular synthesis which organically binds together the general and particular both in characters and situations. What makes a type a type is not its average quality, not its mere individual being, however

profoundly conceived; what makes it a type is that in it all the humanly and socially essential determinants are present on their highest level of development, in the ultimate unfolding of the possibilities latent in them, in extreme presentation of their extremes, rendering concrete the peaks and limits of men and epochs.

True great realism thus depicts man and society as complete entities, instead of showing merely one or the other of their aspects. Measured by this criterion, artistic trends determined by either exclusive introspection or exclusive extraversion equally impoverish and distort reality. Thus realism means a three-dimensionality, an all-roundness, that endows with independent life characters and human relationships. It by no means involves a rejection of the emotional and intellectual dynamism which necessarily develops together with the modern world. All it opposes is the destruction of the completeness of the human personality and of the objective typicality of men and situations through an excessive cult of the momentary mood. The struggle against such tendencies acquired a decisive importance in the realist literature of the nineteenth century.[1]

Lukács finds realism coming into focus at moments of social transition and sees the realist writer as a participant in the processes of change. He defines the objective of realism as the objective of literature, "the concept of the complete human personality as the social and historical task humanity has to solve."[2] Lukács himself sees the tension in Ibsen's drama between the perfection of its form, which he affirms as classic, and a disturbing depiction of reality: "imperfectly its formal perception concealed the inner instability of Ibsen's conception of society and hence of his real dramatic form."[3] Lukács does not develop this concept of Ibsen's instable vision of society and consequent instable dramatic form; but his response is predictable. As a Marxist critic of realism, Lukács sees society as capable of resolution: the writer is a participant in a progressive movement. Ibsen's drama is, on the surface, critical of society; and the figures of the Dean and the Major in *Brand*, Manders in *Ghosts*, even Kroll in *Rosmersholm*, seemed to be personifications of what Ibsen saw as evil and exploitative in society. In one sense, the ethics which these figures voice do provide the restrictions and oppressions which Ibsen's heroes face and attempt to transcend. However, these figures are only pale reflections of the real restriction and oppression experienced by Ibsen's heroes. The demand to renounce sensual pleasure and freedom — which is, surely, the primary ethical restriction voiced by these hypocrites — is much more strongly present within the consciousness of the hero himself. Brand's renunciation of Agnes and Alf, Rosmer's denial of both Beate and Rebekka, Solness's movement away from eroticism into fantasy — all these acts of denial are motivated by internal, not social, demands which voice personal guilt. It would be possible, of course, to argue that the presence of guilt is, indeed, the embodiment in consciousness of the values of the particular society which Ibsen attacks. His insistence that the son inherits his parent's guilt suggests the Freudian concept of the superego as the manifestation of a social or familial restriction within the individual psyche. Certainly this concept is operative in the plays, but guilt in these plays is also something more than the Freudian superego asserting itself. Sexual processes are metaphors for the consciousness of phenomenal experience. Sexuality is the most acute phenomenal experience; within sexual experience *process* — gain and loss, value and distaste, desire and satisfaction, completion and dependence — is all exposed to us. Guilt in Ibsen's drama concentrates in fear of phenomenal experience, fear and rejection. Guilt is a protection from the pain of losing a sense of identity in the flux of phenomenal events; and the impetus to be free of guilt is the energy which develops the individual myth. Ibsen's conception of society is a displacement of his conception of the consciousness. This, perhaps, is why Lukács is disturbed by it. Ibsen's vision of reality is a vision of consciousness and is undeniably pessimistic. The oppressions and restrictions are intrinsic and irredeemable. The final focus in each of Ibsen's major plays is upon a dissolving sense of reality, and the resolution of these plays insists that there is no way to create order outside of the fragile structures of consciousness. Ibsen is guilty of the subjectivism which Lukács decries despite the fact that his apparently realistic forms disguise that intense and "exclusive introspection."

Lukács discusses the formal integrity of Ibsen's dramas as cohesive and efficient in form, producing a classic structure which almost conceals the "inner instability" of his perception of reality. Of course, Lukács interprets this ambiguity as a weakness since that inconsistency undermines the realistic base of the plays. I would argue, of course, from the opposite point of view, seeing the tension created between Ibsen's formal realism and his conceptual subjectivity as a strength. Our age would judge that realism is no longer a sufficiently open dramatic form because it assumes a simplistic approach to experience which is inconsistent with our recognition of the complexity and subjectivity of our response to human experience. In the detail and temporal flexibility of the novel it is more possible to encompass a greater sense of that complexity within a more or less realistic frame. A novel can assume the voice of an introspective consciousness directly, but the conventions of drama present a figure objectively: he is seen and heard as an external object in relationship to the other figures in some environment which is external to the spectator. The process of identification in which the self of the spectator relates to the emotional movements of the play as if they were his own experience breaks down that objectivity. But the imaginative event begins with the spectator seeing and hearing the actors as objects apart from him; and, on one level of consciousness, at least, they remain detached and objective. The experience of identification in which the spectator responds to analogies between his own personal psychic movements and the strategies of consciousness within the play is not based upon a one-to-one relationship between him and the hero. Ibsen begins with an objective realism; and as the play develops and movements of emotional energy are generated, the spectator's identification is distributed among these movements. For example, in *Rosmersholm* the strong desire for a satisfying, integrated relationship with another human being which is free both of guilt and a fear of loss is brought into focus by the characterization of both Rosmer and Rebekka. The spectator identifies not so much with the specific character but with the emotional reality of that desire. The condemnation of that desire as the source of self-destruction and the violation of innocence voices itself clearly in the play as well, and the spectator's repulsion at Rebekka's cunning scheme to destroy Beate is a process of identification with the fear of irrationality and the desire for control which manifests itself in the acts of renunciation made by Rosmer and Rebekka. Also, the deliberately obscure metaphor of the white horses provides a focal point. His conscious imagination denies the reality of such supernatural creatures, laughing with Rebekka at Madam Hespeth. However, the content of the metaphor—the fascination with unknown energy and the equally strong dread of seeing still present that which has been destroyed or overcome—does have reality for him; and the gradual revelation of the substance of that image to both Rosmer and Rebekka is experienced by the spectator as a personal disclosure.

The objective reality of Ibsen's plays seems to present an understandable reality as the plays begin, but the work of these plays destroys that objective comprehension even within the strict formalism of his organized structure. In the works of Beckett, Ionesco, Genet, and Arrabal the poet's personal recognition of the obscurity of experience has produced plays which defy conventional temporal sequence and break down the conventions of character and plot. It is important to realize, however, that Ibsen also works to abrogate those concepts even within the taut structure of his realistic plays. The realism of those plays from *A Doll's House* to *Rosmersholm* is, in itself, a dramatic metaphor. Ibsen seems to say: Reality might appear to take the form which I imitate here, and yet that form is merely a tentative construct of our imagination which allows us to explore the processes in which our imaginations are able to create and respond to certain self-conscious experiences; we must begin with this formal structure because it is necessary to isolate and organize events within some sense of temporal sequence in order to conceptualize experience. Invariably in Ibsen's realistic plays the action is the exposure of the past. Essentially, however, that exposure only takes the form of disclosures of the past; the real revelation is of the quality of the present, and the action is the surfacing of information about the self which had been hidden or disguised in some way. The exposure always isolates the tension between the mythical and the phenomenal. The exposure also reveals the falsity of his personal myth in such a way that the hero cannot partake of the phenomenal experience he desires. The past is not the past in any simple sense in these plays; it is the exposed present: the real identity of Hedvig, the present diseased Alving, the sexuality of Rosmer and Rebekka, the dead Rubek and Irene. The resolution of these plays is the disintegration of the realistic base on which they proceed. Ibsen's drama exposes the invalidity of the external projection of order and reveals the subjective consciousness as the only reality.

The object which we identify as the play, whether it be the text which we read in private or the performance we experience publicly, is the complex stimulus which works upon us to produce the response which is our conception of the play. The complexity and thoroughness of our response depends upon the complexity and thoroughness of the stimuli. I have discussed seven of Ibsen's plays as organizations of images which take us through explorations of certain strategies of consciousness. The structural organization of realism is the method in which Ibsen was most successful in conducting these explorations. We have laid aside, I trust, that attitude which would evaluate these plays on the basis of their closeness to our conception of the phenomena of nature and human behavior. The re-creation of a surface which appeared to be realistic in that sense is Ibsen's medium; the confrontation with the existence of certain processes of consciousness is the significant reality of these plays. The particular density of language and visual image in Ibsen's realistic plays is the result of his exploration of the ambiguous and often obscure workings of consciousness which we have been discussing. This dramatic form provided a structure in which those explorations could take place and voice themselves in such a way that they would stimulate our response. In Strindberg's nonrealistic plays, the playwright attempted to free his spectators from the restrictions of conventional response by using obviously unconventional forms to clarify that his plays were subjective encounters with experience. Ibsen's deliberate concentration and reduction in *When We Dead Awaken* is analogous. However, it is important to realize that both Ibsen and Strindberg were responding to generic literary movements, emphasizing subjectivity, in their nonrealistic plays in the same way in which they were responding to convention in the realistic plays. It is equally important to realize that the multiplicity of detail, especially in the re-creation of an illusion of natural environment which realism demands, affected the development of Ibsen's language, making his imagery assume a narrower focus. In that increased specificity, each individual image informed the larger metaphoric structure more richly, giving this inner structure a greater density and scope. As well, the formal structure of the plays — that apparent cohesiveness which as Lukács notes, leads us to apply the adjective "classic" to the plays — holds our attention in a particular way, demanding that we work through the complications and obscurities in order to re-create in our response the same cohesiveness by understanding that structure and the ways in which the individual part relates to the whole. The ability of Ibsen's realistic structures to provide a deeply subjective experience tells us something, I think, about the failure of expressionism. There is no single expressionist play which we can identify as the masterpiece of the movement and respond to in the theater as an independently significant experience. Expressionism attempts to stimulate the spectator's response in the exploration of basic psychic experiences; and, consequently, the characters are blatantly archetypal. Frequently, the direct exposure of these archetypes does provoke an immediate response; but infrequently is that response profound and densely personal. Because, I think, insufficient detail is fed into the images which should stimulate, there is not enough material for our imaginations to consider and re-form into personal experience. The expressionistic second act of O'Casey's *The Silver Tassie*, for example, is much more probing an experience than most works of German expressionism and its imitations in O'Neill, because the realistic ground of the first act gives us a detailed base on which to build. The images which are blatantly exposed in the unrealistic form of the second act have content for us, and the original and unrealistic juxtaposition of them has meaning to us because of that content.

Ibsen's plays, as well, begin with an identifiable ground of reality in which certain images develop a highly complex content, and while the realistic base dissolves, it has served its purpose by feeding detail into those images which then can cease to function realistically.

Ibsen's plays resolve with no identifiable ground of reality which is fixed and certain between playwright and spectator other than the existence of consciousness itself. Reality seen as phenomena is an incomprehensible flux; reality seen mythically is an illusory vision. The plays from Ibsen's middle realistic period use the conventions of external realism to explore the essential drama of consciousness. Their popularity and the popularity of their superficial limitations have misled us. The realistic form of these plays is just that, a form, an external structure in which Ibsen could work out the processes of the mind with which he was dealing through the resolution of certain metaphors. His use of the realistic form is obviously ambiguous since while these plays seem to assume a realistic base of experience which can be examined scientifically, the endings of the plays deny that possibility. The development of realistic literature at the close of the nineteenth century was an extremely complex phenomenon. Such literature adopted the attitudes of natural science and philosophy and addressed itself to the study of environment and human nature, attempting to find new principles of behavior in a world which was the manifestation of natural processes and not the expression of divine will. However, despite the increasing awareness of the complexity and even incomprehensibility of experience, realism based itself upon the reactionary assumption that the actual nature of human experience could be understood and reproduced in art. The basis of realism is the concept of a world which can be understood. Erich Auerbach discusses the uneasy position of realism at the end of the nineteenth century and the beginning of the twentieth as the final movement of a literature grounded in a clear reality. Although he does not apply this generalization to Ibsen, the relevance of his point is clear:

> As recently as the nineteenth century, and even at the beginning of the twentieth, so much clearly formulable and recognized community of thought and feeling remained in those countries that a writer engaged in representing reality had reliable criteria at hand by which to organize it. At least, within the range of contemporary movements, he could discern certain specific trends; he could delimit opposing attitudes and ways of life with a certain degree of clarity. To be sure, this had long since begun to grow increasingly difficult. Flaubert . . . already suffered from the lack of valid foundations for his work; and the subsequent increasing predilection for ruthlessly subjectivistic perspectives is another symptom.[4]

The disintegration of the central criteria and categories on which to base realistic structures to which Auerbach points is evident in the earliest moments of the development of realistic drama in the nineteenth century, at least in the work of the major playwrights. Throughout its development realism is an ambiguous dramatic form. Realism attempts to confront the nature of experience directly, but those honest confrontations encompass the incomprehensibility of that experience; the realistic work seems to assume that it is possible to represent or imitate reality accurately at the same time as it faces the obscurity of its subject.

Even in the work of Hebbel, Büchner, and Musset — three playwrights whose work is thought to signal the development of realism in modern drama — the concept of a shifting, transitional, chaotic human condition is strong. Woyzeck has become one of the most significant examples of the passive hero whose experience is determined by an equivocal reality. The various bases on which he operates dissolve for him. He suffers the attack of a nature and a society which he could never comprehend, and his victimization has become the prototype of suffering in modern drama. *Maria Magdalena* concerns a society in transition, but Hebbel's vision of change is so aggressively destructive that shifting social values destroy the younger generation and leave the father in a state of ignorance, unable to comprehend his painful experience and his participation in the events which have killed his children. In Musset's *No Trifling with Love*, the two lovers play a game of courtship, acceptance and denial, reacting against the external demand imposed upon them to be lovers. They recognize that their game is not reality, and the denial and suffering they enact are not painful to them because it is a game or a dance; and yet the young peasant girl cannot separate game from reality, and she kills herself when she realizes that the game is unreal. The reality of that death destroys both the game of the lovers and the real love it imitated. The subtle transitions in Musset between game and reality is a comic-ironic anticipation of much of the explorations of the tension between the real and the illusory in modern drama.

It is interesting that realism as a serious dramatic form was extremely short lived. Auerbach's statement points to the source of its disintegration. Ibsen, Strindberg, and Hauptmann all explored the possibilities of realism; and because of their inability to accept the fallacy of a consistent base of reality, moved away from realism into a more subjective drama which based itself upon the concept of an equivocal and incomprehensible reality. Unable to contain the complexity of reality within the restrictions of realism, they dramatized the only reality they could formalize—the subjective workings of consciousness. The other great "realist" in nineteenth-century drama, Anton Chekov, wrote within a form which gave the external appearance of realism, but his plays insist that the characters which comprise his lonely and disabled communities are each imprisoned in a private and painful isolation—that each is unable to share the reality of the other. There is neither interaction nor communication in Chekov's dramas—only the pathetic collision of private mythologies.

Realism for Ibsen was a formal container which gave him the freedom to explore the relationship of the self and its concept of environment with some kind of artistic discipline. However, the work of the plays destroys that formal container, dissolving the assumption that reality can be fixed and understood. Unfortunately, most of Ibsen's imitators have been influenced by the formal container and not the subjective work of the dramas themselves. However, the influence of Ibsen the realist is largely within popular drama. No major playwright, with the possible exception of the late O'Neill, has worked within the tradition of Ibsen's realistic plays. Shaw's imitations were imitations of such a subjective conception of Ibsen that they do not count. Imitations of Ibsen's realism abound in amazing proliferation, but, for the most part, these reworkings are secondary—either popular dramas filling normal emotional needs in an escapist commercial theater, or pretentious social dramas, like those of Arthur Miller, which are admirable in intent and ordinary in realization.

When We Dead Awaken is certainly a nonrealistic play, and yet its form is clearly the extension of Ibsen's use of the form of realism. The density of the environment of the realistic plays comes from Ibsen's concentration of detail, the close and detailed exploration of a smaller space into which the large spatial metaphors of the "seething abyss" and the "infinite arch" were compressed. In When We Dead Awaken, the concentration remains (although the actual scene encompasses a real valley and a real height) but the verbal and pictorial density is given up. The details of the landscape are reduced to a bare minimum—each resonant and yet abstracted. Part of what is abandoned is the need to give each metaphor a rational, psychological plausibility. It is as if Rubek's life consisted of nothing else other than his experience with Irene and Maja and Ulfheim; the breadth of the world is reduced to this strange and yet typical group of four figures. Each object — the champagne, the food fed to the animals, the knife, the metaphoric key; each conversation; each aspect of the scene — the spa, the forest, the heights, the children playing, inform the tension between the mythical and the phenomenal directly. The whole of Ibsen's dramas of consciousness is contained in the simplicity of this play. Earlier I made the statement that *Brand, Emperor and Galilean*, and *Peer Gynt* were more simple than the realistic plays; the simplicity of *When We Dead Awaken* is quite different. In these earlier, more open plays the simplicity derives from the expansion; the particular concerns are more generalized — in the scope and diffusion of the image of empire in *Emperor and Galilean*, for example. In this generalization their concerns remain more vague and tentative. In *When We Dead Awaken* the particular concerns are compressed into a reduced number of images which develop with complexity but which allow the reader to focus upon their presence and strategy.

The world of *When We Dead Awaken* is very small; it contains some sense of the immediate area, the fjord, the valley, the forests, the mountains above the forest. The Lake of Taunitz is remembered, and there is some vague sense of a world beyond which brings Rubek acclaim and which contains the museums which hold "The Resurrection Day." But the reduced world of the play is the only one which has any significance. Rubek and Maja discuss their arrival in a description which illustrates the degree of abstraction in Ibsen's development of the environment of this play:

> I noticed how silent it became at all the little roadside stations. I heard the silence . . . and that assured me that we had crossed the frontier — that we were really at home. The train stopped at all the little stations — although there was nothing doing at all . . . but all the same the train stopped for a long, endless time. And at every station I could hear that there were two railway men walking up and down the platform — one with a lantern in his hand — and they said things to each other in the night, muffled, and dull, and meaningless.

This is the quality of the external world of *When We Dead Awaken*, a limbo or void in which actions, words, or gestures which may have had some former content are enacted. The only meaning which is to be wrought out of it is the experience of these four people. The scene is the phenomenal ground of their experience, and that ground is alien, hostile, and apparently meaningless. Rubek's sense of his experience is projected in that description of the journey "home" as an inconsequential, pointless series of waits at stations — places in which people enact scenes of relation and communication and significance where none exists.

The most complete extension to date of Ibsen's use of a self-defined scenic metaphor as the complete environment of the play is the scene of Beckett's plays. In these plays the nature of the self is disclosed by its relationship to its phenomenal environment, and that world is reduced to a few crucial elements — an almost barren landscape or an almost empty room. Despite that reduction, the substance of experience itself is projected in the relationships between these figures and the objects and places they use. As in Ibsen's, the content in Beckett's drama is a tension between two primary strategies of consciousness — that movement which seeks to retain identity in a ritualistic, formal use of objects and patterns of behavior external to the self, and at the same time desires a complete renunciation, a denial of the phenomenal, a giving up of consciousness itself — the "peace" or "wilderness" for which Winnie longs and fears.

Beckett shares an unresolvable paradox with Ibsen: the inability of the self to accept the mythical as the real and the inability of the self to apprehend the real without the form of the myth. For both playwrights, the paradox results in the strange transformation of basic metaphors. In the resolution of each of Ibsen's major plays the primary image of form dissolves into an image of formlessness: the Ice Church becomes the avalanche, the "infinite arch of heaven" in which silence became sound becomes alive with the dead martyred children demanding vengeance and sacrifice; the image of freedom and sanctuary traps and kills Hedvig; Rebekka, the source of light and freedom and innocence, lures Rosmer into the rushing water of the millrace.

There is, however, an interesting difference between the relationship between external form and actual content in the plays of Ibsen and Beckett. The strict formalism of Ibsen's realism is an ordered structure whose cohesive framework we can identify and hold in mind during the course of the play, and this affirmation of order in some way protects us from the basic recognition of the plays; at least it provides us with a base which is secure enough to support us while the work of the play gradually destroys it. Beckett's plays are as strictly formal, but one aspect of their form is their insistence upon their artifice; they identify themselves as play, as formal games, arguing in some sense, against the movement of the plays emotionally. In both cases, however, the formal structure attempts to distance us (although not completely) from the despairing recognition of the play.

Ibsen's conscious formal development was an attempt to free his plays of restrictive and artificial conventions; his obvious effort was the dissolution of all which would stand between the experience of the play and the spectator's response. The convention of the box set with its sense of a complete and self-contained environment exposing its fourth wall to the spectator's imagination is built upon a concept of emotional intimacy between the plays as a whole and the consciousness of the spectator. That form of drama attempts to isolate the event of the play in a specific and private relationship between the play and the spectator, consciously ignoring, as far as possible, the artificiality of that event as it occurs within the actual theater. Ibsen never played upon the artifice of the work after his fanciful use of theatrical and formal metaphors in *Peer Gynt*, in which he uses the theatrical as a conscious rhetorical device and exploits certain comic and romantic conventions. He worked consistently after that play to create private and exclusive worlds which did not bear obvious relationship to dramatic or theatrical conventions. These private and self-contained worlds, as we have seen, deal with his basic drama of consciousness. They provide a phenomenal ground in which the individual consciousness can explore its function. The use of this metaphoric environment as such a private phenomenal ground is precisely the technique of Samuel Beckett. It is far more significant that Ibsen is the precursor of Beckett's subjective drama than that he is "the father" of the patent objectivity of realistic popular drama which follows his formal structure only externally.

Beckett, of course, is able to use the metaphor of the stage and the play in his dramas of consciousness. While his environments are self-contained and insistently private, he clarifies that they are artificial worlds set up upon an actual stage. Beckett writes in a time when, as I have said before, a realistic structure would distance the spectator more than an obviously artificial one because the realistic perspective would be dismissed as inadequate to contain a profound response to experience. Beckett writes within a conventional demand that the work of art be *real*, that is, that the work of art identify itself authentically as a work of art, not as the duplication of an experience which occurred someplace else. In the late nineteenth century, as Auerbach comments, it was possible to create the illusion that there was an identifiable ground of reality which the spectator and the playwright could share. Ibsen's plays do begin upon that illusory ground, but their content works to destroy it.

Notes

1. Georg Lukács, *Studies in European Realism* (New York, 1964), p. 6.
2. Lukács, p. 7.
3. Lukács, p. 131.
4. Erich Auerbach, *Mimesis: The Representation of Reality in Western Literature,* trans. Willard Trask (Garden City, 1953), pp. 486–87.

Ibsen and Romanticism
The Argument and Its Reassessment

Ibsen the Romantic
E. M. Forster*

"My book is poetry, and if it is not poetry, then it will be."
— *Ibsen to Björnson*

Ibsen was a poet during the earlier part of his life. He began as a lyricist, and his first plays are either in verse or are inspired by an imaginative contemplation of the past. When he was about forty, a change occurred, the importance of which has been differently estimated. Certain critics, both friendly and hostile, regard it as a fundamental change. They argue that with *The League of Youth* the real or realistic Ibsen begins to emerge, the singer dies, the social castigator is born, the scene clarifies and darkens, and ideas come to the front which do not necessarily contradict previous ideas, but which are given a prominence that entirely alters the dramatic emphasis. We pass the epic to the domestic. Peer Gynt becomes Hjalmar Ekdal, and Brand as Gregers Werle tears the spectacles of illusion from his eyes, and they work out their tragedy, not among forests and fjords, but in a photographic studio opening into a sort of aviary. The aviary contains a few dead Christmas trees, also a water trough, some rabbits but no bears, one wild duck and that a damaged one. We could not be further from romance, the critics say, and turn, if we are friendly, to the character drawing, the technique, and the moral and social issues; if they are hostile, to the squalor. "Somewhere in the course of the battle of his life Ibsen had a lyric Pegasus killed under him," writes Brandes. "Novel and perilous nonsense," wrote the *Daily Telegraph*. The critics agree in thinking that the poetry, if ever there was any, has gone.

Has it gone? Can the habits of forty years be set aside? Of twenty years — yes; most people are romantic at twenty, owing to lack of experience. As they grow older life offers various alternatives, such as worldliness or philosophy or the sense of humor, and they usually accept one of these. If, in spite of more solid temptations, they still cling to poetry, it is because a deep preference has to be satisfied. Ibsen was a poet at forty because he had that preference. He was a poet at sixty also. His continued interest in avalanches, water, trees, fire, mines, high places, traveling, was not accidental. Not only was he born a poet — he died one, and as soon as we try to understand him instead of asking him to teach us, the point becomes clearer.

He is, of course, not easy to understand. Two obstacles may be noted. In the first place although he is not a teacher he has the air of being one, there is something in his method that implies a message, though the message really rested on passing irritabilities, and not on any permanent view of conduct or the universe. In the second place, he further throws us off the scent by taking a harsh or a depressing view of human relationships. As a rule, if a writer has a romantic temperament, he will find human relationships beautiful. His characters may hate one another or be unhappy together, but they will generate nobility or charm, they will never be squalid, whatever their other defects. And the crux in Ibsen is that, though he had the romantic temperament, he found personal intercourse sordid. Sooner or later his characters draw their little knives, they rip up the present and the past, and the closer their intimacy the better their opportunities for exchanging pain. Oswald Alving knows how to hurt his mother, Rosmer his mistress, and married couples are even more favorably placed. The Helmers, the Tesmans, the Wangels, Solnesses, Allmers, Borkmans, Rubeks — what a procession, equally incapable of comradeship and ecstasy! If they were heroic or happy once, it was before the curtain rose, and only survives as decay. And if they attain reconcilation, like the Rentheim sisters, the curtain has to fall. Their intercourse is worse than unfriendly, it is petty; moral ugliness trespasses into the aesthetic. And when a play is full of such characters and evolves round their fortunes, how can it possibly be a romantic play? Poetry might perhaps be achieved if Ibsen's indignation was of the straight-hitting sort, like Dante's. But for all its sincerity there is something automatic about it, he reminds us too often of father at the breakfast table after a bad night, sensitive to the defects of society as revealed by a chance glance at the newspaper, and apt to blame all parties for them indiscriminately. Now it is the position of women that upsets father, now the lies people tell, now their inability to lie, now the drains, now the newspaper itself, which he crumples up, but his helpers and servers have to retrieve it, for bad as are all political parties he must really see who got in at Rosmersholm. Seldom can a great genius have had so large a dose of domestic irritability. He was cross with his enemies and friends, with theater-managers, professors, and students, and so cross with his countrymen for not volunteering to help the Danes in 1864 that he had to go to Italy to say so. He might have volunteered in person — he was in the prime of life at the time — but this did not occur to him; he preferred instead to write a scathing little satire about a Norwegian mother whose son was safe at the front. And it is (if one may adopt the phrase) precisely the volunteer spirit that is absent from his conception of human relationships. He put everything into them except the strength of his arm.

"Not a great writer . . . almost great, but marred by this lack of generosity." How readily the phrases rise to the lips! How false they are! For this nagging quality, this habitual bitterness — they are essential in his greatness, because they beckon to the poetry in him, and carry it with them under the ground. Underground. Into the depths of the sea, the depths of the sea. Had he been of heroic build and turned to the light and the sun, his gifts would have evaporated. But he was — thank heaven — subterranean, he loved narrow passages and darkness, and his later plays have a romantic intensity which not only rivals the romantic expansion of their predecessors, but is absolutely unique in literature. The trees in old Ekdal's aviary are as numerous as a forest because they are countless, the water in the chickens' trough includes all the waves on which the Vikings could sail. To his impassioned vision dead and damaged things, however contemptible socially, dwell for ever in the land of romance, and this is the secret of his so-called symbolism: a connection is found between objects that lead different types of existence; they reinforce one another and each lives more intensely than before. Consequently his stage throbs with a mysteriousness for which no obvious preparation has been made, with beckonings, tremblings, sudden compressions of the air, and his characters as they wrangle among the oval tables and stoves are watched by an unseen power which slips between their words.

A weaker dramatist who had this peculiar gift would try to get his effect by patches of fine writing, but with Ibsen as with Beethoven the beauty comes not from the tunes, but from the way they are used and are worked into the joints of the action. *The Master Builder* contains superb examples of this. The plot unfolds logically, the diction is flat and austere, the scene is a villa close to which another villa is being erected, the chief characters are an elderly couple and a young woman who is determined to get a thrill out of her visit, even if it entails breaking her host's neck. Hilda is a minx, and though her restlessness is not so vulgar as Hedda Gabler's it is quite as pernicious and lacks the saving gesture of suicide. That is one side of Hilda. But on the other side she touches Gerd and the Rat-Wife and the Button-molder, she is a lure and an assessor, she comes from the non-human and asks for her kingdom and for castles in the air that shall rest on solid masonry, and from the moment she knocks at the door poetry filters into the play. Solness, when he listened to her, was neither a dead man nor an old fool. No prose memorial can be raised to him, and consequently Ibsen himself can say nothing when he falls from the scaffolding, and Bernard Shaw does not know that there is anything to say. But Hilda hears harps and voices in the air, and though her own voice may be that of a sadistic schoolgirl the sound has nevertheless gone out into the dramatist's universe, the avalanches in *Brand* and *When We Dead Awaken* echo it, so does the metal in John Gabriel Borkman's mine. And it has all been done so competently. The symbolism never holds up the action, because it is part of the action, and because Ibsen was a poet, to whom creation and craftsmanship were one. It is the same with the white horses in *Rosmersholm*, the fire of life in *Ghosts*, the gnawing pains in *Little Eyolf*, the sea in *The Lady from the Sea*, where Hilda's own stepmother voices more openly than usual the malaise that connects the forces of nature and the fortunes of men. Everything rings true and echoes far because it is in the exact place which its surroundings require.

The source of Ibsen's poetry is indefinable; presumably it comes from the same place as his view of human nature, otherwise they would not harmonize as they do in his art. The vehicle in which poetry reached him — that can easily be defined; it was, of course, the scenery of western and south-western Norway. At some date previous to his Italian journey he must have had experiences of passionate intensity among the mountains, comparable to the early experiences of Wordsworth in the English lakes. All his life they kept returning to him, clothed in streams, trees, precipices, and hallowing his character while they recriminated. In *Brand* and *Peer Gynt* they filled the stage; subsequently they shrank and concentrated; in the two last plays they again fill the stage and hasten the catastrophes by a shroud of snow. To compare Ibsen with Wordsworth is to scandalize the faithful in either camp, yet they had one important point in common: they were both of them haunted until the end of their lives by the romantic possibilities of scenery. Wordsworth fell into the residential fallacy; he continued to look at his gods direct, and to pin with decreasing success his precepts to the flanks of Helvellyn. Ibsen, wiser and greater, sank and smashed the Dovrëfjeld in the depths of the sea, the depths of the sea. He knew that he should find it again. Neither his satire nor his character drawing dwelt as deep; neither the problems he found in human conduct nor the tentative solutions he propounded lay at the roots of his extraordinary heart. There, in that strange gnarled region, a primeval romanticism lurked, frozen or twisted or exuding slime, there was the nest of the Great Boyg. The Great Boyg did not strive, did not die, lay beneath good and evil, did not say one thing more than another: "Forward or back, and it's just as far; / Out or in, and it's just as strait." What do the words mean, and, apart from their meaning, are they meant to be right? And if right, are the prayers of Solveig, which silence them for a moment, wrong? It is proper that we should ask such questions as these when focusing on the moral and social aspect of his work, and they have been brilliantly asked and answered by Bernard Shaw. But as soon as we shift the focus the questions go dim, the reformer becomes a dramatist, we shift again and the dramatist becomes a lyric poet, listening from first to last for the movements of the trolls. Ibsen is at bottom Peer Gynt. Side whiskers and all, he is a boy bewitched: "The boy has been sitting on his mother's lap. / They two have been playing all the life-day long." And though the brow that bends over him can scarcely be described as maternal, it will assuredly preserve him from the melting ladle as long as books are read or plays seen.

Introduction: "Ibsen the Romantic"
Errol Durbach*

The quotation marks around the title of this book and of this Introduction indicate an idea for investigation rather than a position confidently asserted — but they also acknowledge the fact that the topic is already over fifty years old. E. M. Forster's essay "Ibsen the Romantic" first appeared in 1928, with its image of the dramatist as a "boy bewitched" (side-whiskers, irritability and all) by a primeval romanticism lurking in the "strange gnarled region of his heart." The later plays, writes Forster, "have a romantic intensity which not only rivals the romantic expansion of their predecessors, but is absolutely unique in literature . . . his stage throbs with a mysteriousness for which no obvious preparation has been made, with beckonings, tremblings, sudden compressions of the air, and his characters as they wrangle among the oval tables and stoves are watched by an unseen power which slips between their words."[1] Trolls mutter, white horses charge, ghosts glide, the sea lures, and the dead and damaged objects of our civilisation are refashioned (like those in the Ekdal loft) into a land of romance. And, even if Ibsen's romanticism lacks a source that Forster can easily identify, its primary vehicle, he suggests, must surely have been the mountain scenery of Norway, where Ibsen would have experienced a "passionate intensity . . . comparable to the early experiences of Wordsworth in the English lakes."[2]

"Romanticism," as Forster's essay ultimately defines it, is an idea vaguely synonymous with "poetry," and closely associated (although, admittedly, in a manner difficult to apply to Ibsen) with beautiful human relationships. ("Though he had the romantic temperament," says Forster, "he found personal intercourse sordid."[3]) It also includes that familiar world of marvellous "romantic" Gothicism, of faery-lands forlorn, permeated by the powerful natural forces of fire, water, and avalanche. But what Forster takes no account of in his definition is Ibsen's habitually *ironic* attitude towards these elements of Romanticism: his sense that faery-lands forlorn may be destructive and regressive myths (as the Ekdal loft surely turns out to be), and that mountain experiences may as frequently prove epiphanies of horror as Wordsworthian revelations of infinitude. As for Norway's landscape, there is more mountain gloom than mountain glory in the frozen glare of the ice-peaks and glaciers that tower

*Originally published in *"Ibsen the Romantic"* (London: Macmillan, 1982), 1–8. Reprinted by permission of the author.

behind the final agonies of *Ghosts;* and the scenery of sentimental National Romanticism — that geography of mystical purity and spiritual refreshment — is demolished as early as *Brand*, where, as James McFarlane puts it, "the repudiation of Romanticism's Nature is abrupt and vehement."[4] Even in the last plays, where the protagonists once more struggle magnificently up the peaks of promise towards transfiguration, the region they finally inhabit is the Ice Church of inhuman aspiration, where death is the only revelation. On the same evidence that Forster adduces for his image of Ibsen the Romantic one could argue for its antithesis.

The problem is obvious: there are as many conceptions of Romanticism as there are critics of Romantic literature, and as many Romantic Ibsens. When Maurice Valency, for example, describes the confessional element in Ibsen's drama as the "special sort of masochism we call romantic," or the "romantic impulse" of Hedda Gabler as "a disease,"[5] it is clear that we are intended to understand Romanticism as that peculiar form of decadence so defined by Goethe and detailed by Mario Praz in *The Romantic Agony*. It would be possible, if not very instructive, to compile an entire lexicon of "Romantic" Ibsens to demonstrate the semantic confusion and the multiplicity of romanticisms, which make any discussion of the topic perilous. One remains grateful, nevertheless, to those critics who have worked through the tangle of specifically Norwegian forms of Romanticism to locate Ibsen's indigenous or local affinities: *Nasjonalromantikken* or National Romanticism of the early historical drama, which Ibsen was later to despise as pernicious fictions; *Huldreromantikken* or "Faery" Romanticism of folkloric tradition, which Ibsen satirised in Julian Poulsen, that Bunthorne of sham Romanticism in *St John's Night*, and *Nyromantikken* or Neo-Romanticism of the 1890s, typified in Hamsun's article "Fra det ubevidste Sjæleliv" ("From the Unconscious Life of the Mind") and already anticipated in Ibsen's psychological studies of Rebekka West and Ellida Wangel.[6] Some of these local romanticisms were undoubtedly a late blooming, in the remote North, of European Romantic themes — Brian Downs points to the Rousseauistic features of National Romanticism in, for example, the celebration of peasant nobility and the image of a pure historical past untainted by the vices of modernity. And it is possible to find in the emergence of an independent Norway in 1814, after her emancipation from four centuries of Danish rule, a late historical paradigm of the political hopes which shaped the Romantic sensibilities of France and England in the age of revolution. The social conditions in Norway, of course, were vastly different. There was no oppressed peasantry, and no industrialism. But the American and French revolutions had already pointed the way for a democratic constitution which would affirm the sovereignty of Norway (despite her political status as a "gift" to Sweden), and a nation was in the process of being reborn in the spirit of bloodless revolution. Ibsen wrote his first play, *Catiline*, in response to the revolutionary political climate of

1848; and it is possible to chart the course of his political concerns from the fervour of *Catiline* to the tragic failure of liberal idealism in *Rosmersholm*, where the reactionary backlash is most keenly felt, and so project a revaluation of his Romantic hopes analogous to the European response to the collapse of post-revolutionary idealism. It is clear, at any rate, that the phases of European Romanticism are recapitulated in the development of Norwegian cultural history, and that literary influences filtered gradually northwards to inspire a group of writers already responsive to these new currents of feeling: Wergeland, Welhaven and Asbjørnsen in Norway; and Oehlenschläger, Johan Ludvig Heiberg and Henrik Hertz in Denmark. Ibsen, as Brian Downs points out, "was not a sudden, causeless phenomenon, born in a hyperborean desert with no traceable ancestry, but stood well in the stream of the ethical, religious, political and sociological thought of his time."[7] This is an aspect of the Romantic Ibsen that I must leave to those more competent to evaluate his role in the various romanticisms that comprise Norwegian literature from the 1830s to the 1860s.

And what of Ibsen the Romantic *dramatist?* It is one of those curiosities of theatrical history that, when Ibsen's *Ghosts* was staged at the Théâtre Libre in Paris, Sarah Bernhardt was also playing Sardou's *Cléopâtre* in the "romantic" *fin de siècle* style (and applying, it is said, a *real* asp to her bosom). Once again, definitions of Romanticism bifurcate: on the one hand the epitome of decadent exoticism, and on the other the exemplar of those metaphysical concerns which, as Terry Otten argues in his study of the Romantic drama, are the hallmark of the English Romantics. "Shelley," he writes, "perhaps unconsciously, was moving towards a new kind of drama, a drama which by the end of the century was to find full expression in Ibsen's late symbolic dramas."[8] And what makes the new drama quintessentially "Romantic," as Otten defines the term, is its refusal to affirm *external* criteria of social morality (as in the Shakespearian mode), and its protagonist's strenuous search after a moral order *within* to counter the cosmic emptiness and the chaos around him. For Shelley and for Byron, as for Ibsen after them, there is no order and no God — except in so far as their protagonists are prepared to conceive of Him. This is a far cry from Forster's vision of Ibsen's romanticism. Ibsen as Romantic *dramatist* is seen in quite another guise: as one standing in direct relationship to European Romanticism, without intervenient local influences, participating in and shaping its mythologies, and finally projecting its spiritual concerns into the images and archetypes of the twentieth century.

This is the Ibsen who emerges in Brian Johnston's recent study as "a post-Romantic artist who still remained loyal to Romantic aspirations: who, though he saw everywhere the betrayal of revolutionary and Romantic ideals, still held onto the impossible goal of a 'revolution in the spirit of man' . . . a militant Romantic who is subversively smuggling the explosive

Romantic powers into the pragmatic bourgeois world that had turned its back upon them."[9] This image of Ibsen the Romantic once again, it seems to me, takes too little account of the ironic, sceptical, at times counter-Romantic and anti-Romantic temperament which sees all too clearly a bourgeoisie grasping at romantic possibility and, in the very attempt to make it viable, devastating and destroying life itself. What Johnston argues most convincingly, however, is for Ibsen's centrality to the moral intelligence of the late nineteenth century, and his close affinity with Hegel's ambitious programme of Romanticism: nothing less than the redemption of man's alienation from himself and from nature by rediscovering "the total human spirit within the conditions of the Present."[10] It is an elaborate and finely detailed argument; and, even if one cannot accept the direct and immediate influence of the late German Romantics on Ibsen, his cultural affinities with Hegel, Schelling, Schiller and Goethe are either a matter of astonishing coincidence, or a consequence of his complete absorption of the ideas, images and spiritual concerns of the *Zeitgeist*. These archetypes of Romantic literature have been brilliantly synthesized, as Johnston notes, by M. H. Abrams in *Natural Supernaturalism*; and merely to compare Abrams's paradigm of the Romantic quest in the poetry and romances of late eighteenth-century Germany to Ibsen's *Peer Gynt* is to recognise Peer's participation in the alienated Romantic hero's search for a recovered sense of pristine unity in himself and in society:

> In Novalis' romances the process of representative human experience is a fall from self-unity and community into division, and from contentment into the longing for redemption, which consists of a recovered unity on a higher level of self-awareness. This process is represented in the plot-form of an educational journey in quest of a feminine other, whose mysterious attraction compels the protagonist to abandon his childhood sweetheart and the simple security of home and family (equated with infancy, the pagan golden age, and the Biblical paradise) to wander through alien lands on a way that rounds imperceptibly back to home and family, but with an access of insight (the product of his experience en route) which enables him to recognize, in the girl he left behind, the elusive female figure who has all along been the object of his longing and his quest. The protagonist's return home thus coincides with the consummation of a union with his beloved bride.[11]

The general narrative framework, the dramatic events, the symbols and metaphors that link Ibsen to Novalis and Goethe are so inescapable that one is inclined to accept, on the basis of this evidence alone, a Teutonic variant of Ibsen the Romantic. Indeed, Peer's explicit reference to Goethe's *Faust* might seem to confirm, unequivocally, Ibsen's conscious reliance upon German Romanticism for the themes and ideas of his own Faust drama: "To quote a famous author," says Peer, " 'Das ewig weibliche ziehet uns an!' " (III, 349). Peer has not quite called to mind the original line; but, even if he had, the image of the redemptive woman is most inappropriately conferred upon the carnally seductive Anitra.[12] Nor, as James McFarlane argues, is *das Ewig-Weibliche* embodied, without irony, in the figure of the blind and aged Solveig — Peer's fantastic projection of a female wish-dream to shelter him against the Buttonmoulder, the inescapable reality of death.[13] But, it seems to me, the anti-Romantic or counter-Romantic implications of this Goethean archetype are manifest throughout the body of Ibsen's drama, from Lyngstrand's flaccid vision of eternally waiting womanhood to old Foldal's pathetic belief "that somewhere out in the wide wide world, far away perhaps, there is to be found the true woman" (VIII, 189). For Ibsen, the Romantic notion of Eternal Womanhood, *das Ewig-Weibliche* — a constellation of abstract ideals which man may strive towards but never possess — ultimately serves only to pervert the reality of sexual relationships and the satisfaction of desire. Faust may be saved by his refusal to yield to the illusions of fulfillment in the world; but Borkman and Rubek, by the same token, are damned for interposing the metaphors of Romantic questing between desire and human experience. And the women in their lives cry out against this essential lovelessness which fashions them into bloodless images of an infinitude beyond attainment. The dramatic structure of *Peer Gynt* may conform to the paradigm of the Romantic quest. But the voice that speaks from within this structure is a dissenting voice, that "other" Ibsen[14] who both participates in and stands apart from the European tradition towards which he gestures, the Romantic Ibsen and the counter-Romantic.

What I want to examine in the chapters that follow are the tensions between these two Ibsens, the impulses that pass from one to the other, and the paradoxical simultaneity of Romantic and counter-Romantic attitudes which make Ibsen a Romantic of extraordinary individuality, both celebrant and critic of a vision potentially redemptive and potentially ruinous. The Romantic Ibsen I have in mind (and whom I shall discuss in his own terms) is not Forster's poet — which is not to deny the poet in Ibsen, but rather to locate his romanticism in a drama of spiritual distress, in his protagonists' search for consolation in the face of death, and their attempt to rediscover a world of lost Paradisal hopes in the mythology of Romanticism. Redemption from cosmic nothingness, from meaninglessness — this is the nature of the Romantic quest which Ibsen's people share with those of Byron, Stendhal, and Jens Peter Jacobsen. Hugo von Hofmannsthal, writing in 1891, was among the first of Ibsen's critics to link his dramatic concerns with a pervasive European mood; and the composite picture of the Ibsen hero that he sketched in his essay is far closer to my sense of Ibsen the Romantic than Forster's image of the boy bewitched. The people in Ibsen's drama, wrote Hofmannsthal, are possessed by a desperation to restore meaning and style to life, anxious (like Niels Lyhne, Jacobsen's hero) not only to write poetry "but instead oneself become the stuff of poetry,"[15] forever yearning for ancient myths of significance in the modern world and for miracle in a faithless age:

This mysterious element, which is to come and carry one away and give life some great meaning, gives all things new colour and every world a soul — this thing has several names for these people. Sometimes it is the "miraculous" for which Nora longs; for Julian and Hedda it is Grecian, the great Bacchanalia, with noble grace and vineleaves in one's hair; or it is the sea with its mysterious allure; or it is a free life on a grand pattern, in America or Paris. All these things are only symbolical names for something "out there," something "different." It is nothing other than Stendhal's yearning search for the "imprévu," for what is unforeseen, for what is not "weary, stale, flat and unprofitable" in love and life. It is nothing but the dream-longing of the romantics for the moonlit magic wilderness, for openings in the mountainside, for speaking pictures, for some undreamed-of fairy-tale element in life.[16]

The "miraculous" for which the Ibsen protagonist yearns, the faery-world forlorn, Hofmannsthal goes on to suggest, is ultimately to be located in the subconscious, in dim memories of a lost and dream-like childhood "in a kind of enchanted forest from which they emerge insatiably homesick and peculiarly insulated."[17]

I want, in the chapter that follows, to define even more carefully the nature of that lost world in the plays of Ibsen, the myths and archetypes and attitudes that shape the Romanticism of his protagonists — and the counter-Romantic vision which dramatises their tragic failure to transpose these fictions and symbols of significance into the realities of life.

Notes

1. E. M. Forster, "Ibsen the Romantic," repr. in James McFarlane (ed.), *Henrik Ibsen: A Critical Anthology* (Harmondsworth, 1970) p. 233.

2. Ibid., p. 234.

3. Ibid., p. 232.

4. James McFarlane, Introduction to *The Oxford Ibsen*, III (London, 1972) 17.

5. Maurice Valency, *The Flower and the Castle* (New York, 1963) pp. 123, 200.

6. See James McFarlane, Introduction to *The Oxford Ibsen*, I (London, 1970); Brian Downs, *Ibsen: The Intellectual Background* (Cambridge, 1946), and *Modern Norwegian Literature* 1860–1918 (Cambridge, 1966); and Ronald Popperwell, *Norway* (New York, 1972).

7. Downs, *Ibsen: The Intellectual Background*, p. ix.

8. Terry Otten, *The Deserted Stage: The Search for Dramatic Form in Nineteenth-Century England* (Athens, Ohio, 1972) p. 14.

9. Brian Johnston, *The Ibsen Cycle: The Design of the Plays from "Pillars of Society" to "When We Dead Awaken"* (Boston, Mass., 1975) Preface, n.p.

10. Ibid., p. 316.

11. M. H. Abrams, *Natural Supernaturalism: Tradition and Revolution in Romantic Literature* (New York, 1971) p. 246.

12. I am grateful to Dr Patricia Merivale for showing me her paper "*Faust* and *Peer Gynt*: Ironic Inversions." "It is useful no longer to wonder if Peer's misquotation . . . could be

a slip of Ibsen's memory," she writes. "It is simply the most explicit clue to Ibsen's deliberate employment of the Faustian structure to invert, ironically, the Faustian theme."

13. McFarlane, "Introduction" to *The Oxford Ibsen*, III, 29–30.

14. For a detailed discussion of Ibsen's "otherness," see Inga-Stina Ewbank, "Ibsen on the English Stage: The Proof of the Pudding is in the Eating," in Errol Durbach (ed.), *Ibsen and the Theatre* (London, 1980).

15. J. P. Jacobsen, *Niels Lyhne* (1880), quoted in Hugo von Hofmannsthal, "Die Menschen in Ibsens Drama," repr. in McFarlane, *Ibsen: A Critical Anthology*, p. 134.

16. Hugo von Hofmannsthal, op. cit., p. 134.

17. Ibid., p. 135.

Ibsen's Dramatic Form
The Reconsideration of
Elements of Structure

Hedda Gabler

John Northam*

So extensive is the draft material for this play, that, together with an analysis by Halvdan Koht, it fills more than one hundred and fifty pages in *Samlede Verker*, volume XI (pp. 397–553). Briefly, it consists of a complete draft entitled "Hedda" (pp. 402–95) which will be referred to in this chapter as "the draft"; within the draft is a set for Act II which was later abandoned. Then there are two note-books whose entries are so fragmentary and scattered that it is difficult to arrange them chronologically with any great accuracy; in any case they provide little information about visual suggestion. Three further sets of material were composed after "Hedda" had been written. Our attention will therefore be directed principally to "Hedda" as being the first dramatic draft, and infrequent reference will be made where points of special interest arise to the other material.[1]

The set of Act I in the play is full of significant detail:

A spacious, handsome, and tastefully furnished drawing-room, deco-
rated in dark colours. In the back, a wide doorway with curtains drawn
back, leading into an inner room decorated in the same style as the
drawing-room. In the right-hand wall of the front room, a folding door
leading out to the hall. In the opposite wall, on the left, a glass door,
also with curtains drawn back. Through the panes can be seen part of a
veranda outside, and trees covered with autumn foliage. In front, by the
wall on the right, a wide stove of dark porcelain, a high-backed arm-
chair, a cushioned foot-rest, and two footstools. A settee, with a small
round table in front of it, fills the upper right-hand corner. In front, on
the left, a little way from the wall, a sofa. Further back from the glass
door, a piano. On either side of the doorway at the back a what-not
with terracotta and majolica ornaments. — Against the back wall of the
inner room a sofa, with a table, and one or two chairs. Over the sofa
hangs the portrait of a handsome elderly gentleman in a General's
uniform. Over the table a hanging lamp, with an opal glass shade. — A
number of bouquets are arranged about the drawing-room, in vases and
glasses. Others lie upon the tables. The floors in both rooms are covered

*Originally published in *Ibsen's Dramatic Method* (London: Faber, 1948), 147–71.

with thick carpets. — Morning light. The sun shines in through the glass door. Miss Juliana Tesman, with her bonnet on — and carrying a parasol, comes in from the hall, followed by Berta, who carries a bouquet wrapped in paper. Miss Tesman is a comely and pleasant-looking lady of about sixty-five. She is nicely but simply dressed in a grey walking-costume. Berta is a middle-aged woman of plain and rather countrified appearance.

The first impression is one of contrast between a dark, artificial and elegant interior, and a bright, though autumnal, exterior. The cold darkness of the inner room is emphasized by the dull white[2] lampshade. The draft contained everything except the shade.

A note of warm life is struck by the flowers, but there is something to be noticed about them; they inundate the room, spreading to the tables. Their profusion is embarrassing.

Both of the women are plainly linked by their costume and general appearance with the exterior rather than the elegant interior, but Ibsen makes the association quite obvious by means of an illustrative action (we recall *Pillars of Society*):[3]

MISS TESMAN: . . . But let us see that they get a good breath of the fresh morning air. . . . (*She goes to the glass door and throws it open.*)

Even before Hedda appears, she is assigned a place in relation to the set. In the centre of the wall of the inner room hangs the portrait of General Gabler[4] — the centre of the stage as the audience sees it, and very much part of the interior. Miss Tesman draws our attention to it: "Well, you can't wonder at that — General Gabler's daughter! Think of the sort of life she was accustomed to in her father's time. Don't you remember how we used to see her riding down the road along with the General? . . ."

In the draft, Ibsen did not mention the word "General" and so missed the connection:

MISS RISING: Well, you can't wonder at that. Think of the sort of life she was accustomed to in her father's time.

It may be objected that Hedda can scarcely have had time to impress her personality on the rooms, for it was only the night before that she arrived from a six-months' honeymoon tour with George Tesman, the old lady's nephew. Ibsen, however, takes pains to make Hedda responsible:

MISS TESMAN: But bless me, Berta — why have you done this? Taken the chintz covers off all the furniture?

BERTA: The mistress told me to. She can't abide covers on the chairs, she says.

George Tesman is connected with the bright exterior by his bright and cheerful appearance: "*. . . humming to himself . . . He is a middle-sized, young-looking man of thirty-three, rather stout with a round, open, cheerful face, fair hair and beard. He wears spectacles, and is somewhat carelessly dressed in comfortable indoor clothes.*"

His colouring does not suit with the dark interior, nor does his inelegance. We are not told what colour hair Miss Tesman has, but her age would suggest white or grey. Hedda contrasts with both these light tones:[5] ". . . *She is a woman of nine-and-twenty. Her face and figure show refinement and distinction. Her complexion is pale and opaque. Her steel-grey eyes express a cold, unruffled repose. Her hair is of an agreeable medium brown, but not particularly abundant. She is dressed in a tasteful, somewhat loose-fitting morning gown.*"

Her cold refinement links her with the interior;[6] it is interesting to note that her complexion is described in terms similar to those used for the lamp-shade in the inner room; the lamp is "*mat, mælkefarvet,*" "dull, milk-coloured"; Hedda is of a "*mat bleghed,*" a "dull pallor" and neither term appeared in the draft.

The draft also omitted all reference to Hedda's hair, which makes a double impression; one of pleasant colour, which might have infused the whole picture but for the second impression, that of sparsity.[7] As for her dress, it is so tasteful as to demand no attention; it is not a strikingly colourful gown. And here we look outside the draft for evidence of the care with which Ibsen experimented with definite characteristics before resigning himself to the mercy of the producer: in the draft, Hedda simply wore "a morning gown" [6]; an entry in one of the two notebooks, which was probably made after the completion of Act I of the draft, had: ". . . *Dressed in a loose morning-gown, white with blue trimmings. . . .*"

When Ibsen wrote out some alternative jottings to parts of the draft, he made Hedda's colouring even more positive and forceful: ". . . *She is dressed in a tasteful morning-gown in which light blue and red are the predominant colours.*"

It is strange that, after taking such pains, Ibsen was not more precise in his final directions.

We already know quite a lot about Hedda from the set and her personal appearance. An illustrative action expands our knowledge. Hedda greets her aunt coldly, and then sees the open door: ". . . Oh — there, the servant has gone and opened the veranda door, and let in a whole flood of sunshine."

This dislike of the sun sums up the difference between the two parties on the stage and emphasizes the division contained in the set. But (and this matches the ambiguity of her pleasant but not abundant hair) Hedda will not have the sun quite excluded:

MISS TESMAN (*going towards the door*): Well, then we will shut it.

HEDDA: No, no, not that! Tesman, please draw the curtains. That will give a softer light.

TESMAN: All right — all right — There now, Hedda, now you have both shade and fresh air.

Hedda, it seems, dislikes the direct impact of the bright outer world. Her distaste for exuberance is shown when she complains of the flowers:

". . . Yes, fresh air we certainly must have, with all these stacks of flowers—"

All of which serves not merely to separate Hedda from the other people, but also to alienate our sympathy. And yet there is the obstinate fact of her agreeably coloured hair which suggests warmth and vitality. We see Hedda's cold dignity stifled by the affectionate welcome given her by the Tesmans, as we see the room swamped with bouquets; we see her curtain off the outer world, but not exclude it completely.

The doubt arises: can she beat off this embarrassing intrusion into her elegance? Tesman thrusts upon her his old slippers wrapped in newspaper, and she snubs him; but it soon becomes clear to Miss Tesman and to the audience that Hedda is expecting a baby. She can disentangle herself from the old lady's adulation, but the baby represents an inexorable invasion of her privacy which no amount of cold aloofness can repel. Her reaction is illuminating: *"She goes out by the hall door. Tesman accompanies her. . . . In the meantime, Hedda walks about the room, raising her arms and clenching her hands as if in desperation. Then she flings back the curtains from the glass door, and stands there looking out. . . ."*

This action, which was lacking in the draft, suggests that, under stress, Hedda is capable of a sudden change from her normal calm dignity. In terms of the set, it suggests that although she is normally content to look through curtains, she will occasionally face the bright outer world; but in no friendly sense, for out there she sees only the autumn leaves: "They are so yellow, so withered."

Our estimate of Hedda is becoming more precise; we see her as a woman of frustrated potentialities whose customary self-control is apt to give way under pressure. She rejects the warm emotional life of the Tesmans, and so aggravates her frustration by her aloofness. The reason why she will not join in the bright world is given us visually; Hedda refuses Tesman's request that she should be nice to his old aunt:

TESMAN: Well, well. Only I think now that you belong to the family, you——

HEDDA: H'm—I can't in the least see why—— (*She goes up towards the middle doorway.*)

—towards, that is, the portrait of her father, whose presence seems to make the room peculiarly her own;[8] this impression is strengthened by her decision to move her piano out of the large room into the smaller. The limits of her world, social and emotional, are laid down for her by her late father's eminence. In the draft this suggestive movement of Hedda's was missing—she went directly to her piano, which stood to one side of the room.

Hedda's isolation is emphasized when Mrs. Elvsted enters; for they are totally different in character. This Ibsen establishes rapidly; in the first place, Mrs. Elvsted is made responsible for some of the flowers in the room, which Hedda dislikes. The connection is strongly made:

> HEDDA (*taking up the bouquet from the piano*): . . . Can you guess whose card it is? . . . The name is Mrs. Elvsted.

Almost at once Berta enters: "That lady, ma'am, that brought some flowers a little while ago, is here again. (*Pointing.*) The flowers you have in your hand, ma'am." The contrast is deepened by Thea's appearance: "*Mrs. Elvsted is a woman of fragile figure, with pretty, soft features. Her eyes are light blue, large, round and somewhat prominent, with a startled, inquiring expression. Her hair is remarkably light, almost flaxen, and unusually abundant and wavy. She is a couple of years younger than Hedda. She wears a dark visiting dress, tasteful, but not quite in the latest fashion.*"[9]

Her blondness ranks her with the Tesmans, leaving Hedda's isolation by colour more marked. Her bright hair and light eyes emphasize Hedda's restrained coldness. The abundance of her hair is plainly an exuberance to be contrasted with Hedda's comparative sparsity. She lacks Hedda's poise and strength, but she has light and warmth. As we look, we do not separate our judgement of her appearance from our estimate of her character. Light-weight or not, she wins our approval.

The dark dress prepares us for the revelation that the lady is troubled. The draft gave no information about Mrs. Elvsted's appearance at all.

In the play, this strong visual distinction between the two women gives force to the more subtle distinction of character which is unfolded, bit by bit, during the rest of the scene. There is a danger that this antithesis might lose its force through familiarity, but Ibsen occasionally redirects our attention. For example, after Thea has revealed that she has come to town to look for her step-children's tutor, Lövborg, an erratic genius and potential rival to Tesman for academic honours, Hedda at once suspects a hidden love-affair between this woman and her old flame; professing friendship, she worms her way into Thea's confidence, but just before the *tête-à-tête* really begins, Ibsen points out the antipathy which prompts the whole interrogation. Hedda reminds Thea how friendly they were at school. Thea replies: ". . . When we met on the stairs you always used to pull my hair. . . . And once you said you would burn it off my head" [14].

This startling revelation, which was not in the draft, moves Hedda's character into sharper focus. Here the hints of frustration and outburst take on a wider and more sinister significance; Hedda is shown to be aware of her own deficiency and ready to take extreme, wild measures to efface it. One other impression is generated; as Hedda drags Thea's secret out of her, there is something a little feverish in the way she enjoys the spurious intimacy of the "cosy chat." She admires Thea's courage in leaving her husband to follow Lövborg, but she plainly would not dare do the same. Her attitude of eager curiosity veiled with propriety recalls the earlier illustrative action with the curtain. She indulges her frustrated instincts vicariously, but the instincts are still there, in her agreeable brown hair, in her curiosity, in her sudden throwing open of the curtains in torment; and behind everything hangs the portrait of her father, the General, the social and hereditary force which dooms her to stultifying isolation.[10]

It is interesting to note that when, during their talk, Thea mentions a rival for Lövborg's love, Ibsen is at pains to specify this rival's vivid, positive colouring [15], as though her red hair were to serve as a symbol of her straightforward sexuality (Mlle Diana is euphemistically called a singing-woman); we are certainly tempted to see in her another strong contrast to Hedda and Ibsen succeeds in making us look again at the revealing difference between Hedda's hair and Thea's. This is a touch added after the writing of the draft.

At last a darker colour appears: *"Brack is a man of forty-five: thick-set, but well-built and elastic in his movements. His face is roundish with an aristocratic profile. His hair is short, still almost black, and carefully dressed. His eyes are lively and sparkling. His eye-brows thick. His moustaches are also thick, with short-cut ends. He wears a well-cut walking suit, a little too youthful for his age.[11] He uses an eye-glass, which he now and then lets drop."*

We now have on one side the light-haired, warm-hearted figures; in the centre, Hedda with her ambiguous hair, at once agreeable and sparse, and her conflicting emotions; and on the other side, Brack, the dark epitome of vigour. Brack is distinct in kind from the others, in degree from Hedda. This impression is immediately verified when we see how she responds to his dark virility; she laughs and is merry for the first time since the play began. The draft did not describe Brack.

One more strand completes the pattern of Hedda's character. Recalling the striking image of the burning hair, we begin to notice that Hedda is becoming closely associated with the stove in the set; at the beginning of her conversations with Thea "(*She forces Mrs. Elvsted to sit in the easy-chair beside the stove.*)" — so that the mention of burning occurs in an appropriate place. Later, when she learns how Thea has reformed Lövborg, she sees her out of the house, and then returns to hear Brack and Tesman discussing him:

TESMAN: Well, you see, dear—we were talking about poor Eilert Lövborg.

HEDDA   (*glancing at him rapidly*): Oh, indeed? (*Seats herself in the arm-chair beside the stove and asks indifferently*): What is the matter with him?

It has been plain that she is still interested in Lövborg; her action, connecting her once more with fire, hints vaguely at danger—a hint missed by the draft, which did not mention the stove at this point. Ibsen's concluding symbol at the end of Act I, leaves us in no doubt as to the peril. Tesman has just heard from Brack that not only is he in debt, but his prospects of a professorship are by no means secure now that Lövborg has started to write again:

> TESMAN: It would be out of the question for us to keep a footman, you know.
>
> HEDDA: And the saddle-horse I was to have had— . . . (*Goes up the room.*) Well, I shall have one thing at least to kill time with in the meanwhile. . . . (*In the middle doorway, looks at him with covert scorn.*) My pistols, George.
>
> TESMAN: . . . Your pistols!
>
> HEDDA (*with cold eyes*):   General Gabler's pistols. (*She goes out through the inner room. . . .*)

This shows us, in physical action, Hedda the daughter of her father rather than her husband's wife. When sordid matters of vulgar finance crop up she retreats towards the portrait which makes the inner room a sanctuary for her. We are also warned that, when she is frustrated, Hedda can employ dangerous weapons for her relief. Thus, at the first curtain, we have a clear picture of a woman whose repression of her natural instincts from mistaken ideas of social superiority leads her into a situation in which the crushing boredom of her alliance with mediocrity is made bearable only when she can indulge a rather feverish interest in other peoples' love affairs. She has lost the art of mixing with the world, but not her interest in it. The use of fire and fire-arms as symbols suggests that this vicarious living may prove an inadequate safety-valve for the strong, almost masculine, pressures within her.

The end of Act I in the draft was incomparably weaker:

> TESMAN: Well, Hedda—you and I must have a serious talk.
>
> HEDDA: Not now, Tesman, I assure you I haven't time . . . I must go and change my dress before lunch. (*She goes towards the door on the left.*)
>
> TESMAN: But you take this as if it didn't matter at all.
>
> HEDDA (*turns in the doorway*):   Why should I not? You are so fond of saying that the strongest always win. (*She goes out.*)
>
> TESMAN (*grasps the back of a chair and gazes uneasily before him*): The strongest, yes. . . .

The first act showed us Hedda triumphant; the Tesmans were put in their place; Thea's confidence was won; Brack arrived to enliven her boredom; but the baby, and time (made highly significant thereby) are beyond her control. The set of Act II emphasizes some of these impressions:

> *The room at Tesman's as in the first Act, except that the piano has been*
> *removed, and an elegant little writing-table with book-shelves put in its*
> *place. A smaller table stands near the sofa on the left. Most of the*
> *bouquets have been taken away. Mrs. Elvsted's bouquet is upon the*
> *large table in front. — It is afternoon.*
>
> *Hedda, dressed to receive callers, is alone in the room. She stands by the*
> *open glass door, loading a revolver. The fellow to it lies in an open*
> *pistol-case on the writing-table.*

We note that Hedda's piano has been moved into the privacy of the inner room; in its place is the writing-table whose elegance would proclaim it hers, even if it were not associated with her most personal possessions, the inherited pistols. Hedda's victorious assertion of her inviolable individuality is also mirrored in the removal of the over-exuberance of welcoming bouquets. She has toned down the set.

Ibsen's first sketch of a set for Act II was crossed out by him:

> *Tesman's garden with a view out over the fiord and the islands. Large,*
> *old lime-trees on both sides. Under a tree on the right a garden-seat with*
> *a table. In the centre a fountain set round with flowering plants. The*
> *garden slopes down towards the back. Evening light. Hedda dressed to*
> *receive callers, is sitting on the bench with a sunshade in her hand. Her*
> *straw hat is lying on the table. Presently Judge Brack comes up from the*
> *back wearing a hat and carrying gloves and stick.*

Why was this set abandoned? Tennant suggests that this is another instance of Ibsen's dramatic economy.[12] It is at least possible that Ibsen rejected the outdoor set, with its lively colours and its openness, because it destroyed the feeling of confinement which he was striving to realize in the draft. The garden can tell us nothing about Hedda.

His next attempt, in the draft, was much closer to the play:

> *The room at the Tesmans' as in the First Act, except that the piano has*
> *been removed, and an elegant little writing-table and an étagère put in*
> *its place. Some of the bouquets have been removed from the table and*
> *placed in the inner room. It is afternoon. Hedda, dressed in a tasteful*
> *afternoon gown, is alone in the room. She stands by the open door of the*
> *veranda, loading a revolver. The other lies in an open case on a chair by*
> *her side.*

Three points are to be noted: the first is that two pieces of furniture competed for interest as successors to the piano; the second is that some of the flowers, symbols of unwanted affection, were moved into Hedda's sanctuary; the third is a point of minute detail; in the play we accept the writing-desk as peculiarly private to Hedda because it replaced her piano and because her pistols were on it; in the draft, the pistol-case was on the chair — the focusing of attention was not so clear. It seems, therefore, that the writing-desk and the flowers are important in Ibsen's final conception of the scene; certainly they were not used lightly.

To return to the play: the most interesting developments are the open door and Hedda's occupation. They remind us of her former veiled interest (tinged with hostility) in the bright exterior, and of her reaction to pressure — her sudden throwing open of the curtains. This new position of open antagonism suggests to us that increased pressure has produced a more marked reaction. Hedda is prepared to come out from behind the curtains, but in a dangerous mood.

It is typical of her ambiguousness that her hostility extends to her friend:

> HEDDA (*raises the pistol and points*):   Now I'll shoot you, Judge Brack!
>
> BRACK: No, no, no! Don't stand aiming at me!
>
> HEDDA: This is what comes of sneaking in by the back way. (*She fires.*)

In this passage Brack, like the Burgomaster in *An Enemy of the People*, is characterized as a crafty person, for the phrase "gå bagveje" has a double meaning which embraces trickery.[13] The door therefore takes on a moral significance.

The draft omitted this piece of information.

It also omitted another which tells us something about the relationship between the two people:

> BRACK (*gently takes the pistol out of her hand*): Allow me, madam! . . . (*Lays the pistol in it* (sc. *the case*) *and shuts it*). Now we won't play at that game any more today!

Brack the crafty can disarm Hedda without her being aware of his power over her. In the draft she put her pistol away herself.

The increased pressure on Hedda is explained: she is bored. No visitors — even Tesman is out. After her momentary reaction, the door is closed again to emphasize her confinement.

Hedda's association with the window is stressed again; she talks to Brack of the tedium of life with a pedant whom she accepted to avoid being left on the shelf. Tesman enters and reminds her, unconsciously, for he is ignorant, of the inevitable intrusion of the baby she carries:

> TESMAN: And you can't imagine, dear, how delighted Aunt Julia seemed to be — because you had come home looking so flourishing!
>
> HEDDA: (*half aloud, rising*):   Oh, those everlasting Aunts!
>
> TESMAN: What?
>
> HEDDA (*going to the glass door*):   Nothing.

In the draft she turned towards the stove, but in the play this action is reserved for a more appropriate moment, which presents itself immediately afterwards, when Hedda tries to explain her earlier rudeness to Miss Tesman: "(*Nervously crossing the room*): Well, you see — these impulses come over me all of a sudden; and I cannot resist them. (*Throws herself*

down in the easy-chair by the stove). Oh, I don't know how to explain it."
This action, prepared for by the earlier association of Hedda with the
stove, serves to illustrate the dangerous nature of these sudden impulses
(we remember Thea's hair) and the heat which smoulders beneath a cold
surface. It will be noticed that in the play Hedda moves between two
distinct symbols; in the draft she wanders about the room before returning
to the stove.

As she and her surreptitious admirer converse, we become more
aware of the utter emptiness of Hedda's life. With an eye on a possible
threat to the triangular relationship he contemplates, he hints delicately at
approaching motherhood:

> BRACK: Are you so unlike the generality of women as to have no turn
> for duties which———?
>
> HEDDA *(beside the glass door):*   Oh, be quiet, I tell you! — I often think
> there is only one thing in the world I have any turn for.
>
> BRACK *(drawing near to her):*   And what is that, if I may ask?
>
> HEDDA *(stands looking out):*   Boring myself to death.

Pressure and reaction again. Outside the window are signs that the months
are passing.

As Tesman gets ready to go off to a lively party at Brack's, Lövborg
arrives in response to Tesman's invitation. His appearance is instructive:
". . . *He is slim and lean; of the same age as Tesman, but looks older and
somewhat worn-out. His hair and beard are of a blackish brown, his face
long and pale; but with patches of colour on the cheek-bones. He is
dressed in a well-cut black visiting suit, quite new. He has dark gloves and
a silk hat. He stops near the door, and makes a rapid bow, seeming
somewhat embarrassed.*" In his personal colouring we perceive the rake,
and also another contrast to the fair-haired Tesman and Thea. In his new
suit we see the gloss of his recent reclamation by Thea;[14] and in his
smartness, a point in common with Hedda.

The draft had: ". . . *He is dressed in a well-cut black visiting suit,
quite new, the frock-coat rather long. He has light brown gloves . . .*"
Ibsen has expunged two hints of inelegance which would have repelled
Hedda.

Tesman, plainly frightened of Lövborg as a rival, as plainly shows his
inferiority, whereupon Hedda's disgust at her situation increases — once
again Ibsen uses the window:

> TESMAN: How odd now! I should never have thought of writing
> anything of that sort.
>
> HEDDA *(at the glass door, drumming on the pane):*   H'm — I daresay
> not.

Tesman is delighted with the result of his talk with Lövborg:

> Hedda! Just fancy — Eilert Lövborg is not going to stand in our way!

HEDDA (*curtly*):   Our way? Pray leave me out of the question. (*She goes up towards the inner room, where Berta is placing a tray . . . on the table*).

—once again that gesture of withdrawal towards her father's portrait, when there is danger of being implicated in sordid family matters.

Lövborg, reformed by Thea, refuses to join the other two men as they sit and drink in the inner room; their presence is no violation of Hedda's sanctuary, because they enter at her invitation.

Her talk with Lövborg, as they feign interest in a picture album, makes explicit many of the hints and suggestions offered visually earlier in the play. For example:

> HEDDA: But now I will confide something to you. . . . The fact that I dared not shoot you down— . . . —that was not my most arrant cowardice—that evening.
>
> LÖVBORG (*looks at her a moment, understands, and whispers, passionately*): Oh, Hedda! Hedda Gabler! Now I begin to see a hidden reason beneath our comradeship! You and I—! After all, then, it was your craving for life——
>
> HEDDA (*softly, with a sharp glance*):   Take care! Believe nothing of the sort!

Here we have the pistols specifically used to ward off intruders, as Hedda fired on Brack, and yet her attitude towards intrusion is not unfriendly, so long as she can control it. This conversation gives a more precise outline to her character: she has been driven by her dread of scandal (after all, her father was a General) to indulge her interest in forbidden things surreptitiously:

> HEDDA: Do you think it quite incomprehensible that a young girl— when it can be done—without any one knowing— . . . should be glad to have a peep now and then, into a world which— . . . which she is forbidden to know anything about . . . ?

Lövborg has been used as a second-hand source of erotic experience—he told her of his escapades and she was in some measure gratified. As usual, however, Ibsen supports his exposition in words with some form of visual emphasis. Hedda's role as emotional middle-man is set before us when Mrs. Elvsted arrives[15] to meet Lövborg:

> MRS. ELVSTED (*takes a chair and is about to seat herself at his side*): Oh, how nice it is here!
>
> HEDDA: No, thank you, my little Thea! Not there! You'll be good enough to come over here to me. I will sit between you.

—and through her they make gentle love to each other. But one gesture keeps us aware of Hedda's true attitude towards the emotional richness in which she dare not participate:

LÖVBORG (*after a short pause, to Hedda*):   Is not she lovely to look at?

HEDDA   (*lightly stroking her hair*): Only to look at?

Hedda, the sadist, really wants to burn off that irritating hair; we feel that some equally wild reaction is about to occur. It occurs when Hedda deliberately goads Lövborg into drinking and accepting Brack's invitation to his party. She destroys Lövborg's faith in Thea, so that the power of controlling him should pass to her; she wants, for once in her life, to have power to mould a human destiny. At the end of the act, the hidden fires break out again:

> HEDDA: Oh, if you could only understand how poor I am. And fate has made you so rich! (*Clasps her passionately in her arms.*) I think I must burn your hair off, after all.
>
> MRS. ELVSTED: Let me go! Let me go! I am afraid of you, Hedda! . . .
>
> HEDDA: Nonsense! First you shall have a cup of tea, you little stupid. And then — at ten o'clock — Eilert Lövborg will be here — with vine-leaves in his hair. (*She drags Mrs. Elvsted almost by force towards the middle doorway.*)

The draft made no mention of the hair, but it did end like the play, with Hedda dragging her victim into her sanctuary, in the light of a lamp which Berta had just brought in. The promise of the opening symbol in Act II has been fulfilled — Hedda, under pressure of boredom and approaching motherhood, has thrown back the curtains and taken a hand in destiny; plainly, her intervention is dangerous to others; to herself it could be equally dangerous, if Brack should slip in by the back way and disarm her. But the act ends brightly and triumphantly, so that Act III is in sharp contrast:

> *The room at the Tesmans'. The curtains are drawn over the middle doorway, and also over the glass door. The lamp, half turned down, and with a shade over it, is burning on the table. In the stove, the door of which stands open, there has been a fire, which is now nearly burnt out. Mrs. Elvsted, wrapped in a large shawl, and with her feet upon a foot-rest, sits close to the stove, sunk back in the arm-chair. Hedda, fully dressed, lies sleeping upon the sofa, with a sofa-blanket over her.*

A cold and dreary set, which admirably mirrors Mrs. Elvsted's misery when she awakes; her hopes that Lövborg would return early and sober from the party have vanished. Ibsen sends Berta in to draw our attention to the smoking lamp and the dead fire. Thea lacks the energy to let in the sun or kindle a flame; Hedda is different. It is to be noted that whereas at the beginning of the play she told Miss Tesman that she could not sleep, now, in circumstances which have prostrated Thea, she has slept quite well. She is enjoying her intervention in life; she can see Lövborg, not sober, but inspired to freedom with wine. She packs Thea off to bed, and shows her determination to face the world by means of the familiar gesture: "*Hedda goes up to the glass door and draws back the curtains. The broad daylight streams into the room. . . .*"

This action, which the draft omitted, is followed closely by another which reminds us of the force which drives Hedda on: ". . . *Hedda kneels on the foot-rest and lays some more pieces of wood in the stove.*"

One other detail of the set becomes more significant as the curtains are thrown open; for the first time in this play, Hedda's sanctuary is closed; the emphasis of the set is on the bright exterior, just as, for the first time in her life, Hedda has decided to intervene in life, without regard to convention; she has left her retreat.

Tesman arrives with the tale of Lövborg's renewed drunkenness, but to Hedda that is just a sign of what she considers her liberating influence; more important, he brings with him the manuscript of Lövborg's new book, the produce of the other woman's influence. Tesman wavers weakly about returning the manuscript, but makes no strong objection to Hedda's taking charge of it, while he runs off to his aunt's death-bed.

His place is taken by Brack, who, in order to cripple a dangerous rival for his corner of the proposed triangle, has come to tell her of Lövborg's second fall into debauchery. Hedda is quite willing to attribute his drunkenness to "inspiration" — plainly her inspiration — until a woman enters the case. Lövborg, it seems, ended up at Mlle Diana's; Ibsen emphasizes the red hair, and we recall that she has earlier been a rival for Lövborg's attention. Hedda's attitude now changes, and when she hears of a noisy quarrel and arrest, she realizes that her intervention has failed:

> HEDDA (*gazing straight before her*):   So that is what happened. Then he had no vine-leaves in his hair.

In the draft there was no hint of this shock to Hedda's ambition; she merely remarked that it would have been interesting to see the episode.

But Hedda's disillusionment is not yet complete; she has, the set tells us, left her sanctuary. A threat begins to develop: Brack's craftiness becomes less than amusing, as he reveals his determination to be the only "cock in the basket."

> BRACK (*nods slowly and lowers his voice*):   Yes, that is my aim. And for that I will fight — with every weapon I can command.
>
> HEDDA (*her smiling vanishing*):   I see you are a dangerous person — when it comes to the point.
>
> BRACK: Do you think so?
>
> HEDDA: I am beginning to think so. And I am exceedingly glad to think — that you have no sort of hold over me.

Just how far Hedda has moved from her former proud isolation is shown by a tableau which contrasts strongly with an earlier one; in Act II, Brack's surreptitious entry was met by pistol fire; in Act III he leaves quite secure in his strength, a change which is not lost on Hedda:

BRACK: Good-bye, Mrs. Hedda. (*He goes towards the glass door.*)

HEDDA: Are you going through the garden?

BRACK: Yes, it's a short cut for me.

HEDDA: And then it's a back way, too.

BRACK: Quite so. I have no objection to back ways. They may be piquant enough at times.

HEDDA: When there is ball practice going on, you mean?

BRACK (*in the doorway, laughing to her*):   Oh, people don't shoot their tame poultry, I fancy.

HEDDA (*also laughing*):   Oh, no, when there is only one cock in the basket——

(*They exchange laughing nods of farewell. He goes. She closes the door behind him.*

(*Hedda, who has become quite serious, stands for a moment looking out. Presently she goes and peeps through the curtain over the middle door.*

The threatening aspect of the scene was missing from the draft.

Hedda is not prepared to retreat; Lövborg arrives to tell Thea that they must part—Hedda has succeeded in one part of her plan. They must part because he has destroyed, so he says, his book, their spiritual "child." At the word, Hedda breathes: "(*Almost inaudibly*) Ah, the child——."

She is jealous of this tangible result of the other woman's inspiring influence over Lövborg, with whom she has failed. She also recalls the different sort of child, of a very different father, which she is burdened with. Jealous of the "pretty little fool" who has broken Lövborg's courage to live in splendid defiance of convention, she prompts him to a beautiful death. She gives him one of her father's pistols to shoot himself—beautifully. Then she turns to the hated "child," in a scene which brings together all the earlier references, verbal and visual, to fire, burning of hair, all the hints of violent, dangerous reaction to emotional frustration, hatred of her unborn child—here, in action, is Hedda's open defiance of the world, and a symbol of her first incriminating act:

LÖVBORG: Good-bye, Hedda Gabler.

(*He goes out by the hall door.*)

Hedda listens for a moment at the door. Then she goes up to the writing-table, takes out the packet of manuscript, peeps under the cover, draws a few of the sheets half out, and looks at them. Next she goes over and seats herself in the armchair beside the stove, with the packet in her lap.

Presently she opens the stove door, and then the packet.

HEDDA (*throws one of the quires into the fire and whispers to herself*): Now I'm burning your child, Thea!—Burning it, curly-locks! (*Throw-*

ing one or two more quires into the stove): Your child and Eilert Lövborg's. *(Throws the rest in.)* I am burning—I'm burning your child.

Hedda has intervened in life; she has moulded a man's destiny and destroyed the product of a more fruitful association. She is ready to retreat as her dominant instinct of privacy reasserts itself. This impression is derived from the set of Act IV:

> *The same rooms at the Tesmans'. It is evening. The drawing-room is in darkness. The back room is lighted by the hanging lamp over the table. The curtains over the glass door are drawn close.*
>
> *Hedda dressed in black, walks to and fro in the dark room. Then she goes into the back room and disappears for a moment to the left. She is heard to strike a few chords on the piano. Presently she comes in sight again, and returns to the drawing-room.*
>
> *Berta enters from the right, through the inner room, with a lighted lamp, which she places on the table in front of the corner settee in the drawing-room. . . . Hedda goes up to the glass door, lifts the curtain a little aside, and looks out into the darkness. . . .*

In strong contrast to the previous set, interest is centred on the inner room by the unusual lighting. The outer world, the "back way," is curtained off. We see Hedda enter her sanctuary; its essential privacy is emphasized when we hear her private piano. This pantomime lasts long enough for these impressions to sink in, then Ibsen reverts to more normal lighting. But before a word is spoken, Hedda reaffirms in action her renewed timidity—by peeping out into the darkness.

Reference to the draft shows that just those points which have been judged significant were late refinements:

> *The same room as the Tesmans'. It is evening. In the drawing-room a lighted lamp stands on the table in the corner to the right. The hanging lamp in the inner room is also lighted.*
>
> *(Hedda walks to and fro in the inner room and disappears for a moment to the left. She is heard to strike a few chords on the piano. Presently she comes in sight again, and enters the drawing-room.)*
>
> *(Berta enters from the right, through the inner room, with a lighted lamp, which she places on the writing table. . . .)*

The rooms were equally lighted; we know nothing about the curtains, but even if they were drawn, the effect of altered emphasis was not so strong as it is in the play. We did not actually see Hedda enter her sanctuary, nor did she peer into the darkness.

To return to the play: it is clear that, whatever her wishes, Hedda cannot retreat. She may have burnt Thea's child, but she is soon reminded of her own, which represents an infringement on her privacy that cannot be evaded and that must inevitably increase with time. Ibsen was right in making her pregnant, not to provide just another reason for her beha-viour[16] but as a symbol of encroachment by powers beyond her control; her condition subsumes all the other pressures being brought to bear on her and endows them with its own force and inevitability.

We are reminded of the heat which lies beneath her cold demeanor by yet another association with the stove:

TESMAN: Let me have the manuscript, Hedda! I will take it to him at once. Where is it?

HEDDA: (cold and immovable, leaning on the arm-chair):   I have not got it.

This recalls both the fact and manner of her participation in life, for the chair is the one she sat in to burn Lövborg's book. The draft did not contain this illuminating action.

The pressure grows, for even a despised husband must be kept quiet; she tells him that she did it for love of him; she lets him, at last, into the secret that she is expecting a baby. But these devices, so far from relieving the pressure on her, increase it, for they subject her to the absurd gratification of her husband:

HEDDA: Don't shout so. The servant might hear.

TESMAN (laughing in irrepressible glee):   The servant! Why, how ab-surd you are, Hedda. It's only my old Berta! Why, I'll tell Berta myself.

HEDDA (clenching her hands together in desperation):   Oh, it is killing me, it is killing me, all this!

She is sustained by the belief that she has influenced Lövborg towards a noble death, but her supports are knocked away, one by one, and the pressure grows: she realizes that Thea still surpasses her in courage and warmth, but she can still cling to the belief that she has brought about one noble deed.

Her triumph is reduced when the literary "child" comes to life again from notes which Thea has kept; and her sense of emotional inferiority is heightened when the "pretty fool" attracts into her sphere the despised husband and moves even a clod to devote his life to the reconstruction of the lost work; such a spirit in so vulgar a creature surprises her:

TESMAN: We shall manage it! We must! I will dedicate my life to this task.

HEDDA: You, George. Your life?

At this point, a startling thing happens: Hedda's sanctuary is occu-pied. Hitherto it has been used as a thoroughfare to the inner rooms of the house, but no one has stayed in it for long except on her orders (as Berta) or by her invitation (as Tesman, Brack and Thea). Now the inner room is to be invaded by two despised influences:

TESMAN: Where shall we sit? Here? No, in there, in the back room. Excuse me, my dear Judge. Come with me, Mrs. Elvsted. (*Tesman and Mrs. Elvsted go into the back room. She takes off her hat and cloak. They both sit down at the table under the hanging lamp, and are soon deep in an eager examination of the papers. Hedda crosses to the stove and sits in the arm-chair.* . . .)

We are once again reminded of the hot violence that lies hidden in her.

While Tesman's use of the room represents visually one aspect of the retaliation for Hedda's deed, Brack exerts a more direct pressure in the outer room. He demolishes Hedda's sustaining illusion; so far from shooting himself beautifully in the temple or breast, Lövborg was shot accidentally in the bowels during a squabble at Mlle Diana's. Hedda's intervention has failed utterly:

HEDDA (*looks up at him with an expression of loathing*): That too! Oh, what curse is it that makes everything I touch turn ludicrous and mean?

Failure does not remove the pressure. Brack tells her that her pistol has been found on the body. Tesman and Thea move to occupy the most personal piece of furniture on the stage, Hedda's writing-desk; the retreat is left open. Hedda takes the pistols into the inner room and returns to sit by the symbolic stove, with Brack in a position of superiority: "(*Hedda goes over to the stove, and seats herself on one of the footstools. Brack stands over her, leaning on the arm-chair.*)"

He points out the alternatives: silence on his part and compliance from Hedda, or a scandal in the courts where she will be coupled with Mlle Diana as a woman in the case. This is the most extreme pressure, and her reaction is equally extreme, as we have come to expect: ". . . Subject to your will and your demands. A slave, a slave then! (*Rises impetuously.*) No, I cannot endure the thought of that! Never!"

Brack may laugh, but we have been warned. Her mind made up, Hedda can imitate Tesman's hated intonations, and touch Thea's envied wealth of hair, because she can now escape from her humiliation.

The final scene recalls the earlier business with the curtains which served to characterize Hedda: "(*Hedda goes into the back room and draws the curtains. A short pause. Suddenly she is heard playing a wild dance on the piano.*) The sound tells us better than words can of the sudden wildness in her. Her drawing the curtains reminds us of the scene in Act I when she had the curtains drawn to shade the sun.[17] Tesman summarizes the pressure brought to bear on her, and we see again her typical gesture of reaction:

TESMAN (*runs to the doorway*):   Why, my dearest Hedda — don't play dance-music to-night! Just think of Aunt Rina! And of Eilert too!

HEDDA (*puts her head out between the curtains*):   And of Aunt Julia. And of all the rest of them. — After this, I will be quiet. (*Closes the curtains again.*)

And there we have Hedda, in terms of the curtain symbol used so often throughout the play—the wild spirit making a brief appearance and then retiring, beaten, to a final refuge with her General father, the cause of her tragedy and its ultimate solution. The draft weakens the effect of the pantomime by not letting Hedda appear for the last time.

"Good God!—people don't do such things."—says Brack as he realizes that she has killed herself—beautifully. But then, Brack never knew her as well as we do.

If this analysis is correct, then the play is neither comical[18] nor clinical.[19] Comedy has a part, and so has piercing observation, but the sum is greater than both these together. We have seen "that supposedly undramatic thing, the picture not of an action but of a condition,"[20] restored to dramatic life by becoming the progress of a condition; we have seen natural endowment, smothered by social conditions to a mere smoulder,[21] grow hot from concealment until it bursts into sudden flame. But Hedda is no longer the poet she might have been,[22] she does not inspire—she destroys; and when her self-assertion implicates her beyond withdrawal, her distorted strength, her "demonic substratum"[23] is turned upon herself. We withhold our affection, admire her courage, and pity, surely, her suffering, pointless though it may be, in a predicament for which the blame rests, not upon her, but upon the forces represented by the General.

The frustration has been kept before us largely by means of visual suggestion, so that if we agree with Edmund Gosse that "there is no poetic suggestion here, no species of symbol," it is only because he means by this "white horse, or gnawing thing, or monster from the sea";[24] our informative details have been infinitely small, and ordinary; but they have been organized so precisely, into patterns so self-consistent, that through them we have become aware of the development of a character whose main failing was inarticulateness—a poet denied self-expression. Through visual suggestion we have come to know the stifling pressures and the fierce reaction; Hedda was not a cold woman; she seemed colourless, but she was white-hot. We have been reached, not by the novelist's technique operating solely through the mind, but through the eyes; never was Ibsen more a practising playwright than he was when he created *Hedda Gabler.*[25]

"We have studied our author under difficulties, for it is impossible to read him without perceiving that merely book in hand we but half know him—he addressed himself so substantially to representation."[26]

Notes

1. Extensive excerpts from "Hedda" are translated in *Archer*, XII, pp. 384–457, which also contains a brief selection of the other material, pp. 381–4. The play is translated in *Archer*, X.

2. See p. 150.

3. Comparison of these two uses of illustrative action provides ample evidence of the progress Ibsen has made in this particular technique. Overt symbolism has completely disappeared.

4. "The title of the play is *Hedda Gabler.* My intention in giving it this name was to indicate that Hedda as a personality is to be regarded rather as her father's daughter than as her husband's wife." Letter to Moritz Prozor, 4th December 1890. *Breve*, II, p. 193; *Correspondence*, p. 435.

The constant use of Hedda's maiden name performs another function: it emphasizes the gulf between her former and present state. "Gabler" has an aristocratic ring (while he was fumbling for it in the drafts, Ibsen toyed with the name "Rømer," but he had already used this, in the form "Boldt-Rømer" to arrive at the equally aristocratic "Rosmer" in *Rosmersholm*); "Tesman," on the other hand, has the unfortunate connotation of "worthlessness"; "tes" means "almost useless."

5. In a letter of 14th January 1891, Ibsen wrote: "George Tesman, his old aunts and their faithful servant Berta, together form a picture of complete and indissoluble unity. They have a common mode of thought, common memories, a common outlook on life. For Hedda they represent a power hostile and contrary to her fundamental nature. And so they must represent a mutual harmony in presentation." *S.V.*, XVIII, p. 280. The Norwegian original is contained in Appendix.

6. Jennette Lee actually sees Hedda as a pistol, by virtue of her appearance! "It is easy to understand her now — a pistol, deadly, simple, passionless and straight." *The Ibsen Secret*, p. 26.

7. Plate XVI in *Ibsen* by Lugné-Poë shows Eleanora Duse as Hedda at the National Theatre in Oslo. She is wearing her own hair, which is dark and abundant.

8. There is confirmation of this in jottings made by Ibsen between the completion of *Hedda* and the writing of the play proper. There he brings Act I to an end in this way: "Tesman and Hedda in brief conversation. Hedda goes into her room." *S.V.*, XI, p. 519.

9. It has been objected that however illuminating may be the physical details of Ibsen's characters, these features cannot be counterfeited by actors differently endowed. In fact Ibsen demands no more of the actor than competence in make-up. Reference to any book on make-up (for example, *The Art of Make-Up* by Helena Chalmers [Appleton & Co., New York, 1930]) will show what can be done. Ibsen himself was well aware of the value of appearance and of the means of achieving it: he wrote to H. Schrøder, 27th December 1890: "There is just one thing that bothers me, and that is that Mr. Reimers corresponds so little in appearance to the picture I wanted people to get of Eilert Løvborg. But with the help of make-up and costume no doubt quite a lot can be done to remedy that." *S.V.*, XVIII, p. 270. The Norwegian original is contained in Appendix.

10. Ibsen was more explicit in the jottings he made after "Hedda" had been started. Under the heading "Optegnelser" in *S.V.*, XI, p. 515, he makes Hedda say: "Remember I am the child of an old man — and a decrepit man at that — or at least a decaying one. Perhaps that has left its mark." The Norwegian original is contained in Appendix.

11. The hint of warning given by his too youthful appearance is faint, but it is reinforced by his name: Brack means "brackish," "fallow."

12. *Ibsen's Dramatic Technique*, p. 28.

13. See *Archer*, X, p. 62, note: also *The Proverb in Ibsen*, by Ansten Anstensen (Columbia University Press, 1936), p. 214. Note 996.

14. Ibsen has used clothes in this way before, in *Emperor and Galilean*, for example: ". . . *Prince Julian . . . his court-dress sits badly upon him . . .*" *Archer*, V, p. 8.

15. In evening dress. Perhaps Ibsen would have been wiser if he had described it. Henry James wrote in a letter of 7th October 1892: "Miss Achurch was so much better in the first act than at any moment of the D. H. (*Doll's House*, performed 5th October 1892) that

one hoped a real *coup* for her—but she went to pieces swiftly in lemon-coloured satin (!!!) . . . She makes a loud, showy, belle-femme, Medusa-Thea." *Theatre and Friendship* by Elizabeth Robins (Jonathan Cape, London, 1932), p. 71.

16. "I will not say that Ibsen understood the psychological relations which present-day science has taught us to see. An indication that he did not is in the excessive number of reasons that he gives for Hedda's actions." *Koht*, p. 257. Professor Downs notes that Ibsen did not commit himself, either in the case of Hedda or Ellida, to the idea that pregnancy was responsible for their behaviour. See *Ibsen — The Intellectual Background* by Brian Downs (C.U.P., 1946), p. 162, footnote.

17. It is interesting to note that in the draft the curtains in Act I were to have been venetian blinds [6]. Did Ibsen make the alteration in order to connect the window with the curtain over the middle doorway?

18. "*Hedda Gabler* is probably an ironical pleasantry." Henry James, *The Scenic Art*, ed. Allan Wade (Rupert Hart-Davis, London, 1949), p. 250. Dr. Bradbrook considers the play a sardonic comedy: *Ibsen the Norwegian* p. 119.

19. "*Hedda Gabler* is simply a spectacle of life from which we retire with a shock." Weigand, *The Modern Ibsen*, p. 244.

20. *The Scenic Art*, p. 250.

21. "J'ai voulu, me répondit-il, montrer ce que produit le contact de deux milieux sociaux qui ne peuvent s'entendre." *Hedda Gabler, traduit par M. Prozor* (Paris, 1891), p. 5.

22. "Eleanora Duse has created Hedda over again, as a poet would have created her, and has made a wonderful creature whom Ibsen never conceived, or at least never rendered. Ibsen has tried to add his poetry by way of ornament, and gives us a trivial and inarticulate poet about whom float certain catchwords . . . vine-leaves in the hair." *Eleanora A. Duse* by Arthur Symons (Mathews, London, 1926), p. 98. It is clear from this that Ibsen makes his point, but it is considered an unsympathetic one, and is therefore changed.

Ibsen's own notes contain the following: "There is poetry deep down inside Hedda. But the environment frightens her. Just fancy, making a laughing-stock of herself!" *S.V.*, p. 501. "Brack is well aware that it is H.'s repression, her hysteria, which is really the motive force in all her behaviour." *S.V.*, p. 510. The Norwegian originals are contained in Appendix.

23. Ibsen's phrase (*det dæmoniske underlag*) occurs in a letter to H. Schrøder, 27th December 1890, *S.V.*, XVIII, p. 270.

24. *Ibsen* in *Literary Lives* series, ed. W. Robertson Nicoll (Hodder and Stoughton, London, 1908), p. 190.

25. "But towards the end of his life, Ibsen became less of a dramatist and more of a novelist. . . . Ibsen's sense of significant detail soon overestimated the capacity of any stage or the attention of any audience." Tennant, *Ibsen's Dramatic Technique*, p. 77. Dr. Bradbrook's conclusion is more acceptable: "In *Hedda Gabler* the screw is turned so tightly that Ibsen has achieved the perfect specimen piece — *Hedda Gabler* is so finished a production that it brought Ibsen himself to a full stop, and he began again in a new way. . . ." *Ibsen the Norwegian*, p. 97.

26. *The Scenic Art*, p. 245.

The Exposition

P. F. D. Tennant*

In primitive drama exposition is bound to be crude, as with the Greeks and with the medieval church drama, because the play represents myths or legends which are already known to the spectators, and therefore the devices of suspense and surprising revelation are unnecessary. The exposition in these cases took the form of direct narrative. It survived in literary drama until the eighteenth century and can be seen on the popular stage at the present day. "I am the villain of the piece," followed by a roll of drums and purple lights, one of the conventions of exposition in Victorian melodrama, is of exactly the same nature as the narrative introduction in morality plays. "Asides," stage whispers and explanatory monologues are a form of this primitive narrative exposition in literary drama.

The monologue exposition, a form of introductory prologue, lived on after the middle ages in the literary comedies of Holberg, in Lessing's and Goethe's drama and in Scribe's plays, so that we are not surprised to find Ibsen's first play, *Catilina*, following the same principles. The transition from religious to secular drama was, however, accompanied by a new demand for realistic illusion, and in obedience to these demands the naïve narrative exposition tended to become more sophisticated and realistic. D'Aubignac advised the French classical dramatists to avoid the monologue and to use other devices, such as confidants, conversations between master and servant, and discussions between servants alone.

Ibsen makes use of confidants very frequently. Mrs. Linde is Nora's confidant in *A Doll's House*, and Dr. Herdal acts as Solness's confidant in *The Master Builder*. But the *pièce à thèse* in France had already transformed the confidant into the *raisonneur* character. The raisonneur-confidant recurs often with Ibsen in his modern plays: Dr. Rank in *A Doll's House* and Dr. Relling in *The Wild Duck* are two outstanding examples. But in his later work Ibsen eliminated these mouthpiece characters almost entirely, beginning with *Rosmersholm*. Confidences between master and servant were a traditional element of *bourgeois* drama and more particularly of comedy. This method of exposition occurs twice with Ibsen in his modern plays, in *Hedda Gabler* and *Rosmersholm*. Conversations between servants alone, as in the case of *Romeo and Juliet*, are used for the purposes of exposition by the great majority of dramatists, and were particularly favoured by Goethe and Schiller and the German domestic dramatists Iffland and Kotzebue. Ibsen adopted this type very early in *Lady Inger*, where it is obviously inspired by Shakespeare, and later on in *The Wild Duck*, where Pettersen the butler and a hired servant from outside clumsily recapitulate the preamble to the Werle-Ekdal family

*Originally published in *Ibsen's Dramatic Technique* (Cambridge: Cambridge University Press, 1948), 89–109. Reprinted by permission of Humanities Press International, Inc.

history before the guests leave the dining-room after dinner. This is Ibsen's nearest approach to the ungainly method so much exploited by Dumas fils of letting characters tell one another things they obviously know already. Such expositions are usually avoided by Ibsen.

In avoiding direct narration, exposition came to depend very largely on allusion, direct or indirect, or on inadvertent remarks. In *The Merchant of Venice* Portia's love for Bassanio is confirmed by a slip of the tongue when she says (Act III, Sc. 2): "One half of me is yours, the other half yours, / Mine own, I would say." S. Freud has pointed out a similar instance in Schiller's *Wallenstein*. Subtleties of this nature are also used by Ibsen. In *Rosmersholm* Rosmer reveals his intimate relations with Rebekka when he, in the presence of Rector Kroll, refers to Rebekka by her Christian name and then corrects himself to "Miss West." Allusions are also necessary not only for revelation of relationships between people but to preserve the continuity of the action. The unity of action in *Ghosts*, for instance, is a result of the suspense and expectancy aroused by breaking off questions and postponing their answers till the ensuing act. Act II is closely bound to Act I by the question asked by Manders at the end of the latter, concerning Regine's identity. This is revealed in Act II and the action is accelerated until it is checked at the end of the act by another question. Will Mrs. Alving have the courage to free herself from the ghosts that haunt her and tell the truth to Osvald without ideals suffering in consequence? In Act III she tells the ungarnished truth, only to find that her ideals of uprightness were only another ghost, and the play ends with the tense question of whether she will be able to rid herself of this last obsession and give Osvald the fatal dose of morphia.

Continuity of time is preserved in *The Wild Duck* without the necessity of descriptive stage directions. In Act III Gina says to Hjalmar: "I am only expecting the two sweethearts who are to be taken together. . . . I booked them an appointment for this afternoon when you'll be having your nap." Act IV opens with Gina at the door saying good-bye to her clients on the stairs, and the room is so arranged that one can see a photograph has just been taken. Thus without any further indication we realize that the act begins on the afternoon of the same day as Act III. Ibsen's method of exposition is always most careful in preserving the continuity of acts by allusions such as these.

The most characteristic feature of Ibsen's technique of exposition is, however, his use of what may be called the retrospective method, a technique employed by Sophocles, by Racine and to a certain extent by Hebbel. That is to say, he prefers to begin his tragedy just before the catastrophe and to make the dialogue unravel the preceding events in retrospect, instead of presenting the actual events in succession on the stage. This type of exposition concentrates the action into a very small space of time, in conformity with the realistic desire to observe the unities. It is also, as it happens, a type of exposition favoured by the traditional fate-tragedy, the dramatic conflict in all cases being between past and present, the sins of the past contrasting violently with the calm atmosphere of the present and swiftly destroying the idyll as retribution approaches. The dramatic contrast between the beginnings and endings of Ibsen's plays is dependent for its effect on this type of exposition. In *Pillars of Society* the false atmosphere of calm at the sewing party is dispersed as the past is revealed step by step and brings about the fall of the self-righteous consul. In *Ghosts* the play opens with Regine watering flowers, in *Rosmersholm* Rebekka is arranging flowers in the morning-room as the curtain rises, and in *Hedda Gabler* Aunt Julia arrives in the first scene to greet the young married couple with a bouquet. Nothing could however be more characteristic of Ibsen than the endings of these plays, Osvald going mad, Rebekka and Rosmer throwing themselves into the mill-race, and Hedda shooting herself.

The first instance of this type of exposition is to be found in the historical play *Warriors of Helgeland* (1857), though the dramatic revelations of many of the earlier plays concern past sins. The method was then dropped and not used again until 1877 with *Pillars of Society*. From now on, with one exception, in the comedy *An Enemy of the People*, Ibsen never abandons this technique and he evolves a formula for its application which is particularly characteristic of his style. He presents first of all an idyllic picture of a household living its everyday life. Then this little fenced-in world is suddenly broken into by a visitor from the world outside. He or she is an old friend of the family who has not been seen for several years. These meetings of old friends are the pivot of nearly all Ibsen's plays and they are followed up by a perfectly natural exchange of recollections and inquiries about the intervening period during which the friends have not seen one another. It is these inquiries which open up old wounds and bring about the catastrophe. An exposition of this nature is obviously more realistic than most since it eliminates the necessity of asides and explanatory monologues, because the characters can tell one another what they otherwise would have to communicate direct to the audience. It can also deal with almost unlimited periods of time and extensions of space without exerting the spectator's imagination to any great extent. In plays like *Pillars of Society*, *Ghosts*, *Hedda Gabler* and *When We Dead Awaken*, although the drama is enacted in a restricted space (in the same room in the first three, in the same district in the last) the action actually concerns not only local events, but happenings in America, Paris, a European tour, and on the Starnberger See. The time extension is also great, and becomes progressively greater as Ibsen himself grows older and feels the power of the past over his conscience. The earlier modern plays concern young people, while the later plays are definitely based on a conflict of youth and age, so that in Ibsen's last work we find the old sculptor atoning for sins which he had committed as a very young man.

There are certain technical difficulties, of course, in this type of exposition which Ibsen often found it hard to surmount. Persons who have not met for a long time are inclined to involve themselves in explanations which would be tedious on the stage and would hold up the action. Dumas fils and Scribe had a ready solution by which they made them into schoolfriends. Ibsen, however, simplified this by very often relating the characters to one another so that there is no need of introduction. The mechanism creaks at points, and the cold light of reason reveals improbabilities which are hidden to an absorbed audience. In *The Wild Duck*, for instance, Gregers has not seen Hjalmar for seventeen years, and his warm friendship is a little hard to explain when we realize that he knows nothing of Hjalmar's occupation, nor of his wife or their fifteen year old daughter; but Ibsen here covers his tracks by allusions to a correspondence between them which has come to a standstill.

This type of exposition is also helped out by the device of repetition which has already been referred to when discussing the use of fate, the fatal objects, words and actions which are associated with the repetition of fatal catastrophes. Heredity also plays its part here, as in *The Wild Duck*, where Ibsen at the last moment introduced the element of Hedvig's weak eyesight, which immediately refers the spectator to Werle's weak eyes and arouses the suspicion, which is later confirmed, that Hedvig is Werle's illegitimate daughter. In this case Ibsen makes very effective use of dramatic irony. In Act II Hjarlmar tells Gregers that Hedvig may become blind. Gregers asks him to explain it and Hjalmar remarks with a sigh: "Heredity, of course." Gregers starts back and exclaims, "Heredity!" thinking with the audience of his own weak-sighted father. But Hjalmar has no suspicions and attributes Hedvig's bad eyesight to her great grandmother, not realizing the real connection until the end of the fourth act. Previously the only clues were to be found by doing a little mental arithmetic with the dates of Hjalmar's marriage and Hedvig's birth. In the same way, in *Rosmersholm*, the fact that Rebekka is Dr. West's illegitimate daughter is demonstrated indirectly by a comparison of dates. The skillful use of allusion is seen again in the latter play when we realize how Rebekka has unwittingly committed incest and been her father's mistress, solely from her expression of unspeakable horror when Dr. West is revealed as her father. A brilliant use of allusion is seen again in the case of *Hedda Gabler*, in which play Hedda's pregnancy is communicated to the spectator without any direct reference, simply by Hedda's behaviour and her annoyance when Tesman compliments her on getting plump. It is not till some time after that Aunt Julia and later Tesman realize her condition and mention it in veiled language. Allusion again is all-important in *The Wild Duck*, for the duck itself is hardly seen and only gains significance by allusion and description.

Ibsen's manipulation of exits and entrances also assists the exposition and increases the suspense of the gradual revelations. In the drawing-room drama of Ibsen's predecessors, new characters were introduced in order to help out the action by bringing in a letter, taking a message or imparting new information. Ibsen introduces new characters in order to break off the conversation and create suspense by putting off revelations until the catastrophe is due. Traces of this method can be found in his early Bergen work, but it was not evolved to technical perfection until the writing of *Emperor and Galilean*. Instances in the later plays abound. Reference has already been made to the suspense caused by the endings of the acts in *Ghosts*. A similar suspense is brought about by the entrances in *The Lady from the Sea*. Lyngstrand comes in and breaks off the conversation between Ellida and Arnholm just as she is about to confide her strange obsessions to him; just as Ellida is going to tell Wangel about the stranger she is broken off by Bolette and the arrival of the excursion party. Not until the end of the act does she reveal the extent of her fears to Wangel, and then with the arrival of the stranger in the third act the drama begins to develop unchecked. In *Rosmersholm* the action is punctuated by the two appearances of Rosmer's old tutor Brendel, the first at the beginning of the play, which starts the catastrophe, the second at the end, when he gives Rosmer and Rebekka the solution to their dilemma by his indirect references to suicide. These exits and entrances are always well motivated in the later plays, and the characters have given up their tendency to turn up on demand as they did previously.

In order to comprehend the full skill of Ibsen's exposition it is easiest to consider one play in its entirety. *The Wild Duck* is excellent for this purpose, as it is a good example of Ibsen's mature technique. This play covers a period of almost two days on the stage, but the action is taken as representing the precipitation of a tragedy which has been ripening for over seventeen years. The catalyst in the play is Gregers Werle, who returns after having been away for seventeen years. Gradually, by his questions and conversations with various characters, the past is unveiled, a hidden sin is revealed and finds its drastic retribution in the suicide of the little illegitimate girl Hedvig. The action progresses by a series of references to the past which are accompanied by allusions to four other factors. These are namely, Werle's weak eyesight, Hedvig's weak eyesight, the suggestive presence of the duck and the fatal pistol, and they bring about the immediate tragedy. Suspense is achieved by putting off revelations, which are interrupted by the entrance of a character or the end of an act. The time factors and the other four factors referred to are represented on the accompanying chart, which shows diagrammatically how the action progresses by repeated digressions and allusions. The continually interrupted references to the past do not give a full picture of what has happened until Relling describes Hjalmar's youth to Gregers in the beginning of the last act, and then it is left to the last two factors, the wild duck itself and the fatal pistol, to consummate the tragedy in the present.

The following analysis of *The Wild Duck* traces the development of the action as it is diagrammatically presented on the chart:

ACT I. *Werle's drawing-room. Evening.*

Two servants are talking. Werle is celebrating the return of his son Gregers by a dinner-party. Old Ekdal passes through the room to the office, and we learn that this broken old man has once been a lieutenant and previously Werle's business partner, but that he has served a term of imprisonment for some mysterious timber speculation of an illicit nature. He now does copying work for Werle.

The guests leave the dining-room and pass on into the music-room.

Gregers and Hjalmar remain behind. They recall old times and ask questions. They have not met for 17 years. After the disaster to his father, Ekdal, Hjalmar had to abandon his studies and took up photography for a living, with the financial assistance of Gregers's father. On his instigation also he married Gina, Werle's housekeeper, who had looked after the household during Mrs. Werle's fatal illness.

The guests return. We notice Werle has weak eyes and cannot stand the light. They exchange witticisms and Hjalmar is ridiculed.

Old Ekdal, who has been unable to escape from the office, now makes his way out through the room and causes extreme embarrassment to Werle and Hjalmar by his presence. Hjalmar leaves. Mrs. Sørby takes the guests to another room.

Gregers is left alone with his father and reproaches him for leaving the Ekdals destitute. Werle protests that he assists them as far as is compatible with his position without arousing suspicion. Ekdal does copying work for the office, and Werle has made it financially possible for Hjalmar to become a photographer and to marry. Gregers accuses his father of having had illicit relations with Gina and of having disposed of her conveniently by marrying her off to Hjalmar. Werle attributes these rumours to his late wife's neurotic jealousy, denies them and offers Gregers a partnership in the family firm. Gregers suspects a hidden motive, finds his father intends to marry his housekeeper, Mrs. Sørby, decides to leave his father's house for good and announces his intention of fulfilling his life's mission. Curtain. (Suspense caused by Gregers's refusal to say what his mission is.)

ACT II. *Hjalmar's studio. Same evening.*

Gina and Hedvig, the 14 year old daughter, are waiting for Hjalmar to come home. Hedvig is peering with her weak eyes over a book. They discuss household affairs.

Old Ekdal comes home with his work and a bottle of drink concealed in his pocket. Before going into his room he opens the door of the garret and exclaims: "They're all asleep. She's lying in her basket." (First veiled allusion to the duck.)

While the women are discussing him Ekdal comes in again and fetches hot water from the kitchen to make himself a drink, under the pretext of using it to dissolve his clotted ink.

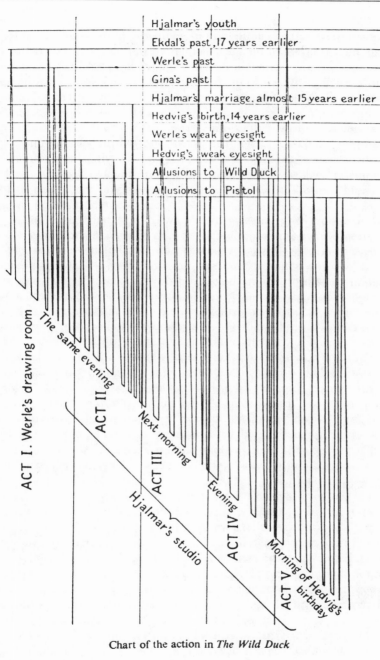

Hjalmar's youth

Ekdal's past, 17 years earlier

Werle's past

Gina's past

Hjalmar's marriage, almost 15 years earlier

Hedvig's birth, 14 years earlier

Werle's weak eyesight

Hedvig's weak eyesight

Allusions to Wild Duck

Allusions to Pistol

ACT I. Werle's drawing room

The same evening

ACT II

Next morning

ACT III

Hjalmar's studio

Evening

ACT IV

Morning of Hedvig's birthday

ACT V

Chart of the action in *The Wild Duck*

Hjalmar returns from the party, Ekdal enters again and they all listen while Hjalmar boasts of his social success and disappoints Hedvig by having forgotten to bring any tit-bits, consoling her instead with the menu. He talks to his father about the inhabitants of the attic (suspense of veiled language) and Ekdal then returns to his room for a drink, pretending to clean his pipe.

Hjalmar then becomes testy, but is soothed by beer and food and finally consents to play the flute.

This idyllic family scene is then broken into by Gregers, who is given a hearty welcome. (Arrival of the messenger from the outside world and transformation of idyll into catastrophe.) Hjalmar confides to him that Hedvig is in danger of becoming blind and that her ailment is hereditary. Gregers thinks immediately of his own father, but Hjalmar is referring to Hedvig's great-grandmother. They eat sandwiches and drink beer. Hjalmar tells Gregers that Hedvig is fourteen and that her birthday is in two days' time. He also explains rather awkwardly, but with a certain sense of sly pride, that he has been married fifteen years all but a few months. Old Ekdal enters and they all sit down and eat together.

Ekdal then goes and opens the garret to show Gregers the wonders it contains, and points out in the dark the pigeons and rabbits and the wild duck in its basket. The doors are then shut. (First direct allusion to the duck.)

The duck was wounded by Werle out shooting and it was given to Ekdal by the butler. Ekdal goes to sleep. Gregers agrees to rent one of Gina's rooms as a lodger and, using Ekdal's words, he expresses his desire to be a well-trained retriever so as to bring wounded wild ducks to the surface when they dive to the bottom. Exeunt Gregers and Hjalmar.

Gina is puzzled, but Hedvig suspects a meaning in Gregers's symbolical language. Hjalmar returns full of satisfaction at having got his old friend as a lodger, and in spite of Gina's premonitions of disaster he assures her of a bright future.

ACT III. *Hjalmar's studio. Next morning.*

Hjalmar tells Gina that Gregers and the two other lodgers, Dr. Relling and Molvik, are coming to breakfast. He sits down grudgingly to touch up photographs. Ekdal enters and they persuade one another to stop working and to play in the garret instead. They open the doors and it is revealed in full sunshine. (Only view of garret and inhabitants in whole play.) The floor and inhabitants of the garret are then concealed from view by a sail-cloth to keep the animals from straying. The upper part is visible through a fishing net. Ekdal enters the garret.

Gina comes in to lay breakfast and Hjalmar immediately insists on using the table for his work. Gina leaves and Hedvig comes in, persuades her father to join Ekdal in the garret and help him move the duck's trough.

She asks to do the photographs for him and he consents when she promises not to strain her eyes. Hjalmar goes.

Gregers enters and talks to Hedvig. They discuss the garret, she tells him of the strange things she has found there, says she often thinks of it as the bottom of the sea. He asks her the strange question if she is quite sure that it is not the bottom of the sea, and Gina enters and breaks off their conversation. (Suspense.)

The table is laid and a shot is suddenly fired in the attic. (First allusion to pistol.) Hjalmar comes out with a smoking pistol and tells Hedvig not to touch it as one of the barrels is loaded. He lays it on a shelf and Gregers looks into the garret and describes the duck which is invisible to the audience. (Allusion.)

Gina and Hedvig go out and leave Hjalmar and Gregers alone. The doors of the garret are shut. Hjalmar confides to Gregers that he leaves to his wife the menial work of the photography business because he himself is occupied with an important photographic invention of a very vague nature with which to fulfil his life's mission, namely the rehabilitation of the family name. He describes the sufferings of his father's disgrace and tells of the fatal pistol with which he and his father had both almost committed suicide. Instead of ending his life he had determined to dedicate it to a mission, to make the name of Ekdal famous by his invention and to make it possible for his father to wear his uniform again. He takes a nap after lunch every day, and hopes for inspiration while his faith in himself is supported by the encouragement of the lodger Dr. Relling. Gregers is just about to tell Hjalmar the truth when he is interrupted by Gina and Hedvig bringing in the breakfast and the arrival of the guests Relling and Molvik. (Suspense.)

The latter have been on the razzle the night before, and when Ekdal emerges from the garret with a newly flayed rabbit-skin Molvik's stomach is turned and he has to leave the table. Relling flatters Hjalmar, who preens himself on his family happiness, while Gregers protests. Relling threatens to eject Gregers if he will not hold his tongue, the latter turns to leave and at the door meets his father (surprise), who asks to speak to him alone. The others withdraw discreetly.

Werle refers to the mission of which Gregers had spoken in his last conversation and warns him that he will not help Hjalmar by revealing to him the circumstances of his marriage. Gregers refuses to renounce his mission and Werle leaves.

The others return and Gregers expresses a wish to go out for a walk with Hjalmar. Relling advises against such a course, but Hjalmar goes and Hedvig is left perplexed at all the inexplicable complications.

Act IV. *Hjalmar's studio. Afternoon of same day.*

Gina and Hedvig are waiting for Hjalmar to return from his walk.

Hjalmar enters. He has been enlightened about the past by Gregers. He is peevish and touchy and threatens to strangle the wild duck, a gift soiled by Werle's hands. He promises the distressed Hedvig, however, that he will refrain and tells her to go out and get some fresh air.

Hjalmar faces Gina alone (*scène à faire*) and she confesses to her former relations with Werle.

Gregers enters in high spirits, but is distressed when he finds that his action has not met with the desired result.

Relling comes in and curses Gregers for his interference and begs them all at any rate to be careful of Hedvig who is at the strange and impressionable age of puberty.

Mrs. Sørby breaks in upon them, announces that she is leaving in order to get married to Werle. Relling, an old flame of hers, leaves dejected and invites Hjalmar to join him and Molvik in a drinking bout to drown their sorrows. Mrs. Sørby explains Werle's need of a wife because of his approaching blindness. Hjalmar is surprised, and she goes with his assurances that he intends to repay with interest all that he has received from Werle and to assert his independence. Gregers praises Hjalmar for his moral idealism and Hjalmar expresses a sense of regret that Werle, and not he, should finally contract the ideal marriage.

Hedvig comes in, Mrs. Sørby has given her a present which she is not to open till her birthday. Hjalmar insists on opening it on the spot and it turns out to contain a deed of gift to Hedvig from Werle. Hedvig reads it and at the sight of her weak eyes Hjalmar sees her relationship to Werle; he becomes frantic and she is told harshly to get out of his sight and go out of the room. He tears the deed of gift in half, and then challenges Gina, asking if Hedvig is his child or no. She confesses she is uncertain, he decides to leave the house. Hedvig's distressed pleadings are unheard and Hjalmar stamps out of the room. Gina follows him and Gregers is left alone with Hedvig.

Gregers suggests to Hedvig that she will regain her father's affection if she sacrifices the duck for him. Gina comes back to say that Hjalmar has gone out with Relling and Molvik, and Gregers leaves with a reminder to Hedvig to remember the duck.

ACT V. *Hjalmar's studio. The morning of Hedvig's birthday.*

Old Ekdal goes into the garret, and Gina and Hedvig are waiting for Hjalmar to come back. Gregers comes to inquire after him and Relling enters to say that he is asleep, snoring in his room. Gina and Hedvig exit and leave Gregers and Relling alone.

Relling undermines Gregers's belief in Hjalmar's ideal personality, and analyses him as the product of an upbringing by two maiden aunts, of admiration by those around him; a conglomerate of other people's ideas and expressions, a person who cannot survive without illusion as the stimulating principle of life. Hedvig enters and Relling leaves.

Gregers reminds Hedvig of his suggestion about sacrificing the duck and he leaves as Ekdal emerges from the garret. Hedvig asks him the best way to shoot a duck and he tells her. He goes into his room and she fingers with the pistol on the shelf and replaces it as her mother comes in. Hedvig goes to see to the coffee in the kitchen, and Hjalmar at last enters.

He has come to collect his belongings before leaving for good, and rejects all Hedvig's advances when she looks out of the kitchen. He turns his back on her and goes into his room, followed by Gina.

Hedvig in despair suddenly remembers her promise to Gregers, exclaims, "the wild duck," takes the pistol from the shelf and hurries into the garret.

Hjalmar and Gina return. He looks for his pistol, finds it has gone and supposes his father is using it in the garret. He proceeds to eat the food which Gina has prepared, then decides to remain at home a day or so, and finally sets about sticking together the deed of gift which he had torn the day before.

Gregers enters and Gina leaves. He assures Hjalmar of Hedvig's devotion and promises that he will be given proof of it; Hjalmar in turn expresses his affection for Hedvig, but demands a sign. He wonders what answer she would give if she were asked to sacrifice her life for his. A shot is heard from the garret. (Dramatic irony.) Gregers utters an exclamation of joy believing that she has persuaded Old Ekdal to shoot her duck. But suddenly the old man comes out of his room. They then open the doors and find that she has not shot the duck but herself.

Relling responds to their cries for assistance and states that she is dead. The drunk Molvik enters and lends an atmosphere of macabre humour to the scene. Hjalmar and Gina, united in their sorrow, carry out the corpse and leave Relling to pronounce a cynical epilogue in his last words to Gregers, the bungling idealist.

The Wild Duck gives a good example of Ibsen's method of exposition, and his expositions are some of the most characteristic features of his technique. In his use of monologues and asides his general tendency is to evolve realistic conventions. In the treatment of the general features of his exposition this tendency has also been obvious. What we now accept as plain conventions, the retrospective analysis, the manipulation of exits, entrances and curtains to cause suspense and tension, the idyllic beginning and the drastic ending, the use of the meeting and the introduction of the conventional character from the world outside, these were all conventions adopted in the name of realistic illusion, and these conventions were elaborated in conscious reaction to an equally rigid form that had dominated the theatre previously. Ibsen's method of exposition was of great consequence for the theatre of his successors, and it was adopted wholesale by imitators in England such as Shaw, Galsworthy and Granville-Barker.

The use of asides is associated in particular with conventionalized French intrigue drama. It owes its origin to comedy, and has been handed down as a useful means of exposition from classical times, being in turn adopted by Italian, Spanish and English authors. Molière and Holberg have exploited its effects in modern times perhaps more than any comic dramatists of repute. The function of the aside is to throw light on a situation or to reveal any motive or intentions which may be obscure to the audience. It is essentially a secret between the actor and the audience, and is understood not to be heard by the other characters on the stage.

Asides were an unknown thing in tragedy. But the *bourgeois* drama of the eighteenth century revelled in them. This element of comic machinery had clung to the sentimental comedies of Steele, and, as this form of play gradually evolved into the *bourgeois* tragedy, the aside still remained as an essential feature. The first famous *bourgeois* tragedy, Lillo's *London Merchant*, has no less than twenty-three asides. With the standardization of the *drame* in France the aside became incorporated into the technique of the stage in tragedy as well as comedy. The intrigue drama of the nineteenth century, in the hands of its great exponent Eugène Scribe, adopted the aside as a technical convention. The first reaction against the artificiality of the aside came from Dumas fils, who claimed by its suppression in *La Dame aux Camélias*, *Diane de Lys*, and *Le Demi-Monde* to have attained a greater illusion of reality. Gottsched and, later, Lessing as early as 1750 demanded a realistic motivation for the aside (*Beitr. zur Hist. und Aufnahme des Theaters*) and the German *bourgeois* dramatists Kotzebue and Iffland were in fact the first European dramatists to moderate their use of it. Hebbel, though he uses it rarely, never abandons it altogether.

Ibsen's early works reveal a complete dependence on the traditional Scribe technique in the use of asides. His first two works *Catilina* and *The Warrior's Barrow*, and the fragmentary two acts of *The Ptarmigan of Justedal*, do not however contain in all more than five asides, whereas in his short political satire *Norma*, one of the four asides is introduced with a note for special comic effect. It was only after his contact with the practical theatre that Ibsen realized the stage effectiveness of the aside. On his European study tour in 1852 he wrote a comedy, *Midsummer Eve*, which has no less than some twenty-five asides. His next play, *Lady Inger of Østråt*, contained more than twice that number (fifty-nine), and there are few things which show so strikingly Ibsen's advance in realistic technique as the revised edition of that play in 1874 in which the number of asides were reduced to five in all. The same was the case with the play that followed, *The Feast at Solhaug*. In the original version this short play contained twenty-one asides which were all excluded in the revised edition of 1883. The next play, *Olaf Liljekrans*, written in 1856, is the last play to contain asides, in the stage directions. *The Warriors of Helgeland*, written in the following year, inaugurates the complete elimination of asides from

Ibsen's work. After Brandes had criticized the nature of the dialogue in *The Pretenders* and Ibsen had revised the play with particular attention to realistic illusion, he wrote to Brandes (June 26th, 1869) speaking of the corrections he had made and thanking him for his criticism. He referred to work on a play in hand (*The League of Youth*) which he said "is written in prose and as a consequence has a strongly realistic colouring. I have treated the form with care and amongst other things have succeeded in the achievement of managing to do without a single monologue, yes, even without a single aside." These remarks have led many people to date Ibsen's so-called realistic technique from this play. As far as monologues and asides are concerned we see, however, that they were reduced and eliminated much earlier. But while the stage direction aside disappears from the text, we find its function being substituted by stage whispers and thinking aloud. Stage whispers are an advance in objectivity because they no longer permit the character to act as a direct mouthpiece of the author. The aside breaks the continuity of the drama by reason of its undramatic nature as a commentary or explanation of the action by the author. The stage whisper, on the other hand, is realistically motivated. The characters continue the action by whispering to one another, not by confiding in the audience, with the intention that the audience shall hear what they are saying, while they appear to be speaking so that other characters on the stage shall not overhear them. Thinking aloud is merely a formally realistic development of the aside. It differs from the monologue in that the character is not alone on the stage and from the aside in that the character appears to talk to himself and does not address his remarks direct to the audience. With Ibsen it becomes even more realistic in later plays, when it is overheard by another character and is used for the development of the dialogue.

The way in which the stage whisper and thinking aloud replaced the aside may be seen by comparing the original and the revised versions of *Lady Inger of Østråt* and *The Feast at Solhaug*. In the 1857 edition of *Lady Inger* there are fifty-nine asides. In the 1874 edition there are only five. Twenty-three asides were completely suppressed, but seventeen were formally replaced by stage whispers, and fourteen by thinking aloud. In the 1855 edition of *The Feast at Solhaug* there were twenty-one asides. In the 1883 edition there were none. Two were suppressed completely, thirteen were replaced by whispers and six replaced by thinking aloud.

Effective illustrations of Ibsen's development with regard to the aside may be found in comparing plays of two different periods. In *Olaf Liljekrans*, which was written in 1856, we can find a snatch of dialogue such as the following: Olaf and Ingeborg meet in the mountains. They have run away from one another and a search party is heard approaching. Each is convinced that the other is in command of the search party which is hunting for them.

INGEBORG (*aside*).   He must have ridden ahead.

OLAF (*aside*).   She must have come up here with her father to search for me.

INGEBORG (*aside*).   But I will not go with him.

OLAF (*aside*).   I refuse to move from here.

At the beginning of the third act of *Ghosts*, when everyone is returning home after the fire, Mrs. Alving, Regine and Manders are followed by Engstrand.

REGINE (*asks*).   What's the matter?

ENGSTRAND   Oh, it all came of that there prayer meeting, you see. (*in a low voice*) Now, my child, we've got the fellow! (*aloud*) And to think that it should be my fault that a thing like this should be Pastor Manders' doing!

In this case Engstrand is revealing his duplicity to the audience, not by addressing them a direct aside, but by preserving the illusion and whispering to his daughter. Here we see plainly how the conventional aside underwent with Ibsen a transformation so as to conform to the scheme for producing the illusion of the fourth wall.

The stage whisper itself undergoes many transformations as Ibsen becomes a progressively more versatile technician of the stage. It is used to increase the illusion of space on the stage which becomes characteristic from the writing of *A Doll's House* onwards. This is the first of Ibsen's plays in which we have a sense of the architectural plan of the house in which the play is performed, and this is due to the dialogue rather than to the setting or stage directions. The architectural plan is filled out by characters speaking off stage, before they enter, by references to other rooms while on the stage, by talking on stage to persons off stage and by whispering on stage so that persons off stage shall not hear. The garret in *The Wild Duck* is only revealed to the audience once during the performance, but allusions to its nature and contents produce a complete illusion of reality. We never see the mill-race or the bridge in *Rosmersholm*, but we know exactly where they are.

Ibsen adapted to his own ends the clap-trap settings of romantic melodrama with its trap-doors and secret passages, and with him this eerie atmosphere of locality was assisted with asides and stage whispers.

Hedda Gabler opens with a scene between Miss Tesman and the maid Berte, who both speak in whispers, thereby creating a feeling of suspense and indicating the imminent proximity of Hedda and Tesman. Likewise in *The Wild Duck* Gina speaks to Hedvig in a low voice so that old Ekdal shall not hear in the room next door. *The Master Builder* begins with an exchange of whispers indicative of the approach of Solness himself on the scene. There are endless instances of the realistic stage whisper to create suspense and a sense of space, beginning with *A Doll's House* and continuing to the end of Ibsen's work.

In order to avoid the improbable use of whispers on a restricted stage, Ibsen enlarges the stage, very frequently with the help of an inner room, and parades his characters backwards and forwards, leaving them on the fore-stage for opportunity to talk aloud of subjects which persons on the inner stage must not hear. When a person from the inner stage approaches them they react by changing the subject of conversation, not by a melodramatically whispered warning. In *Hedda Gabler* we have excellent instances of this. Hedda is seated on the fore-stage with Løvborg, exchanging reminiscences under the pretext of showing him photographs of her honeymoon tour. Whenever Tesman comes in from the inner room, where he is seated with Brack, she changes the subject of conversation without any intervening whisper and continues speaking in the same tone about the photographs. In the last act there is a similar scene. Tesman and Thea Elvsted are together at one side of the room piecing together Løvborg's work, while Brack at the other side of the room is blackmailing Hedda. In this case they converse aloud, but begin and conclude their conversation in whispers.

Ibsen also develops the stage whisper to complete realism, that is the whisper which is neither heard by characters on the stage nor by the audience. This again loads the atmosphere with suspense though it is a matter for the actor to give it its full dramatic significance.

In *Rosmersholm* Rebekka is talking to Rosmer, and Madam Helseth asks to speak to her. Rebekka asks her to wait, but she insists on a few words. Then the directions are as follows: "Rebekka goes to the door. Madam Helseth gives her a message. They whisper together. Madam Helseth gives a nod and goes out." Rosmer then asks agitatedly, "Was it anything for me?" Rebekka replies, "No, it was only about household matters. Now you ought to go and take a walk in the fresh air, Rosmer. You ought to take a really long walk." Only after a long conversation does he finally go. When he has gone out Rebekka calls for Madam Helseth and Rektor Kroll is shown in.

Another form of realistic whisper used by Ibsen is a development of the dumb-show whisper. It is the whisper which is inaudible to the audience but which is communicated to them by the audible reply of the person to whom it is addressed. Thus in *The Wild Duck* we read the following: Hedvig (puts her arm round Hjalmar's neck and whispers in his ear). Hjalmar. "No. No bread and butter now." This type of whisper does not recur often in Ibsen's plays. It has been adopted by later dramatists for telephone conversations.

These are the variations which the aside undergoes in its contribution to the realistic illusion of Ibsen's plays. It disappeared in its most primitive form in 1857 with *The Warriors of Helgeland*, the first play in which he used the technique of retrospective exposition. It was probably the adoption of this type of exposition which permitted a descriptive treatment of plot and character that made the omission of the aside possible, but it was above all Ibsen's insistence on the illusion of realism that made the exclusion of the aside a matter of technical principle.

The monologue in its most primitive form was used both in tragedy and comedy as a convenient means for narrative exposition. Its function was such in the Greek and Roman theatre, in the mystery and morality plays and in the popular Italian farces. The Renaissance extends its function. Shakespeare and Racine both use the reflective monologue to help the action in the course of the play. The French classical dramatists were advised by d'Aubignac to avoid the monologue exposition and to divide the task between one of the protagonists and his confidant. In the sentimental *bourgeois* drama of the eighteenth century we find the same state of affairs as with the aside. The plays bear marks of their double origin. In comedy the narrative monologue remained as a legitimate device long after it had been abandoned in tragedy, and, as such, it was transferred to the *bourgeois* drama, becoming in fact a sort of lengthy aside. The reflective monologue was also incorporated with *bourgeois* tragedy; but as psychology gradually becomes subordinate to intrigue the monologue loses its function, and either is shortened to the length of one exclamation or is developed merely into a tirade of sentimental emotion. Moore's play, *The Gamester*, which ranks high among plays of this type, gives admirable instances of the standardization of the monologue into the two types, the narrative and explanatory on the one side and the emotional on the other. Stukely, the villain, when unable to reveal his evil machinations to the audience with the aid of asides, uses the explanatory monologue to help the intrigue. Beverley, the victim, on the other hand, regularly gives vent to his emotion in monologues of self-reproach, especially before his suicide and prolonged death at the end of the play. These two types of monologue were adopted by the intrigue dramatists of the nineteenth century, and only after coming into intimate touch with their work did Ibsen realize the effectiveness of the explanatory monologue on the stage.

The monologues in *Catilina* are reflective and stand under the influence of Shakespeare, Schiller and Oehlenschlæger. Only after his European tour in 1852 do we find in Ibsen's comedy, *Midsummer Eve*, the first instances of using the monologue as an aid to exposition. The first monologue of this type in Ibsen's work is spoken by Mrs. Berg at the end of the first scene of the latter play (*Eft. Skr.* I. 375), when she reveals the fact that there are some important papers to be found and concludes with the words: "I must find out for certain, I cannot rest until I have done so."

The same is the case with *Lady Inger* and *Olaf Liljekrans*. The latter play contains the last full-length "aside" monologue in Ibsen's work (*Saml. Vaerker*, 1902, Vol. X, p. 157). In this monologue Olaf informs the audience that Alfhild is the daughter of Ingrid, who eloped many years ago with a wandering musician Thorgjerd. This dispels the illusion that she is a fairy and prepares the way for his betrothal to her at the end of the play.

With *The Warriors of Helgeland* we meet with a new technique, as in the case of the aside. The explanatory monologue is abandoned, the monologue is reduced in length to a few words, finally taking the form of epigrammatic generalities to round off an act, and, but for the fact that it is spoken with the character alone on the stage, it is identical with what has earlier been defined as "thinking aloud." (In the illustrative table with monologue and "thinkings aloud" recorded in brackets are those which can scarcely be distinguished from one another. They have been recorded as identical on the graphs.) The only plays after *The Warriors of Helgeland* to use conventional monologues were *The Pretenders* and the two epic verse dramas, *Brand* and *Peer Gynt*. Ibsen consciously eliminated both monologues and thinking aloud from *The League of Youth*, but there are only two plays written afterwards which eliminate both of these devices completely (*An Enemy of the People* and *Little Eyolf*), and it seems that Ibsen never made up his mind completely on this point. He is consistent in curtailing the length of the monologue, but sure enough, both explanatory and reflective monologues recur in his later plays, as may be seen from the figures in the illustrative table.

The second act of *A Doll's House*, for instance, begins with the charming monologue which so penetratingly reveals Nora's state of mind and her naïve nature, ending with the words: "Oh, nonsense. Of course he won't take it seriously. Nothing of the kind could possibly happen. It is impossible. I've got three small children." And when the blackmailer Krogstad leaves her, Nora peeps through the door leading to the hall and in an explanatory monologue describes to the audience how he drops the incriminating letter in the box. A similar descriptive monologue appears in *Rosmersholm* at the end, when Rosmer and Rebekka have left to commit suicide in the mill-race and Madam Helseth stands at the window talking to herself as she watches them go. But it must be remembered that this type of monologue is not an intrigue device; it is not used to unravel a complicated situation, but like the messenger of classical tragedy has the function of describing action which it is not convenient to present on the stage.

It seems that Ibsen realized that the abolition of the monologue was just as artificial as the abolition of verse in his later plays. He accepted it as a legitimate device and modified it to fit his scheme of realistic illusion, but he never cast it aside altogether. Strindberg reinstated the monologue for the very reason that almost made Ibsen abandon it, namely realistic motivation, and it must be conceded that the realistic illusion of his one act play *The Stronger* is in no way impaired by the fact that the whole play is one long monologue. Ibsen, however, was too submissive to the conventions of his own technique to launch out on such experiments.

IBSEN'S DRAMATIC TECHNIQUE

STATISTICAL TABLE OF ASIDES, STAGE WHISPERS, MONOLOGUES AND
THINKING ALOUD IN IBSEN'S PLAYS

Play	Asides	Stage whispers	Mono- logues	Thinking aloud
Catilina	1	2	11	7
The Warrior's Barrow	3	0	3	0
The Ptarmigan of Justedal	2	0	4	0
Midsummer Eve	25	13	7	4
Lady Inger of Østråt {	59 (1857 ed.) 5 (1874 ed.)	26	11	21
The Feast at Solhaug {	21 (1856 ed.) 0 (1883 ed.)	24	5	9
Olaf Liljekrans	34	20	6	8
The Warriors of Helgeland	0	13	(3)	2
Love's Comedy	0	8	0	2
The Pretenders	0	18	5	(3)
Brand	0	11	14	7
Peer Gynt	0	8	25	1
The League of Youth	0	14	0	0
Emperor and Galilean I	0	29	0	1
II	0	7	0	1
The Pillars of Society	0	13	0	1
A Doll's House	0	7	(7)	0
Ghosts	0	4	(4)	0
An Enemy of the People	0	6	0	0
The Wild Duck	0	9	0	2
Rosmersholm	0	(1)	(2)	0
The Lady from the Sea	0	8	(2)	0
Hedda Gabler	0	(17)	(3)	0
The Master Builder	0	9	(1)	0
Little Eyolf	0	7	0	0
J. G. Borkman	0	3	(6)	0
When We Dead Awaken	0	4	(3)	0

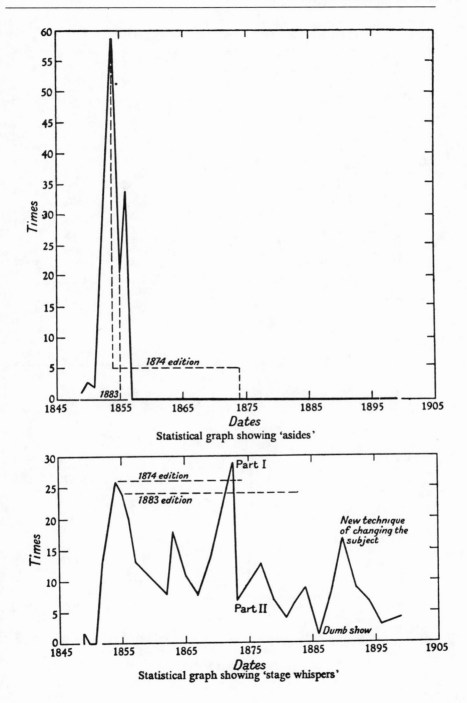

Statistical graph showing 'asides'

Statistical graph showing 'stage whispers'

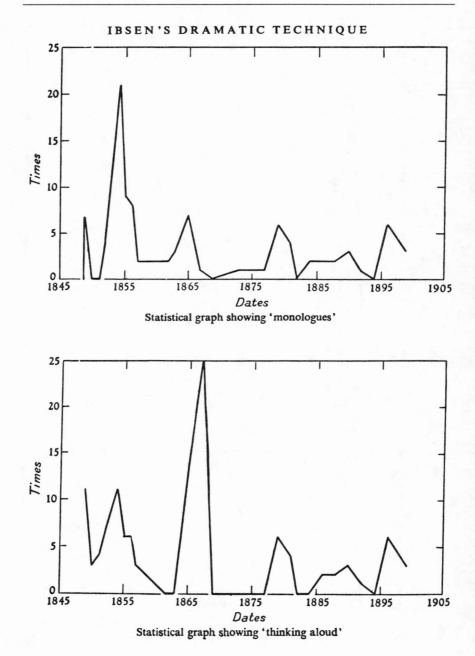

IBSEN'S DRAMATIC TECHNIQUE

Statistical graph showing 'monologues'

Statistical graph showing 'thinking aloud'

112

"The Play-within-the-Play" in
Ibsen's Realistic Drama   Daniel Haakonsen*

Something has happened in Ibsen's scholarship since our first International Ibsen Seminar held in Oslo in 1965. Without too much over-simplification we can say that research into Ibsen's work at that time — five years ago — was well along in its second main phase. The first phase was initiated by Georg Brandes and was continued by critics and scholars right up until the appearance of Halvdan Koht's great biography. During this period interest was centered on Ibsen the iconoclast, the man who laid bare bourgeois society and its morals. But even while these concerns dominated, discoveries were being made in other areas, e.g., symbolism, indicating another approach to Ibsen. And at about the middle of this century Ibsen scholarship entered upon a new phase in which interest in the symbolism of his plays played a decisive part. The playwright's idealism was also emphasized during this period, just as much as his criticism of society and his removing the masks of moral rectitude worn by members of society. This is where we were at the time of the first Ibsen Seminar five years ago.

But in the past few years the pendulum has swung back again. In the Nordic countries at any rate, there has been a steadily increasing tendency to regard all of Ibsen's idealism as ironic, at least whenever expressed by his main characters. Ibsen, we are told again, was primarily concerned with exposure of falsehood and critical comment. There is no time to go into all the points of view advanced in this third phase of research, which is partly a return to Phase One. I shall content myself by referring to a few important points made by the Danish Professor Aage Henriksen in his article entitled "Henrik Ibsen som moralist" ("Henrik Ibsen as Moralist") which appeared in *Kritik XI* (1969), opinions further reinforced by the same professor in a guest lecture given at the University of Oslo earlier in the same year.

In both places Henriksen quotes and identifies himself with Georg Brandes, who maintained that "a remarkable suspicion of idealism and moralism (en storartet, ideel eller moralsk Mistænksomhed), was Ibsen's muse." (*Kritik XI* p. 69). Ibsen felt strongly that his talents should be directed towards criticism and exposure of falsehood. When it appears that the main characters in his realistic plays are idealists, as occasionally happens, the reason is, simply, that Ibsen wished his plays to be produced in the theatre. Because of this, he had to compromise with the spirit of the times and allow his characters to appear on stage as idealists. But Ibsen himself believed all the while that their apparently lofty moral idealism was false and should be exposed, and to that end he established a literary

*Originally published in *Contemporary Approaches to Ibsen*, vol 2 (Oslo: Universitets-forlaget, 1970 / 71), 101–17. Reprinted by permission of the author.

form which created one impression in the theatre and another, completely opposite, impression from careful reading and study of the texts. When a normal audience has seen one of Ibsen's plays performed on the stage, it will retain an impression of having seen characters with an idealistic bent. But the scholar who is able to study the play at his leisure and can see various parts of the dialogue in context realises that this impression is but an illusion. What the author presents to the attentive reader is, in fact, a caricature of idealism, an exposure of the kind of idealism which holds theatre audiences. An instance quoted by Henriksen in support of his argument is the following: in *The Master Builder* Hilde persuades Solness to append his recommendation to Ragnar Brovik's drawings. This appears to be a warm and generous action on the part of Solness. But if one examines the arguments used by Hilde to persuade him, one discovers that they are designed to pander to his egocentricity. Solness does not modify his desire to dominate at all; he simply affords it an edifying justification (p. 82).

Now, what interests me especially in Aage Henriksen's article is his analysis of Ibsen's art of dialogue. We shall examine this analysis more closely, since it is a natural lead-in for the subject I shall treat myself.

As we have seen, Henriksen maintains that the real meaning of Ibsen's plays cannot be comprehended by the theatre audience: "Hidden from even the most perceptive theatregoers, this meaning exists only for the reader, who can leaf back through the pages, read again, and thereby disrupt the passage of time" (p. 74). This implies, of course, that Ibsen's dialogue must contain both an overt and a hidden meaning, otherwise it could not be interpreted in opposite ways. Henriksen speaks of "camouflaged connections" (kamouflerede sammenhænge) in the plays. He maintains that "the . . . ambiguity in Ibsen's later plays arises from . . . a life-long preoccupation with . . . dialogue." He then explains more precisely why Ibsen's characters speak ambiguously: "The basic situation is this: when a person says something to another in the hope of achieving something, he makes the fulfillment of his wish dependent on the will of the other. Obviously then, if a person wants to get his way, it is wise to conform or tailor his desires to the requirements of the world in which he hopes to have them fulfilled. Ibsen has made a study of this kind of wordly wisdom, which necessitates a kind of manoeuvering or steering of others." ("Det er dene styring og denne klogskab, som Ibsen har gjort til et studium") (p. 75).

So Ibsen's characters camouflage themselves in their speeches in order to be accepted by, and to influence and steer, others. This use of camouflage is directly opposed to the author's highest moral standard, which is "to speak and act in accordance with one's true intentions" (p. 70).

The nature of Ibsen's dialogue, the subject under discussion here, has interested me for a number of years. And when, from time to time, I have discussed the camouflage in lectures, I have connected it with the "play-within-the-play" on Ibsen's stage. But then I had to include much more than the kind of "steering" Henriksen mentions. Camouflage is a many-sided phenomenon on Ibsen's stage, and it is worth while taking a moment to become acquainted with it before we ask what purpose it serves.

The point is this: there is hardly a single major character in Ibsen's realistic plays who does not lead a secret existence in addition to the one portrayed on the stage. Most of his characters cover over parts of their past history and their present condition by means of pretense and by withholding important information. They allow significant causes or events to remain in either semi- or complete obscurity. The main characters, for example, nearly always have a hidden past, about which they would prefer others to remain in ignorance. Their pasts have, in turn, a connection with the plans they are now striving to achieve. This is why they camouflage their thoughts, feelings, intentions, and aspirations. It is because of this that they need to play-act to a certain degree when the dialogue touches upon some important aspect of their hidden lives.

The condition is so widespread that one can choose practically at random any major scene in an Ibsen play to illustrate how the dialogue seems to conceal something: there are secrets which one party alone is covering up or those which both parties are concealing from each other. A conversation on the stage may appear to be the essence of harmony and understanding, while in reality it is fraught with great tension. Tension in a particular scene can be due to one cause for one character and to a completely different cause for another.

"When, for example, Nora in the first act of A Doll's House talks to her husband about Krogstad's dubious past, for which he has not made amends, the conversation contains other aspects and deeper tensions than Helmer has reason to suspect. In the first place, Nora has a closer relationship with Krogstad than Helmer realises. And secondly, she conceals the fact that she also has been guilty of a forgery similar to Krogstad's, for which she hasn't made amends either. When Nora hears Helmer's judgment of Krogstad, it has a much more profound effect upon her than Helmer is aware of. For Nora, the conversation concerns more than just an assessment of a person who really means nothing to her. By implication, she is herself being judged by Helmer's opinions. But Helmer is unaware of this, and Nora has to play her cards in such a way that he remains ignorant of the truth.

Another example might be mentioned. In the first act of Rosmersholm Rebekka West leads the spectator to understand that she is not being open with Rosmer in that she spies on him from behind a curtain. A little later she is sitting and talking to Rector Kroll, who steers the conversation towards the subject of her relationship with Rosmer. Kroll would very much like Rebekka and Rosmer to get married, but he has no conception of what this idea means for Rebekka, of what she has in fact done in order to attain this end. He does not suspect that it was precisely this idea which led to the death of his own sister. Therefore, Rebekka must "play-act" during her conversation with Kroll. That is to say, she must control herself and keep up a pretense of disinterestedness; hence, the conversation assumes a completely different character from her point of view than from Kroll's.

This kind of pretense or play-acting is not the exception but the rule. Many of Ibsen's characters lead a camouflaged existence throughout much of the action and only come out into the open shortly before the final curtain. This is the case, for example, with Nora and Mrs. Alving, Osvald and Gregers Werle, Rebekka West and Hedda Gabler.

Obviously this phenomenon is related to the process of revelation in the plays, which is so important a part of Ibsen's dramatic technique in general. Certainly, the gradual revelation of hidden facts is a vitally important part of the action in his realistic plays. And at the same time the camouflage makes possible the revelation of hidden purposes and feelings. Thus the idea of revelation is concerned not only with past history but present states of mind.

However, it would hardly be correct to contend that the dissimulation and camouflage which abound in Ibsen's plays are *merely* necessary conditions for the literary genre he cultivates, a necessary prerequisite for providing something to reveal on various levels, including the psychological.

Ibsen makes other use of the fact that many secrets are concealed in people's words and actions. This gives the actors plenty of scope—a rich, varied, and complex range of emotions to express. In a way, Ibsen offers both his actors and his audience a refined version of Scribe's artifice and theatrical effect. With Scribe, dialogue may be exciting or piquant on the stage because someone is standing behind a door or a curtain. But Ibsen's dialogue may be exciting because his characters may be hiding behind their words, hiding behind the thoughts or plans they express in their speeches. This heightens the theatrical quality of his plays and manifests the histrionic sensibility that Fergusson talks about, a "sensibility" which is just as important for the playwright as a sense of color is to the artist or the sound of words is to the poet. This is the way Ibsen becomes "a poet of the theatre." With all the short speeches assigned to her, just think how boring the part of Hedda Gabler would be to play without the constant sense of ambiguity which the actress must convey through those speeches.

And surely there is a strong correlation between the deceptive speech or play-acting of an Ibsen character and various kinds of verbal symbolism or symbolic actions. If we consider, for example, the scene in which Hedda Gabler has engineered Ejlert Løvborg's departure for the bachelor party and is left alone with Thea Elvsted, it is clear both that Thea has difficulty in understanding Hedda and that Hedda experiences what is happening in quite a different way from Thea. When Hedda talks to Thea, therefore, she is forced to play-act. And for precisely this reason, it is natural for her to use symbols and to utter the line which, symbolically, explains to the viewer why she wanted Ejlert to go off to the party: "You will be drinking weak tea, you little fool. Then at ten o'clock Ejlert Løvborg will come — with vine leaves in his hair." The spectator recognizes, although Thea does not, the hidden implications here. The same thing can be noted when Judge Brack gives Hedda his account of what happened at the party. Hedda has her own expectations and her own standards of judgment which Brack cannot comprehend. Here also it becomes clear that Hedda is play-acting and that using symbolic language comes naturally to her. When Brack tells her about Ejlert's fight with the police, the stage directions state that Hedda "stares vacantly ahead" (*ser hen for sig*); she then speaks: "So that's what happened. Then he didn't have vine leaves in his hair after all." To this Brack replies, obviously confused: "Vine leaves, Mrs. Hedda?"

We can also see in *John Gabriel Borkman* how a similar situation, one where a character "play-acts" in relation to another who is unable to see things in the same light, occasions symbolic dialogue. In the last act Foldal comes back and finds Borkman in the snow. Foldal has been tainted by the rich society in which his daughter now finds herself. Borkman is not so impressed and is more concerned about what is missing in such a society on a human level. But he does not want to deny Foldal his pleasure and therefore employs the following metaphorical form of speech:

> FOLDAL   (*clapping his hands together*). Just think how my little Frida sat in that magnificent carriage.
>
> BORKMAN   (*nodding*). Ye-es, Wilhelm. Your daughter has learned to ride well. So has young Borkman. Did you notice those silver bells?
>
> FOLDAL. Why, yes. — Silver bells, did you say? Do you think they were silver bells? Real, genuine silver bells?
>
> BORKMAN. You can be sure of that. Everything was genuine. Both outside — and inside.

It is perhaps worth mentioning that characters are forced to play-act not only because they want to conceal mistakes and crimes. They may also want to conceal ideas, intentions, hopes, and plans of which they are by no means ashamed — quite the contrary in fact. The moment may not be ripe for revealing everything, or the character in question may not want to reveal his ideas, intentions, hopes, and plans to just anybody. A good example of this can be found in *Ghosts*. At one point Pastor Manders says: "A man really does not have to give an account to everyone for what he thinks or reads within his own four walls." "No, of course not. That's what I think too," Mrs. Alving replies. But behind this superficial accord are concealed two different attitudes: Manders wishes to suppress knowledge of what he reads for fear of other people's judgment; Mrs. Alving, on the other hand, disguises her feelings because she considers the process of liberation which she is undergoing to be her own business, not other people's. So then, much of the play-acting in Ibsen's theatre is simply because certain characters do not consider those they are talking to at the time to be sufficiently mature to share in their secret thoughts; this, for example, explains the nature of Hedda Gabler's conversation with Brack about Ejlert Løvborg. Generally speaking, then, the deceptiveness of Ibsen's characters is as much the result of emotions and ideas they personally consider to be highly respectable as the result of actions they want cunningly to conceal in order to manipulate and "steer" others.

One may now ask what this camouflage tells us about Ibsen's characters and especially about their idealism — that is, of course, if the idealism has not allowed itself to be reduced to a simple matter of the ability to steer or manipulate. Since I believe that this question is important enough to consider carefully, I shall attempt to throw light on it from two different angles. First, I should like to study camouflage in specific scenes where it is, in a way, concentrated. Then, I shall consider camouflage in connection with Ibsen's character portrayal in a single play. It is in these short, condensed scenes on one hand and in connection with character portrayal as a whole on the other that a distinct play-within-the-play is discernable.

To begin with, then, we shall cast a glance at certain compact scenes where the camouflage is brought into focus, where we gain a distinct impression that a theatre has been created within the theatre and that what is taking place is a play-within-the-play. I am thinking of such scenes as the comedy Hedda Gabler creates with Aunt Julle's hat and Hjalmar Ekdal's performance after his coming home from Werle's party, of such theatrics as Nora's tarantella and Brendel's self-dramatization during his visits to Rosmersholm. I am thinking also of the grim drama-within-the-drama which takes place at the end of the first act of *Ghosts*: Mrs. Alving conjures up a scene from the past and recites what was said at that time; suddenly we hear Osvald and Regine, re-enacting that scene, repeat the same lines. One could mention many other examples of obvious play-acting scenes in Ibsen's work, i.e., scenes in which the actors build a kind of theatricality into the everyday life they are supposed to represent for the audience.

What function do these scenes perform? They do, of course, entertain the audience and intensify the impression made by the action. The intensification is obvious, since the play-within-the-play introduces an element of life and freedom which stands out against the somewhat colourless background of realism which otherwise predominates in the portrayals of people and their environments. We also get the impression that something else, something momentous, has suddenly happened. The characters have been given the opportunity of revealing something of their real selves, of appearing more independent. And with this, the accepted

social conventions are suddenly broken through, revealing other conceptions of life with their own attendant rules.

But this is not, I believe, the most important function of these scenes.
We note that Ibsen carefully employs the heightened awareness of life
created by them — employs them in the formulation of new surprises. To
begin with, let us quote an example which only concerns subsidiary
characters. In the last act of *The Lady from the Sea* the egocentric young
sculptor, Lyngstrand, implies that he will propose to Hilde when she
comes back, although at that time he is rather more attracted to Bolette.
He doesn't know that he is dying. Hilde, on the other hand, does. So she
replies to his indirect proposal by talking about black clothes and by taking
part without apparent motivation in a kind of futuristic mannequin
charade. She sees herself through her inner eye: "In black up to the neck —
surrounded by a black ruffle — black gloves — and a long black veil behind." Lyngstrand does not understand her but is captivated; he says that
he wishes that he were a painter so that he could paint her as a "young,
beautiful, mourning widow." But Hilde, who knows that they will never
get as far as marriage, replies pitilessly: "Or a young, mourning bride."

The scene is funny, even if Hilde's playing with the narcissistic and
uncomprehending young man is heartless. She portrays herself as the only
kind of bride she could be if she were to commit herself to Lyngstrand. But
amid the humour we realize that Hilde also introduces Death into the
stage; Lyngstrand is unaware that he is being linked with this unobtrusive
travelling companion. This leads me to my real point: Ibsen employs a
peripheral scene as a preparation for something more central in the play.

Wangel and Ellida come in and talk about the English tourist-ship
shortly to arrive. Lyngstrand, in fact, is already able to point out: "There
it is already, Doctor. Come like a thief in the night, one might say — so
completely noiseless and unobtrusive. . . ." The feeling that Hilde has
already created, that there is something beneath the happy surface of life,
is included now in a distinctly threatening context. We might say that the
increased sensitivity to ambiguity, which her little comedy with Lyngstrand created, helps us to be even more aware of the threat from the
great, noiseless ship.

As a rule the connection between the play-acting scenes and what
they foreshadow is simpler. Stockman in *An Enemy of the People* plays his
comedy on stage in the uniform (a special hat and stick) of a Justice of the
Peace, but then an unexpected discovery forces him to lay his status
symbols aside. This means, simply, that the powers-that-be have succeeded
in turning public opinion against him. He no longer represents the power
of the people; he has become, on the contrary, an enemy of the people.

Indeed, we can say in general that the scenes we are talking about
lead towards and prepare us for a reversal (*peripeteia*). They begin as
expressions of the principal character's need for freedom, often taking the

form of revolt against the social conventions that encompass him. But then the scene changes to something quite different. The characters have broken loose from *one* kind of chain only to find themselves bound by an even stronger one. Let us note a couple of examples.

In the first act of her play Hedda Gabler is irritated by her husband's relative, Aunt Julle, who has come visiting much too early in the morning—especially as this is after the first night Hedda has spent in her own house. The well-meaning, though indiscreet, aunt seems to be assuming privileges. Probably with a view to teaching her a lesson that the house now belongs to her, Hedda, and not to Aunt Julle, Hedda enacts a little comedy. She pretends to think that Aunt Julle's hat, which is lying on the chair in the drawing room, belongs to the maid. This wounds the old lady deeply, for, in spite of being well-disposed towards the maid, Aunt Julle has a well-developed sense of class distinction. But Hedda plays the cruel little play within the main action. Suddenly, however, things take another turn. Hedda wanted to get away from her insistent in-laws. But Aunt Julle hears something which makes her think that Hedda is pregnant and therefore assumes the older female's right to protective indiscretion. This first play within the main action quickly changes into a kind of ritual which one must simply accept. With the authority that the situation gives her, the aunt takes Hedda's head in both hands and pulls it down towards her. She kisses Hedda on her hair while she intones a priestly benediction: "God bless and keep Hedda Tesman." Suddenly new laws come into play— biological, familial, and others—which with an automatic right take over Hedda's playing and bind her even more strongly than she was at the beginning.

Another example. In the second act of *The Wild Duck*, Hjalmar Ekdal comes home from a party at the elder Werle's house where he felt distinctly out of place among the more socially at-ease guests. Indeed, the party had been one long humiliation for him. But as soon as he comes home, he quickly recovers. He now plays the part of a veritable social lion, completely at ease; he treats his admiring audience to a wide selection of biting and witty ripostes with which he is supposed to have regaled the rich merchant's sophisticated guests. After some initial domestic unpleasantness, he completes the winning-back of his security in his own small world by playing the flute for his admirers. But suddenly there is a knock at the door, and the game is reversed. From now on, Hjalmar doesn't even feel safe in his own home: he is sought out by an agent from the threatening environment he had just left.

Or consider Ulrik Brendel at Rosmersholm. He makes two appearances, which stand in obvious contrast to one another. The first time he comes and plays nonchalantly with the rector's official title and other conventions; he is his own master on the way to a society he will help to liberate. The next time the laws of that society—laws also which apply to the leaders of the opposition—have caught him in *their* net. When he now plays with titles, "president" or "excellency," with reference to Peter Mortensgaard, it is a morbidly humorous game with a man who has defeated him and sent him out into the night.

A final example of a short scene. At the end of the first act of *Ghosts*, we have become acquainted, indirectly though actively, with Mrs. Alving's "comedy play" (*komediespill*) — the designation is her own — which has the ultimate intention of removing all trace of Chamberlain Alving. And suddenly we glide over into a play imposed on Osvald and Regine without their realising it themselves, a play which shows all Mrs. Alving's efforts have been in vain. The society of ghosts has its own rules, and Chamberlain Alving is just as alive as ever.

So much then for the short, concentrated play scenes. They are, to begin with, an expression of man's freedom. But in many cases they swing over in the opposite direction. The play-within-the-play is first set in motion by the characters themselves, but later on we feel that other powers take control of the action.

This feeling is intensified by studying the play-within-the-play from a somewhat wider angle. The point is that when characters indulge in play-acting and camouflage to the extent they do in Ibsen's drama, their whole lives may be assessed from this point of view. Obviously the consequences are more far-reaching than in the artifice and camouflage of isolated scenes. Nevertheless, the dynamics are the same as we observed before: at first the character himself plays the part; later Life or Fate comes in to direct an action which the characters are forced to participate in if they are to act out their roles to the end and thus be true to themselves.

As an example, let us take the main character's camouflage in *Ghosts*. Mrs. Alving lives in a society which worships the past at the expense of the present. For example, the past insists that the doctrine of the father's traditional authority over his progeny, whatever the father's character might be, should be upheld; at the beginning of the play both Pastor Manders and Engstrand are seen trying to impress this idea on Regine. Another example is the image of God which Pastor Manders paints for the rebellious Mrs. Alving: it is a picture of an autocratic father who demands blind obedience and the fulfillment of all duties; people's lives and happiness do not concern him.

In the community life depicted in the play people follow religious and social norms which they really do not believe in, but which they blindly adhere to. Ideas and prejudices retain their power far beyond their normal life span. But behind the substantial facade of this society, behind the lawful order, a life burns which the older generation tries to suppress. The powerful symbol of the past's control over those living in the present and especially over the young is the kind of disease which is passed on from father to son and which burdens the son with the consequences of his father's life. In the same way, inherited concepts cripple the thought and moral life of man.

Mrs. Alving is opposed to this society, over against the dead pater-familias and all he represents, she places the living son; over against an enslaved morality, she sets freedom of thought and belief. She moves freely about her domain, the estate, because she pays lip service to the rules of society. But she thinks and believes what she likes about the circumstances which surround her, and she aims at freeing her estate from the mastery of the past and at affording her young son a free and worthwhile existence. This is her hope, her ideal, in the play's present.

But Mrs. Alving also "plays" in a way different from simply advancing her own aims behind an acceptable facade. As mentioned before, she has produced a great "comedy-play" in order to pull the wool over people's eyes and to free herself from the heritage of Chamberlain Alving. Ten years after his death she wants to set up an official charitable institution in his memory to show outwardly how worthy he was of the high regard he had earned, but which in reality she had earned for him. This comedy does not belong to the play's past. At the end of the first act Mrs. Alving has to defend herself from a broadside fired by Pastor Manders; in a gripping account she brings to life on the stage the whole truth about her marriage, as well as the whole truth about the face-saving act she has put on over the years. Pastor Manders is so flabbergasted that he has to grab for a chair. The "play" continues in the next act: while Osvald is actually reviving the past, his mother believes that he cannot endure the truth about it. Hence she must continue to camouflage herself — and the truth.

The Mrs. Alving we meet at the beginning of the play is, therefore, an actress who conceals her real self — both the defiant plans and ideas which motivate her and the intentions behind her public actions. And her acting continues until the end of the Second Act, when she rises from the table clairvoyantly: "Now I see how it all fits into place; now I can speak." But suddenly events take an unexpected turn and thrust her into new contexts which she has not originated herself. And these new contexts develop according to a logic all their own.

To understand what has happened we must be quite clear that Mrs. Alving's acting skill is not just a shield for her freedom. This skill is also an attribute of the society in which she lives, and its influence on her is deep-seated. She herself has contributed greatly to the father-cult and to the cult of the past by means of the Captain Alving Memorial Orphanage. She herself gradually acknowledges that the "ghost-morality" and all the inherited conceptions remain in people long after these ideas should have died out. She realises that she must fight with herself in order to fight against them. And, without denying her own guilt, she clearly sees that, without realising it, she herself had been instrumental in triggering the calamities in her husband's life.

Mrs. Alving, then, maintains some solidarity with the society she is rebelling against, and every step she takes in the direction of freedom increases her bondage and suffering. But she refuses to give up. She bravely endures opposition while leaning over backwards in an effort to understand her emancipated son. He leads her rebellion against the deepest taboos of her society. In fact she ends in a border country where it is impossible to judge whether she is faced by genuine taboos caused by fear of inherited morality, or with a transcendent norm, which mankind cannot ignore, a norm protecting human life. Who dare make himself master over life and death?

With tragic irony, what Mrs. Alving desired to achieve by means of the original *komediespill* can now be realised. She wants to exorcise Chamberlain Alving from her life. This can only be done by also ridding herself of her son, who perpetuates his father's unworthy life.

Now it is my contention that the tragedy which begins with Mrs. Alving's own play-within-the-play concludes by drawing her into contexts which are themselves a kind of play: Destiny's play with her, in which she must act a part which is forced upon her and which she cannot avoid without being false to herself. This new part rounds out and completes her earlier role in a completely unexpected way. And I believe that all the camouflage and the whole other dimension caused by the play-acting at the beginning of *Ghosts* help us to feel that the events which take place at the end are something more than just life's coincidences. In the final analysis, man must participate in the drama of his own destiny, created by his own past in conjunction with the logic of existence. It is not a drama for which one is morally responsible in the normal sense of the word, and only the greatest personalities are able to experience existence at the depth (or height) where his drama is played out. The camouflage at the beginning of the play should therefore contribute to the feeling at the end that the hero belongs to a context lifted above the everyday level. But at this point the hero no longer chooses his own role.

The kind of turn we have seen in the action of *Ghosts* is to be found in a number of Ibsen's other plays. Once or twice it is stated directly that a more objective context can be woven out of the lives of the main characters. But generally speaking, the main indication that one kind of play glides over into another is that the same goal which the hero originally pursued is in fact attained, but in a way quite different from that anticipated and planned for. For the sake of completeness it must also be said that in certain instances the camouflage remains unrecognized by the main character himself; here it is more a psychological process of explanation he must go through rather than a tragic-ironical one.

Such a development of the play-within-a-play as I have tried to outline above must be important for the assessment of Ibsen's idealists on a moral plane. If a kind of objective order enters into the picture, leading the characters into its own play, then the main moral question is connected with their readiness to accept this new order of things and consequences which they had not anticipated.

The most general conclusion I myself am inclined to is that the moral problems connected with Ibsen's idealism must be judged in relation to the genre to which his plays belong. The dramaturgic analysis must take precedence; ethical judgments must come after. It is obvious that a writer of tragedies measures human life in terms quite different from a writer of bourgeois plays. For the latter, the conflicts in life can often be a sign of sickness. But the tragic writer may consider it an advantage for a man and a sign of merit if he can understand, experience, and accept the disharmony in human life.

We recall the heroic ideal of the Greek tragic writers. A Greek hero was not one who excelled in virtue of his good deeds, as I believe Gilbert Murray has said. He was a man whom the gods had touched and who courageously accepted their intervention. If we overlook this and consider King Oedipus from a narrow, moralistic perspective, we are far from the world in which Sophocles lived and thought. Similarly I think we may do Ibsen an injustice if we do not ask which literary form his plays belong to and then what moral norms apply to his form.

The conflict of a bourgeois drama like Bjørnson's *The Bankruptcy* (*En fallit*) arises from a fault committed by the protagonist, and harmony is reestablished when the fault is atoned for. But Ibsen's heroes are touched by the gods: they cannot act in a wrong manner without actualising fundamental conflicts of human life. They are not fully responsible for the consequences of their deeds, any more than King Oedipus is fully responsible for killing his father and marrying his mother. Mrs. Alving has her share of blame for her husband's miserable years of married life, but her fault is not proportionate to the horrors of the final scene of *Ghosts*. The conflicts in this tragedy transcend in fact the perspectives of one individual life, even though they are actualised by a single human being.

The same thing is true for the verbal "steering" and the play-acting, indeed for all the camouflage used by Mrs. Alving and other Ibsen heroes. The real context for the play-within-the-play then is not the moral code of bourgeois drama, but the greater tragic stage where man has to measure up to his destiny and effectively play his part in a larger order of things.

Enactment in Ibsen   Oliver Gerland*

Ibsen's critics have identified the reenactment of the past as one of the playwright's basic dramatic principles. Daniel Haakonsen provides an example from the first act of *Ghosts*: "Mrs. Alving conjures up a scene from the past and recites what was said at that time; suddenly we hear Oswald and Regina reenacting that scene, repeat the same lines."[1]

*This essay was written specifically for this volume and is published here for the first time by permission of the author.

Haakonsen calls this moment "a play-within-the-play" and argues that Ibsen uses it for a number of reasons: to entertain the audience; to intensify the impression made by the action; and, principally, to demonstrate that "man must participate in the drama of his own destiny, created by his own past in conjunction with the logic of existence."[2] In other words, Haakonsen suggests that the play-within-the-play structures the audience / reader's perception of the play-without-the-play, or Life, in theatrical terms. Just as an actor is "forced" to play a certain role by the playwright through the drama, so the Ibsen hero (and, one supposes, humanity in general) is forced to play a certain role by Destiny through life.

Given that the behavior of characters is determined by Destiny, Haakonsen calls for a reassessment of Ibsen's idealists on a moral level. For example, he claims that one ought not judge Mrs. Alving according to the moral code of her (or our) society, but according to her readiness to accept the demands of Fate. Like Oedipus, Mrs. Alving cannot be held fully responsible for the consequences of her actions; she is, like the Greek hero, a victim of Fortune. Thus, Haakonsen makes reenactment of the past a means by which Ibsen secures for his realistic drama a metaphysical and moral context proper to Greek tragedy.

Whereas Haakonsen treats reenactment in both metatheatrical and moral terms, Margot Norris analyzes it in terms derived from Levi-Strauss's structural anthropology. She argues that reenactment of the past is the crux of a process of self-therapy undertaken by Ibsen's protagonists to cure neuroses that originate in a mythic crime (an original sin) committed in the past. Having committed the original sin, usually a sacrifice of some kind, such as the sacrifice of love by marriage for money, the protagonist becomes "enthralled to (a) private myth which crystallizes around the painful and guilty experience of his past."[3] Triggered by the visit of someone from the past, the protagonist reexamines his original sin, and "re-enacts the crime in some symbolic fashion, thereby effecting either his forgiveness and redemption or his penitent destruction."[4]

Norris claims that therapy by reenactment is the structural principle that governs Ibsen's last twelve plays, and shows how the middle works can be distinguished from the later ones according to the nature of the reenactment. In the middle plays, according to her argument, the protagonist reencounters the dilemma he has already "resolved" by committing the original sin, and, perhaps, makes a new choice to his moral credit, as, for example, Bernick in *Pillars of Society*. In the later plays, the protagonist reenacts the myth, or "the real or imaginary moment from the past which has become symbolic," for example, Solness's climbing the tower, but this mythic reenactment is never more than a mere gesture, a symbolic action, and so is never truly healing. Thus, Norris hints at an increasing pessimism in Ibsen's later works; whereas in the middle plays the past can be revised, the original sin forgiven, in the later works the past is all-powerful and determining, and the original sin is so grave that characters die in the attempt to cure themselves by re-enacting it.

These interpretations of the reenactment of the past agree in their characterization of the past as that which determines or organizes the present, although the extent of this determination varies from Haakonsen to Norris. In the former's analysis, the past overdetermines the present, forcing characters into patterns already established for them. Thus, Osvald is doomed from birth to imitate the ugly decline of his father. In Norris's analysis, on the other hand, the past determines a general scene to be played that frames the dilemma facing the protagonist in the present. Moreover, the successful playing of the scene determined by the past enables the protagonist to revise that past; thus, we might say that the present determines the past, or, at least, determines how the past affects the present. In Ibsen's final plays, however, the myths against which the protagonists oppose themselves through enactment prove fatal. In these plays, the past cannot be revised and characters are, as in Haakonsen's analysis, predetermined.

Although both Haakonsen and Norris isolate reenactment of the past as a crucial concern, neither examines the dramatic principle as a form of theatrical self-consciousness. To be sure, Haakonsen identifies reenactment as "a play-within-the-play," yet he intends mainly to show how the play-within-the-play works to alter our perception of moral behavior on the stage, and does not ask for other reasons why Ibsen patterns his protagonists as actors, that is, as characters who enact a scene or text from the past. Norris, on the other hand, does not see reenactment at all in theatrical terms, but as a therapeutic strategy, and so, whereas she does provides a fascinating and illuminating account of the protagonist as shaman-for-self, she does not pursue the issue in terms of self-referentiality and self-consciousness.

In other words, neither Haakonsen nor Norris explicitly identifies the past, or, more precisely, a narrative about the past, as a dramatic text to be enacted within the enactment of Ibsen's dramatic text. I suggest that Ibsen conceives his protagonists as actors because he sees in the performance situation a trope for human being in the world: man acts from the text of his past and so is enslaved, but in the acting of it he authors it and so is free. The impulse which drives the protagonist to attempt self-cure qua Norris, or to break from predetermination qua Haakonsen, is the impulse to escape from the text in order to achieve self-authorship. The protagonists of *When We Dead Awaken*, *John Gabriel Borkman* and *The Master Builder* struggle to free themselves from texts they have constructed in the past, narratives which determine their identities in the present. They endeavor to revise or to reconstruct the texts they enact in order to write for themselves new personae and to live new identities. However, because these protagonists are constituted by the very texts or personal myths they must destroy, to reach their end requires their death.[5]

Before beginning a reading of *When We Dead Awaken* with reference to *The Master Builder* and *John Gabriel Borkman*, I need to define more closely what is meant by textual determination, performance, and freedom. Jiri Veltrusky, a Prague School semiotician, demonstrates in his article "Dramatic Text as a Component of Theatre" that two perduring sign systems operate in the theater in a dialectical tension that is essential to theatrical performance. Veltrusky identifies these sign systems as language and acting, the first of which intervenes through the dramatic text, the second of which presents itself through the actor's body (taken in the most general sense). Veltrusky characterizes the relationship between text and body as one of combination and conflict: the dramatic text is a predetermining, linguistic text which "create(s) the most complicated combinations and relationships" of meanings within itself; the actor's body, on the other hand, the purely material bearer of the dramatic text, "tends, because of its overwhelming reality, to monopolize the attention of the audience at the expense of the immaterial meanings conveyed by the linguistic sign."[6] Thus, the actor's body functions not only to signify and to reveal the dramatic text and its play of immaterial meanings, but also to interpret and occlude that text, to write, in the mind of the audience, its own text. Although the dramatic text predetermines the performance to a greater or lesser degree (depending on the type of script, or, more generally, on the type of performance situation) there is always the possibility that the actor will "clash with the semantic requirements of the text"; he may, for example, forget his lines.[7]

The actor's freedom lies not in his humanity, however, which may drop a line or two, but in his materiality which supplements and so presents the author's (and director's) linguistic text. "Supplement" ought to be taken here in the double-edged Derridean sense: that is, the actor's body adds an inessential something to a text supposed complete in itself (as the playwright and poet Henrik Ibsen was at pains to point out);[8] and, as well, the actor's body completes that text. As Derrida has demonstrated in the case of writing and speech, one sign system supplements another only if the latter lacks something which enables the former to be added to it. Thus, writing supplements speech and exposes the lack of presence in speech which logocentric philosophies have taken care to conceal. So, too, the actor's body (acting) supplements the written text (language) and exposes the lack of immateriality in language which philosophers like Veltrusky overlook: acting a text makes clear that meaning begins in the very material which disrupts the immaterial meanings of the simply linguistic text. Veltrusky suppresses the materiality of language to such an extent that he can claim "the sound components on which the linguistic meaning relies are to a large extent predetermined by the meaning itself."[9] In other words, just as the linguistic text is held to predetermine the material bearer of that meaning, the actor's body, so immaterial meaning is held to predetermine the sensory material in which that meaning is conveyed. The theater reverses this relation: the actor's body tends to divert attention away from the linguistic text to itself, and so rewrites the old text while writing its own.

In this view, the theater celebrates the extra-linguistic materiality of the signifier. In the body of the actor is his being beyond the reach and realm of the linguistic text which "predetermines" his performance. In the sign-making capacity of the actor's body, his material being, is room for him to function as both a character inside the dramatic text and as an observer or reader of that text. An analogy may be drawn to language, where, in the material being of a word, its sound, is room for multiple meanings, as with a pun. Thus, the actor's materiality, his flesh and blood, allows him to step outside the universe of characters determined by the dramatic text.

Even though "stepping outside" the linguistic, determining dramatic text, the actor is still "inside" the theatrical text. The theatrical text, composed of both linguistic and extra-linguistic elements, constitutes the totality of signs the spectator derives from the stage. The distance between these different texts, the dramatic and the theatrical, is neatly traversed by the actor's body; the actor's body proves the distinctness of these texts. Hence, although the actor can, as it were, "duck" out of the dramatic text and play against its determining power (actually, point to its determining power), he does so always within the theatrical text as a whole, from which there is no leaving. I have been characterizing the dramatic text as some sort of determining cage from which the actor may escape, and could characterize the theatrical text in similar, immuring terms. Rather, we should view the theatrical text as the area where the actor's freedom, freedom from the dramatic, linguistic text, is represented; in this space, the body's sign-making capacity is affirmed rather than suppressed.

The protagonist of *When We Dead Awaken*, the sculptor Arnold Rubek, operates within a dramatic text he wrote for himself with the making of his masterpiece group, "The Resurrection Day." We may even say that the group itself is that dramatic text, for it appears on the stage only as a narrative, a linguistic structure, which is then enacted or embodied by characters. This issue will be dealt with at greater length later in the essay. Needing to make a masterpiece to establish himself as an artist, Rubek denied the native impulse to touch Irene, his model, for fear that contact would spoil his vision of her and ruin the sculpture which confirmed him in his identity as an artist. Rubek's remorse over this denial of his sexual impulse and his failure to embrace life is depicted in the masterpiece group; that is, "The Resurrection Day" represents the consequences of his desire to make himself an artist. If we consider the sculpture to be a dramatic text, then essential to that text is the role Rubek so desperately wanted to play—being an artist. The action of *When We Dead Awaken* is to escape from this dramatic text and role, that Rubek might write for himself, with Irene, a new identity. The area where

Rubek's and Irene's escape from their personal dramatic text appears is the theatrical text as a whole, which, as it is composed of both linguistic and non-linguistic elements, marks the boundary of the dramatic text. Rubek's and Irene's deaths in the avalanche may represent a real escape from the identities of artist and model established through the linguistic structure of "The Resurrection Day," or they may not. Successful or failed, the attempt to outscale and undo their personal dramatic text can be represented through their bodies only, in the theatrical, non-linguistic text.

During the reading or viewing of a play, one cannot draw such subtle distinctions as that between the dramatic and theatrical texts, though one may well perceive the protagonist's attempt to escape some sort of text, a myth, for example, as in Norris's analysis, or a role or an identity as in Rubek's case. I suggest that Ibsen patterns Solness, Borkman, and Rubek as actors enacting a dramatic text of their own construction from which they attempt to escape. The question is open whether or not these protagonists succeed in their attempts, that is, on another level, whether or not the theatrical text represents an exit from the dramatic text. Ibsen very carefully identifies the personal myths or dramatic texts of these protagonists with the theatrical text as a whole, and so renders ambiguous the plays' fatal conclusions. For example, if Solness's personal text or myth is himself as the master builder, will we ever be able to conclude with certainty that he has escaped from that role or identity, when the work which constitutes him and shows his escape / death is titled *The Master Builder*?

The relevant question is, "How does Ibsen represent, through the text as a whole, the protagonist / actor's escape from his personal text (which, again, may be identified with the text as a whole)?" The most general and accurate answer to this question is that the whole text contains within itself another text, which, like the whole, is enacted, and from which the protagonist tries to escape. In other words, the text contains a synecdoche of itself. In this essay, I show that the synecdochic text is a role or identity which the protagonist has labored to create for himself, a role or identity based in an artifact of his own making. Rubek's masterpiece group, "The Resurrection Day," is such an artifact and, as it appears only as a narrative, such a text.

Three arguments suggest themselves as ways to show that "The Resurrection Day" is a text like that of *When We Dead Awaken*. First is the argument from autobiography which states, in essence, that Rubek represents the author, Ibsen. Critics who have entertained and found useful the patently autobiographical elements of the play suggest that Rubek's statuary stands for Ibsen's corpus, that Rubek's self-incrimination and doubt stands for (or, at least, is helpfully thought of in terms of) Ibsen's crisis near the end of his writing career that in foregoing poetry for prose, he had somehow misused his talents. Given these sets of identifications, artist as author, statuary as drama, to show that "The Resurrection

Day," in part a portrait of the artist in despair, represents *When We Dead Awaken*, wherein the artist / author voices that despair, seems straightforward.

The second argument that "The Resurrection Day" is a dramatic text like *When We Dead Awaken* relies on the working draft of the play which is entitled *Resurrection Day*.[10] Ibsen changed the title once to *When The Dead Awaken* before changing it again to its present form. Clearly, *Resurrection Day* is the progenitor of *When We Dead Awaken*: the latter title is a paraphrase of the former (when can any dead awaken except on Resurrection Day?), deriving as well from one of the most haunting passages in the play. Although such a nominal coincidence is not in itself sufficient to prove that "The Resurrection Day" is a dramatic text of sorts, it does show that the group figured centrally in Ibsen's first ideas about the play: "The Resurrection Day" has been the framing metaphor for the whole since the play's inception.

The third and most pertinent argument that "The Resurrection Day" stands for the text of *When We Dead Awaken* is that the former is enacted within / during the enactment of the latter. In the second act Rubek describes "The Resurrection Day" to Irene, while both are in the physical positions dictated by the narrative: Rubek sits before a stream even as the remorseful man in "The Resurrection Day" does; Irene stands behind him, as "subdued" as the girl in the group, with the realization dawning that Rubek like herself has "died."

This observation does not derive from any production of the play I have seen, but from Ibsen's explicit stage directions, and, more forcibly, from Rubek's pronounced self-awareness that he is representing one of the group's figures. Describing the group, he tells Irene, "Listen now how I have placed myself in the group. In the foreground, beside a spring—as it might be here—sits a man weighed down by guilt."[11] Rubek's self-conscious statement "as it might be here," and placement of himself within the group (presumably, the man in "The Resurrection Day" is a self-portrait) points to the coincidence between the group and the present action, between the past and the present, and between "The Resurrection Day" and *When We Dead Awaken*. More significantly, Rubek's comment indicates that he himself is aware of the coincidence, that he perceives himself as reenacting the past, or, more precisely, as enacting his narration of the group. In short, Rubek conceives of himself as an extension of the guilt-ridden figure; he is the active, present representation of the absent, marble man; a self-conscious actor pointing to his connection with the text he enacts.

Consider more closely Rubek's narrative of the group. Rubek's description places a female figure standing almost in the background, in the foreground a seated man, and in between a score of grotesque human figures with secret animal faces. As Rubek's statement implies, the man in the foreground is a self-portrait of the artist, and, as we know from the play, the woman is a modified version of the figure for whom the youthful Irene posed, perhaps even suggestive of Irene as she appears on the stage. Rubek's self-representation and the foregrounding of that figure makes the piece much more about himself and his guilt than about a glorious resurrection as was originally conceived. His organization of the sculpted figures suggests an interpretation of the work that the play itself reinforces: the group depicts an artist having turned his back on a youthful model, who, though once fresh and ebullient (in "The Resurrection Day" as originally conceived), has been marred, "subdued," saddened by the artist's rejection of her. The artist himself regrets this action and bathes his sculpting hand in a stream in an attempt to wash clean his sin. Between these figures swarm a set of human figures with animal faces, enforcing the man and woman's separation. These grotesque human forms are described in exactly the terms Rubek uses to describe the busts he made between the time of the play, and the time of "The Resurrection Day" group.

The grotesque figures that keep the man and woman (Rubek and Irene) apart represent that which separates the artist from his model, namely, the work of art itself. The tiny figures mediate the artist and his model even as "The Resurrection Day" mediated Rubek's and Irene's relationship. No wonder Rubek is having doubts about the merit of his work. Within his great masterpiece, signifying the masterpiece itself, are the "equivocal" busts which earned for him merely material success. These figures, central to the group, occupy the gap between artist and model and define them; they mark the separation which the artist claimed was necessary to maintain between himself and his model. The action of the play is to collapse that gap, to annihilate the figures standing between Rubek and Irene, that is, to deconstruct "The Resurrection Day" itself.

"Deconstruction" is a term one must use with caution. In this context, I mean simply the breaking down and inversion of existing relations between things. Thus, to deconstruct "The Resurrection Day" is to recover the gap between artist and model the group represents by breaking down the marble-enforced identities, artist and model, and creating new identities, the flesh and blood identities of man and woman. In other words, "The Resurrection Day" is the concrete form of Rubek's perception of himself as artist and Irene as model; it is the codification of these identities, a determining text against which both characters rebel.

"The Resurrection Day" is fundamentally a text, a narrative, a purely verbal structure present on the stage only in so far as it is animated by the actors' bodies just like the dramatic text itself. That Ibsen was concerned about stressing the script-like qualities of the art-object is further evinced by material in an earlier draft later cut. Climbing the mountain with Rubek in the third act, Irene asks, "You want to go up there?" and the sculptor answers, "Together with you. Live Resurrection Day and re-create it in a new likeness . . . in your likeness, Irene."[12] In this earlier draft, Rubek and Irene succeed in their quest for the mountaintop and the light of morning; no avalanche crushes them down. Their enactment of, or "living" of, "The Resurrection Day" dissolves and re-creates the group in a positive, fulfilling manner; the deathly marble statue melts to dewy, resurrected flesh and blood: Rubek's life- and love-denying sacrifice of Irene is recovered / reenacted and, perhaps, forgiven. As Norris's analysis maintains, however, such a positive ending tends to characterize Ibsen's middle rather than his later plays, and, when the playwright altered the ending to show Irene's and Rubek's deaths in an avalanche, the explicit reference to their re-creation of "The Resurrection Day" was removed. Still, we may consider Irene's and Rubek's mountain-climb as an attempt, although, perhaps, a failed attempt, to re-create, become, and overcome the text which determines them.

The attempt to escape old personae and to write new ones is represented by the mountain-climb: only on the mountaintop, out of view of all others, including the audience, can new identities be wrought. Thus, the stage space itself is identified with the text which Irene and Rubek try to escape. Their climb, and the climbs of Solness and Borkman, represent the attempt made by the protagonist to write himself anew, to shed an old identity and to reform the self. The falls and deaths which follow these climbs are ambiguous: they may be interpreted as a victory for the new life, if one takes death to imply a freedom of some sort; or as a statement of failure, if one takes death to be an utter end.

In order to examine *John Gabriel Borkman* and *The Master Builder* in the terms of our discussion of *When We Dead Awaken*, it is necessary to provide the analogous form that patterns all three plays. Each presents the story of a man self-consciously enacting an identity he has constructed for himself in the past. This identity or role is based in an artifact or text he has created at the expense of denying impulses and other roles incompatible with the one he wants to play. This denial, at the root of his personal dramatic text, and the creation of the text itself inevitably hurt a woman (and / or children). At the time of the play, the man is locked into the identity or role he wrote for himself long ago. The woman he hurt (or a representative of her) returns from the past and sparks a reexamination and deconstruction of the deadening identity he now plays. The action of these plays is to overthrow that identity, his being determined by a personal dramatic text (closely identified with the text as a whole which constitutes him), in order to write himself anew.

Rubek, Borkman, and Solness have all established identities for themselves which they self-consciously enact: Rubek is the artist, Borkman the emperor, Solness the master builder. These identities are self-consciously enacted in the sense that each man insists on presenting himself in these terms, which precludes him from presenting himself in any other terms. One thinks of, for example, Borkman's Napoleonic posture upon hearing an unexpected knock, and Solness's playing the master builder for the benefit of Ragnar and Brovik in the next room, while secretly courting Kaja (Act I). We recall *Brand* as well, where the protagonist has to make a choice between being a father and being a priest: the former implies moving his son to warmer climes, the latter implies the boy's death. Brand makes the choice which identifies him as a priest. In Brand's world of "all or nothing," a vocation and the identity concomitant with that vocation preclude any other system for self-conception like the family. Ibsen's last protagonists take this same dictum, "all or nothing," quite to heart. Solness cannot see himself being both a father and a master builder; moreover, the death of the twins which ends his being as a father establishes him as master builder. Neither can Borkman conceive of himself in any terms other than those related to his unachieved empire; he had the opportunity to take Ella, his love, to wife, but being the businessman and empire-builder precluded playing such a role. Similarly, Rubek cannot conceive of himself in any way except as an artist, which implies (or did imply) denial of Irene as a lover.

Rubek's is an interesting case: unlike Solness and Borkman, whose identities or roles seem to be a matter of choice, Rubek claims to have been born an artist, and hopes to be one until he dies. If we take Rubek at his word, the identity / role which he spends the play coming to grips with and attempting to overthrow extends from the womb to the grave. Rubek claims that his being an artist is coextensive with his being at all; being an artist is, simply, being himself, that is, himself as he is self-conscious.

If we take the role which the protagonist aims to escape from and overthrow as emblematic of his self-consciousness, then the "original sin" which establishes that role, here Rubek's denial of Irene, marks the first moment of self-consciousness, when the self realizes its singularity. Framing the analysis in this way, I perceive the protagonist's establishment, enactment, and overthrow of his personal text as a metaphor for the establishment and travails of self-consciousness. Although a digression from our discussion in main, Lacanian psychoanalysis provides an interesting and relevant model with reference to this idea.

For Lacan, the first moment of self-consciousness, or "the primordial precipitation of the I," occurs during the "mirror-stage" when the child, held in its mother's arms before a mirror, identifies itself with the specular image of its body. The subject sees itself for the first time as a Gestalt, a whole, though the child's motor incapacity prevents it from feeling anything but a fragmentation of that whole, Lacan continues "The mirror-stage is a drama . . . which manufactures for the subject, caught up in the lure of spatial identification (in the mirror), the succession of phantasies that extends from (the subject's present) fragmented body-image to . . . a form of its totality . . . to the assumption of the armour of an alienating identity, which will mark with its rigid structure the subject's entire development."[13] Lacan phrases the establishment of the subject's "I" as the development of an alienating armor, a rigid circumscribing structure. Ibsen's protagonists develop exactly this kind of alienating armor or structure as well, the frigid, rigid and determining text which each writes for himself and enacts.

As I hope to have suggested, in *When We Dead Awaken* it is "The Resurrection Day" which places and identifies the protagonist, which is the text of his "I." In *John Gabriel Borkman*, the text or artifact which determines the protagonist's identity is the icy cold, metallic empire of which John Gabriel is the emperor; in *The Master Builder* it is Solness's empire of buildings, homes for human beings, which establishes him as the master builder. Having created the artifact or text, the protagonist enjoys viewing himself as its maker and master, its Author, if you will; yet, the protagonist comes to view the artifact as representing him in an unsatisfactory manner, and undertakes to deconstruct it. His attempt to do so, to end the text's icy determination of him that he might enjoy again the thrill of life in flesh and blood, is the attempt to escape from the text which constitutes him.

As mentioned above, escape from the text as a whole is impossible, because it is impossible to show: what Ibsen does, rather, is to associate the protagonist's enactment of his role with a claustrophobic, static space. This space is the "stage" for the protagonist's role-play, and is left behind as the protagonist struggles against the adamantine shackles of his identity. This struggle is represented in all three plays as the flight from interiors suggestive of death and decay to exteriors of wild height and prospect.

Even before the first line of *The Master Builder* is spoken, Solness's workroom is identified as a suffocating space: the curtain rises and Knut Brovik suddenly gets up from the drawing table as though in distress, comes forward into the doorway breathing heavily and with difficulty, and says, "Oh, I can't stand this much longer!" So, too, in *John Gabriel Borkman*, where the protagonist's quarters are identified as a cage before the protagonist himself appears. Although Rubek's workroom, a cold, damp cellar, never appears on the stage per se, *When We Dead Awaken* opens with a vision of stasis: the curtain rises and Maja sits for a while as though waiting for the Professor to say something, then lowers her newspaper and sighs. Rubek looks up, "Well, Maja, what is it?" and Maja replies, "Listen to the stillness." Rubek and his wife continue on this theme, the silence all around them, even characterizing the air countrywide as "somehow dead."

From the static, cloying interiors smelling of death, the protagonist moves progressively outside and upward into the wild countryside and onto the heights. This trajectory, from low to high, inside to outside, which represents the protagonist's overall movement, is a scenic representation of his attempt to escape from the space ruled by the determining text. For it is only the tower-top or mountaintop which is a suitable space for trading one identity for another: the mountaintop, above the proscenium arch, provides a space beyond representation in the determining text. It is as if the protagonist climbs to the point where God's pen touches the earth in order that he might talk to his Author and exchange one role for another (as Alfred Allmers does during his solitude on the mountain, exchanging his role as a writer for his role as father) or defy his Author and take one role while leaving another behind (as Solness does, leaving behind his role as father and church-builder to become the master builder).

Sexuality is more or less explicitly associated with escape from the text and new writing. I suggest that, for Ibsen, sex relieves the self of its alienating, circumscribing armor, opens it to new perceptions and experiences, and thereby provides an avenue for escape from the text which determines the self. In other words, in flesh and blood, the body, the protagonist may seek and find some respite from the travails of self-consciousness. The structure or artifact that is the basis for his self-conscious being, his personal text, is thus deconstructed through his flesh and blood. We note the similarity of sex to the mirror-stage, where the child innocently flails and frolics in its mother's arms, feeling a fragment of the whole picture before it, excited to try and make itself whole. Moreover, the protagonist's deconstruction of his text through the flesh and blood is like the actor's deconstruction (re-writing) of the text which he enacts through his body. The protagonist's new writing, though it may be associated with sexuality, is also associated with mounting to great physical heights where the Author Himself is supposed to be.

Brand's mountain-climb and death in an avalanche seems to provide the model for the conclusion of *When We Dead Awaken*. Having climbed to the foot of the Ice Church, Brand experiences a conversion of the sort sought by Rubek and Irene. "Serene, radiant and young again," he proclaims,

> Until this moment, what I wanted to be
> Was a tablet on which God might write.
> But from today, the poem of my life
> Shall surge and fountain warm and rich . . [14]

On the mountain, Brand moves beyond one identity, himself as the iron-willed priest, to embrace a second, the free-flowing identity of a poet of life. I suggest that in *Peer Gynt*, the drama Ibsen wrote after *Brand*, the playwright explores and brings to crisis the role of the wandering poet of life, as *Brand* explores and brings to crisis the role of the stone-hearted priest, as *When We Dead Awaken* explores and brings to crisis the role of the life-denying artist. Each of these plays represents essentially the protagonist's deconstruction of his own identity, an identity written and enacted by himself and closely linked with the play as a whole. The protagonist's personal dramatic text is not completely identified with the whole dramatic text, however, as the ambiguous pronouncements at the end of *Brand* and *When We Dead Awaken* show. A function shared by the mysterious voice's "God is Love," and the nun's "Pax vobiscum" is to differentiate the protagonist's synecdochic text from the text it represents.

Notes

1. Daniel Haakonsen, ed., *Contemporary Approaches to Ibsen, August 1970 (The Second International Ibsen Seminary)*. " 'The Play-within-the-Play' in Ibsen's Realistic Drama," by Daniel Haakonsen. (Oslo: Universitetsforlaget, 1971), 109.

2. Haakonsen, "The Play Within the Play," 115.

3. Margot Norris, "Myth and Neurosis in Ibsen's Mature Plays," *Comparative Drama* 10:1 (Spring 1976):4.

4. Norris, "Myth and Neurosis," 5.

5. The notion of the protagonist's personal dramatic text is very similar to Charles R. Lyons's notion of the personal myth, an imaginative construct by which the protagonist organizes his experience. Charles R. Lyons, *Henrik Ibsen: The Divided Consciousness*, (Carbondale: Southern Illinois University Press, 1972), xii. I hope to suggest that this imaginative construct is not only a pattern for consciousness, but, as well, a pattern for the body, behavior. Moreover, considering the protagonist's personal myth a dramatic text opens Ibsen's plays to analysis in terms of self-referentiality and theatrical self-consciousness.

6. Ladislav Matejka and Irwin R. Titunik, eds., *Semiotics of Art*. "Dramatic Text as a Component of Theatre," by Jiri Veltrusky. (Cambridge, Mass.: The MIT Press, 1976), 115.

7. Veltrusky, "Dramatic Text," 113.

8. Ibsen says that he views it " 'as a misfortune for a dramatic work to have communicated to the public initially through the stage. . . . The reception of the piece becomes intertwined with its performance' which 'confuses two completely disparate things.' " Quoted from *European Literary Theory and Practice*, ed. Vernon Gras. "Ibsen's *The Masterbuilder* (1892)," by Ludwig Binswanger, trans. Vernon Gras. (New York: Delta Publishing Co., 1973), 185.

9. Veltrusky, "Dramatic Text," 115.

10. James Walter McFarlane, ed. and trans., *The Oxford Ibsen*, vol. VIII (New York: Oxford University Press, 1977), 356.

11. McFarlane, ed., *The Oxford Ibsen*, 279. (All quotations are from McFarlane's translations in *The Oxford Ibsen*).

12. McFarlane, ed., *The Oxford Ibsen*, 306.

13. Jacques Lacan, *Écrits*, trans. Alan Sheridan (New York: W. W. Norton & Company, 1977), 4.

14. James Walter McFarlane, ed. and trans., *The Oxford Ibsen*, Vol. III (New York: Oxford University Press, 1972), 249.

SELECTED BIBLIOGRAPHY

TRANSLATIONS

McFarlane, James Walter, gen. ed., *The Oxford Ibsen*. 8 vols. London: Oxford, 1962– . Well-translated editions of the plays that also contain useful supplementary information.

Fjelde, Rolf. *Ibsen: The Complete Major Prose Plays*. New York: Farrar, Strauss and Giroux, 1978. Clear and stageworthy translations.

Evert Sprinchorn. *Ibsen: Letters and Speeches*. New York: Hill and Wang, 1964. A useful collection of Ibsen material.

BIOGRAPHIES

Koht, Halvdan. *The Life of Ibsen*. Trans. Einar Haugen and A. E. Santainiello. 2nd. ed. rev. New York: Benjamin Blom, 1971. English version of Koht's work that was published originally in 1928 in Norwegian and revised in 1954. The standard biography until the publication of Meyer.

Meyer, Michael. *Ibsen: A Biography*. Garden City: Doubleday, 1971. An exhaustively researched and finely detailed biography. Meyer's occasional critical analyses are not, however, particularly insightful.

CRITICISM

Adams, Robert Martin. *Strains of Discord: Studies in Literary Openness*. Ithaca: Cornell University Press, 1958. Very revealing discussion of the open form of the resolution of *Ghosts*.

Arestad, Sverre. "Ibsen's Concept of Tragedy." *PMLA* 74 (1959): 285–97. Insightful analysis of Ibsen's relationship to ideas of tragic form.

Binswanger, Ludwig. "Ibsen's *The Master Builder*," from *Henrik Ibsen*, trans. by Vernon Gras and re-printed in *European Literary Theory and Practice*. New York: Dell, 1973. A phenomenological and philosophical analysis of the play.

Bradbrook, M. C. *Ibsen the Norwegian*. New ed. Hamden: Archon Books, 1966. Rev. of 1946 study that attempts to replace the image of Ibsen the realist with a conception of him as a poet in the theater.

Downs, Brian. *Ibsen: The Intellectual Background*. Cambridge: Cambridge University Press, 1946. A clear and incisive discussion of the ideology informing Ibsen's work.

Durbach, Errol. *"Ibsen the Romantic."* Athens: University of Georgia Press, 1982. Places Ibsen in the context of Romanticism and documents his romantic and anti-romantic sensibilities.

Ewbank, Inga-Stina. "Ibsen's Dramatic Language as a Link between His 'Realism' and His 'Symbolism'." *Contemporary Approaches to Ibsen.* Vol. 1. Ed. Daniel Haakonsen. Oslo: Universitetsforlaget, 1965 / 66. Demonstrates the ways in which the realistic placement of critical metaphors provides a symbolic, but not allegoric, structure.

———. "Ibsen and the Language of Women." *Women Writing and Writing about Women.* ed. Mary Jacobus. London: Croom Helm in association with Oxford University Women's Studies Committee, 1978. Excellent analysis of Ibsen's language and gender.

Haakonsen, Daniel. "The Play-within-the-Play in Ibsen's Realistic Drama." *Contemporary Approaches to Ibsen.* Vol. 2. Ed. Daniel Haakonsen. Oslo: Universitetsforlaget, 1970 / 71. Proposes a model of the reenactment of the past in the present.

Hurt, James. *Cataline's Dream.* Urbana: Illinois University Press, 1972. General chronological commentary on the plays from a psychoanalytic point of view based on R. D. Laing.

Joyce, James. "Ibsen's New Drama." *Fortnightly Review,* n.s., (1900): 575–90. Reprinted in James Joyce, *The Critical Writings.* ed. Ellsworth Mason and Richard Ellmann. New York: The Viking Press, 1959.

Kenner, Hugh. "Joyce and Ibsen's Naturalism." *Sewanee Review.* 49 (1951): 75–96. Discusses relationship of Joyce and Ibsen from a New Critical perspective.

Kerans, James E. "Kindermord and Will in *Little Eyolf." Modern Drama: Essays in Criticism.* ed. Travis Bogard and William I. Oliver. New York: Oxford University Press, 1965. A Freudian reading of the play.

Lowenthal, Leo. *Literature and the Image of Man: Sociological Studies of the European Drama and Novel, 1600–1900.* Boston: Beacon Press, 1957. Situates Ibsen within a concept of social history.

Kott, Jan. "Ibsen Read Anew." *The Theatre of Essence and Other Essays.* Evanston: Northwestern University Press, 1984. Especially interesting psychoanalytic interpretation of Hedda Gabler as a lesbian.

Lyons, Charles R. *Henrik Ibsen: the Divided Consciousness.* Carbondale: Southern Illinois University Press, 1972. Phenomenologically oriented study of Ibsen's major plays.

———. "The Function of Dream and Reality in *John Gabriel Borkman." Scandinavian Studies* 45 (1973): 293–309. Related to entry above.

Lukács, Georg. "Historical Novel and Historical Drama." *The Historical Novel.* Trans. Hannah and Stanley Mitchell. Boston: Beacon, 1963. First published in Russian (from the German) in Moscow in 1937. Criticizes Ibsen for his novelistic technique in *Rosmersholm.*

McFarlane, James Walter. *Ibsen and the Temper of Norwegian Literature.* Oxford: Oxford University Press, 1960. A fine critical survey of the plays that responds to their poetic language.

———. "The Structured World of Ibsen's Late Dramas." *Ibsen in the Theatre*. ed. Errol Durbach. London: Macmillan, 1980. Discussion of Ibsen's fictional world as an arena of relationships and meta-relationships (relationship of relationships).

Northam, John. *Ibsen's Dramatic Method*. London: Faber & Faber, 1953. A ground-breaking analysis of the relationship of dramatic language and the visual imagery of performance.

Shaw, George Bernard. *The Quintessence of Ibsenism*. London: Faber, 1913. Establishes the long-lasting image of Ibsen the polemical realist.

Szondi, Peter. *Theories des modernen Dramas*. Frankfurt am Main: Suhrkamp Verlag, 1965. Expands Lukács's argument that Ibsen's structural technique is novelistic rather than dramatic.

Tennant, P. F. D. *Ibsen's Dramatic Technique*. Cambridge: Cambridge University Press, 1948. Clear, formal analysis of Ibsen's functional structure.

INDEX